K

20 016 897 56

2439500702
1919195*

D1588761

University of Northumbria at Newcastle
LIBRARY

MARKETING, COMPETITION AND THE PUBLIC SECTOR:

Key Trends and Issues

Edited by

Henry Tam
MA(Oxon), PhD, FCIM

Published by Longman Information & Reference,
Longman Group Limited, 6th Floor,
Westgate House, The High, Harlow, Essex CM20 1YR
Telephone: Harlow (0279) 442601; Fax: Harlow (0279) 44501;
Telex: 81491 Padlog.

©Longman Group Limited 1994

All rights reserved. No part of this publication may be reproduced,
stored in retrieval system, or transmitted in any form or by any
means, electronic mechanical, photocopying, recording, or
otherwise, without the prior permission of the Copyright owner or
a licence permitting restricted copying issued by the Copyright
Licensing Agency Ltd., 90 Tottenham Court Road, London W1P
9HE.

A catalogue record for this book is available from the British
Library

ISBN 0–582–24447–1

UNIVERSITY OF NORTHUMBRIA AT NEWCASTLE LIBRARY	
ITEM No.	CLASS No.
4001689756	354.42001 MAR

Printed and bound in Great Britain by Bookcraft (Bath) Ltd.

CONTENTS

PART C COMPETITION

PART D MARKETING IN ACTION

I PREFACE

It is generally agreed that the exposure of private enterprise to market forces tends to improve product quality, customer service and overall efficiencies. Where the market engenders undesirable consequences — for example, unemployment, pollution, poverty, insecurity, social alienation — it is accepted that the public sector has a key role to play in maintaining a basic framework of human decency and well-being. But if the public sector is to fulfil its role effectively and efficiently, should it not also be subject to the test of market forces? And yet if it is to open up to market forces, would that process not lead to the same undesirable consequences which the private sector has generated in coping with the pressures of market forces, against which the public sector is supposed to give protection?

This book is concerned with helping politicians, managers, and students of public sector management understand the potential benefits and harm of exposing the public sector to market forces. It examines how the discipline of marketing, which was developed by the private sector to respond positively to the needs of customers in a competitive environment, can be applied to management in the public sector.

The book is divided into four parts. Part A provides a general introduction to the theme of 'Exposing the Public Sector to Market Forces'. Part B deals with *the Customer Focus*. In 'Building a Customer-driven Culture', Charles Daybell sets out the key management ingredients which made Braintree District Council, in the opinion of a wide range of independent assessors, one of the most customer-orientated public sector organisations in the UK. Tom Ling, in 'The Benefits Agency — Claimants as Customers', looks at the difficulties of applying the concept of customer to those who depend on state provisions, and who have little real choice in relation to those provisions. His analysis examines the issues with particular reference to the management approach of the Benefits Agency. In 'Consumerism and Citizenship', John Gyford examines the implications of introducing consumerist language and thinking into the public sector, and the effects this may have on the development of citizenship. The customer focus in the provision of education services is discussed in 'Education and Marketing' by

Mike Clayden with reference to his experience at the Education Authority in Islington. In 'The Customer's Opinions', Brian Gosschalk and Warren Hatter give their views on how market research can help to improve the customer focus of public sector management.

Part C of the book turns to the theme of *Competition*. In 'Health in the Marketplace', David Fillingham demonstrates how the introduction of an internal market in the NHS requires a sophisticated partnership approach, and warns against the crude adoption of commercial techniques. Kieron Walsh gives a comprehensive assessment in 'The Impact of Competition' of the effects which the introduction of competition to the public sector has brought about. In 'The Commercial Environment' Elizabeth Ransom and Serena Simmons highlight the difficulties which different types of public sector organisation have to face in adjusting to the pressures of competition. In 'Preparing for Market Testing', Guy Hollis and Janet Baker review the key issues to be considered in order to maximise the benefits which could be gained from market testing.

Part D looks at *Marketing in Action*. Marketing techniques have to be properly understood before they can be fully utilised by the public sector. In 'Direct Marketing in the Public Sector' Miles Young shows how the principles of direct marketing can be much more widely applied in the public sector. Despite the widespread use of direct marketing in the private sector, it is a management tool which is rarely appreciated by public sector practitioners. On the other hand, although advertising is a relatively more familiar discipline, Gene Wonnacott shows, in 'Achieving Effective Advertising', that there is still a lot which can be done to make advertising more effective. Nicholas O'Shaughnessy and Dominic Wring, in 'Political Marketing in Britain', provide a critical overview of how the marketing approach has been used by political parties in shaping and responding to public opinions. James Kay gives a case study account of the applications of a range of techniques to achieve the social marketing aims of Healthwise, a Regional Health Information Service. Finally, Keith Haarhoff offers an example, in 'Marketing and Economic Development: The Cambridgeshire Unit's Approach', of how the marketing discipline can be utilised in the highly competitive challenge to attract and retain businesses to meet public sector economic development objectives.

I have been most fortunate in being able to bring together a team of distinguished and experienced practitioners as well as leading theorists in the field. I would like to thank all of them for their contributions to this book, which will undoubtedly become a key text for anyone interested in finding out how competitive forces and the marketing discipline should be applied to the management of the public sector.

I would also like to thank Shelley Couper of Longman for her support in getting this project off the ground and steering it through. As for my own part in the project, it was helped along as always by the encouragement of my wife, Celia, and the laughter of our daughters, Jessica and Antonia.

Henry Tam
Risby, West Suffolk
April 1994

NOTES ON CONTRIBUTORS

Janet Baker is a senior consultant with Coopers & Lybrand's Local Government Practice, where she specialises in organisational strategy and design work. She has assisted a wide range of clients in their preparations for compulsory competitive tendering, voluntary competition and market testing. Prior to joining Coopers & Lybrand, she was a management advisor at Berkshire County Council which pioneered large-scale externalisation.

Mike Clayden is Deputy Director of Education at the London Borough of Islington, where he has played a key role in establishing the new Islington Education Service, one of the successor bodies to the Inner London Education Authority. He created Islington's Local Management Scheme which delegates one of the highest proportions nationally of schools' spending. Islington Education now operates many of its services successfully on a trading basis. Before joining Islington, he worked for ILEA for twenty years, including being divisional education officer in three different boroughs.

Charles Daybell was formerly Chief Executive of Braintree District Council, which won a Charter Mark in the Award's inaugural year, and again in 1993, and picked up the first prize in the SOLACE/ P. A. Consulting Total Quality Award in 1992. Charles Daybell has now set up his own consultancy, and his clients include the House of Commons Select Committee on the Environment, and the British Airports Authority. He is a Fellow of the Institute of Management, Fellow of the Royal Society of Arts, Member of the Institute of Directors, and a Liveryman of the Company of Information Technologists.

David Fillingham is Chief Executive of St Helens and Knowsley Health, which incorporates the District and Family Health Service Authorities. He joined the NHS in 1989 as Regional Personnel Manager at Mersey Regional Health Authority. Prior to that he worked in the private sector for Pilkington where he held positions in marketing and personnel. He has a strong interest in the adaptation of private sector business practices to assist with the delivery of high-quality public services.

Brian Gosschalk is Managing Director of MORI. He is responsible for most of MORI's social and political research. He has directed over a hundred surveys for local authorities examining service delivery and customer care issues, and the research on Performance Indicators for the Audit Commission. He is the past Chairman of the Social Research Association.

John Gyford is Reader in Urban Politics and Planning at University College London. His books include *Local Politics in Britain*, *The Politics of Local Socialism*, and *Citizens, Consumers and Councils*. He has eighteen years' experience as a local councillor at district and county level. He is currently leader of the Labour Group on Braintree District Council and Chairman of the Environment Committee on Essex County Council.

Dr Keith Haarhoff is Director of The Cambridgeshire Unit, a pioneering partnership between the private sector and the local authorities in Cambridgeshire. He spent ten years in management consultancy in the oil industry with Shell International and BP before joining the banking industry with J P Morgan. In 1991 he took on the task of establishing what became the Cambridgeshire Unit. Dr Haarhoff has postgraduate qualifications in marketing, finance, and accountancy.

Warren Hatter is a Senior Executive in MORI's Local Government Research Unit and Social Research Institute. He has managed surveys examining customer care in both the public and private sectors. His research work has included a major study of local government employees' views, carried out on behalf of the Local Government Management Board, and studies for the police and armed forces.

Guy Hollis is the Local Government Practice Leader at Coopers & Lybrand. Since joining Coopers & Lybrand in 1984, he has been involved in giving management advice in the UK and overseas, in central and local government, and in the health service, in connection with policy studies, organisational reviews, financial and policy analysis, and IT strategies. He was previously Deputy County Treasurer of Devon County Council.

James Kay is Managing Director of Healthwise, an independent Regional Health Information Service on contract to the Mersey Regional Health Authority. He began his career as a trainer, and developed a specialist interest in drugs and AIDS issues. He has written and published a series of articles, books, trianing materials, and computer programs on drugs and sex education. He also runs training courses on marketing.

Dr Tom Ling is Head of Politics at Anglia Polytechnic University, and a Director of the Centre for Citizenship Development. His research interests concern the relationships between the management of the public sector and wider political processes. He is the author of *Managing the British State Since 1945*, and joint author of *Thatcherism: A Tale of Two Nations*. He was formerly a local councillor on Cambridge City Council.

Nicholas O'Shaughnessy is Lecturer in Marketing, University of Cambridge. He also teaches at the Judge Institute of Management Studies. His published works include *The Phenomenon of Political Marketing* (Macmillan, 1990), and *Light, Liberty and Learning: the Idea of a University Re-visited* (The Education Unit, 1992). He is a former parliamentary candidate and ex-President of the Oxford Union.

Elizabeth Ransom leads KPMG Peat Marwick's Central Government Practice, and has been closely associated with management reforms in government over the last decade. She leads KPMG's work on market testing, and is currently working with the Ministry of Defence on corporate planning in defence agencies. Before joining KPMG, she was a civil servant dealing with science and technology policy and R & D management.

Serena Simmons is a principal consultant in the strategic business management practice of KPMG Management Consulting. She has been involved in many projects helping organisations understand their marketplace and customer requirements, establish service standards, and prepare marketing action plans. She began her career with British Airways, where she was responsible for the promotion of business products. She moved to specialist marketing consultancy, Marketing Solutions, before joining KPMG in 1988.

Dr Henry Tam is Assistant Chief Executive of St Edmundsbury Borough Council. He was formerly Head of Marketing at Braintree District Council. He is a Fellow of the Chartered Institute of Marketing, and was Chairman of the Institute's Public Sector Advisory Panel 1991–92. He is the Founder and Chairman of the Local Government Marketing Network, and an Honorary Director of the Centre for Citizenship Development. His published works include *Serving the Public: Customer Management in Local Government* (Longman, 1993).

Kieron Walsh is Professor of Public Sector Management in INLOGOV at the University of Birmingham. He has conducted research on a wide range of topics in public service management, and acts as a consultant to many different bodies. He has recently completed a major study of competitive tendering in local government — *Competition and Services* (HMSO, 1993). He is presently conducting a study of the impact of contracts in health, social care, and local government.

Gene Wonnacott is Director of the National Association of Public Service Advertisers, which was founded in 1984. He is also Secretary of the Society of County and Regional Public Relations Officers. He was previously Advertising Manager with Somerset County Council, where he established the first local authority in-house advertising agency to obtain official agency recognition from the Periodical Publishers Association. He is a Member of the Institute of Public Relations.

Dominic Wring is Tutor in Politics at Trinity Hall, University of Cambridge. He is currently carrying out research which assesses the growth and impact of commercially derived marketing techniques on the Labour Party. He has also helped with the development of courses in politics at the Anglia Polytechnic University.

Miles Young is Chairman of Ogilvy and Mather Direct, one of the largest direct marketing agencies in the world. His clients have included the Central Office of Information, Lever Brothers, Wall's Ice Cream, Bowater Scott, Mars, and Beecham Foods. He has lectured and written widely on integrated marketing. He is also a Governor at Bedford School, and since July 1993 he has been the elected Leader of Westminster City Council.

PART A
Introduction

Chapter 1

EXPOSING THE PUBLIC SECTOR TO MARKET FORCES

by Henry Tam

■ THE POWER OF MARKET FORCES

Love them or loathe them, market forces have been a major factor in shaping modern social development. Exposure to competitive pressures from rival suppliers has meant that organisations which have hitherto operated in a protected environment, must either improve continuously what they can do for their customers or end up losing out to their competitors.

The quality of life in terms of the affordability, reliability, and variety of goods and services at our disposal has been substantially enhanced by the entrance of new and vibrant suppliers into the marketplace. Although this has to be balanced against the less desirable effects of competition — e.g., unemployment, poverty, social alienation — the final and total collapse of communism means that there is at present no serious alternative to the free market system as the basic model for socio-economic arrangements.

Yet, ironically, if market forces are valuable precisely because they pose a challenge to what might otherwise ossify into rigid and outmoded service patterns, the absence of any real challenge to the free market system itself should raise questions about its ability to adapt and improve without the pressures of competition.

One particular question which those in the public sector need to tackle urgently is how they should respond to the constant stream of proposals to open up public sector management more and more to market forces. Rather than jumping to the conclusion either that anything to do with free market thinking must be damaging for the public sector and society at large, or that exposure to market forces must be good regardless of their actual impact, we should take a closer look at how a competitive market may generate benefits to society under the appropriate conditions.

■ THE RISE OF THE MARKETING DISCIPLINE

Whenever an opportunity arises for a new supplier to enter into a market, the customers in the market will only benefit if either (or both) the existing or new supplier adopt the marketing approach. By 'the marketing approach' we mean an approach which places the anticipation, identification, and satisfaction of the relevant customers' needs at the centre of the supplier's management strategy. In other words, the emergence of new suppliers will not benefit the customers at all unless the competitive situation leads the newcomers or the existing players, or best of all, both, to concentrate on how to offer more benefits to those customers.

The rise of the marketing discipline in the 1950s and 1960s led to a customer-driven spiral of increasing product features, rising quality standards, and improving after-sales care. Many organisations which failed to adopt effective marketing strategies had by the 1970s been squeezed out of their markets. However, market forces can only set the scene for competition. It is ultimately up to those who manage the organisations involved to come up with strategies to win over more customers. If in a given market none of the suppliers is particularly good at marketing, and most are fairly mediocre in their customer focus, the fact that there are a number of them in competition would only result in minor variations which make little difference to the customers.

The recognition that it is the adoption of the marketing approach, and not the presence of market forces themselves, which makes the real difference has important implications. First, we can now see that it is not necessary to expose any organisation to competition in order to secure greater benefits for customers. Provided that an organisation has the vision to see that its future is bound up with how satisfied its customers are with its performance, and it has the management expertise to translate this vision into an effective marketing strategy, it will continuously improve what it has to offer to its customers regardless of what competition may or may not exist. Secondly, we can also see that competition is not itself sufficient to bring about better services. Without sound marketing thinking, competition would leave things pretty much as they are. In fact it is arguable that competition could divert an organisation from its underlying customer focus to fight off short-term problems.

Proponents of the free market system can be expected to retort by pointing out that without the pressures of competition, few organisations would be motivated to adopt, let alone sharpen, a customer focus. This is difficult to deny in the public sector where the concept of putting the customer of public services at the centre of management thinking hardly emerged until the 1980s. What we must not lose sight of now is that the link between competitive pressures and marketing response is a complex one, and anyone wanting to see better public services resulting from more customer-driven management should consider carefully how the rhetoric of the market is to be translated into a meaningful management environment which is genuinely conducive to the marketing approach.

■ TURNING TO THE PUBLIC SECTOR

The public sector is in a fundamental sense different from the private sector because its role is derived precisely from the inability of the latter to sustain a civilised form of human existence without the support of a collective system. It is debatable how much any system of government should be entrusted to do in terms of regulations, controls, protection, and development, but it cannot be denied — except perhaps by the most utopian anarchist — that there must be a mechanism binding on all members of a society to deal with many of the issues which those members individually cannot resolve fairly or effectively.

There will always be a need for a structure of democratic government to deliberate and act on how individuals should pool some of their resources together for their common good. What we are concerned with is therefore how the management of public sector matters can be improved through the adoption of the marketing approach. The approach has evolved in the private sector in response to the pressures of competition, but given that the public sector is inherently different from the private sector, any attempt to create competitive conditions in the public sector must be handled carefully.

What we must bear in mind is that competition is not good in itself. It only brings about benefits if it succeeds in stimulating the organisations concerned to develop effective marketing strategies. In fact market forces can sometimes eliminate from the field those players who were the best at satisfying their customers. Laker Air, for example, was subject to pressure of market forces which eventually ended what many regarded as an airline business which served its customers particularly well. To raise the issue of fair or unfair competition would only serve to illustrate that competitive conditions must be structured correctly if they are to enhance and not undermine customer satisfaction. However, before we look at the difficulties involved in structuring competitive conditions for the public sector, we should examine the concept of customer as it applies to public sector organisations.

■ THE CUSTOMERS OF POLITICAL INSTITUTIONS

The customers of private sector organisations pay for what those organisations have to offer. The more they like what is on offer, the more they purchase, and the more money goes to the organisations to continue their commercial activities. This provides a direct link between the financial and organisational health of private sector bodies on the one hand, and their customers' satisfaction with their performance on the other. In the public sector, the link has to be conceived very differently.

Public sector bodies obtain their funding primarily through tax revenue which must be seen, not as a private payment for some vaguely defined package of personal benefits, but as the citizens' contributions to their collective resources for their common good. How these resources are used for the good of all is then a matter of political judgement and management planning. The 'good of all' must be conceived as more than the sum total of individual satisfaction. One danger of over-stretching private sector analogies is that one could end up suggesting that unless someone benefits personally from a state activity, it cannot be regarded as an activity which is for the good of all. If one cannot see the benefits which go to help the sick and vulnerable in one's society as benefits for the common good, then one would be sliding into a conception of life which is so devoid of civic virtues, compassion, and mutual regard that it would be incompatible with life in a democratic society.

To apply the concept of customer to the public sector, we must anchor it properly to the distinct features of democratic life. The customers of political institutions must not be seen as, and certainly should not be encouraged to see themselves as, individual purchasers of bits of public service for their personal consumption. They are citizens who should judge the public sector in terms of its performance in enhancing the good of all.

The customer focus in the public sector will therefore work if public servants concentrate on evaluating the services they provide with constant reference to the needs and preferences of citizens, who must be given every opportunity to understand and comment on the quality of those services — and the policies which underpin them — so that a virtuous circle of service development evolves through the constant interactions between the public service providers and the citizens they serve.

Unlike the private sector which needs to focus on what level of personal satisfaction customers would pay for, the public sector should focus on working with the customers of political institutions — i.e. the citizens — to define what is the most desirable level of common good for society and striving towards attaining that level. The prime motivation is not greater market share in financial terms, but better realisation of the common good in moral and political terms. This is where the spirit of public service is so important, and why so many of the most outstanding professionals and managers of every generation choose to work in the public sector for what in pure financial and material terms are lesser rewards than that which they could secure in the private sector. It is a mark of the more ignorant critics of the public sector that, never having felt the slightest hint of any spirit of public service in themselves, they constantly blame every weakness in public sector management on the absence of commercial pressures in the system.

The truth is that the marketing approach to management is still relatively new to the public sector. Managers who are committed to serving the common good can nontheless overlook the importance of identifying what citizens really need, as opposed to assuming what they must need. In many cases, it is not the threat of commercial pressures, but sensitive management training which will lead to a better understanding of and readiness to develop a marketing approach.

Charles Daybell, for example, has shown (*see* Chapter 2) that a strong ethos of public service can be integrated with a management strategy which is customer-driven. Braintree District Council become one of the first local authorities in the UK to appoint a Head of Marketing to develop a council-wide approach to putting customers first. In such a context, competition is neither necessary nor helpful. Those who worked at Braintree were empowered to become the best local authority in terms of anticipating and responding to the needs of local people, and they took pride in achieving that objective. Customers' views were constantly sought and services were reviewed and improved in the light of public feedback. The Council's achievements have been recognised by a host of external awards, the latest of which being the *Service Excellence of the Year Award for Not-for-Profit*

Organisations (1994), given by Arthur Andersen Management Today[1].

But it is not always easy to break away from the old hierarchical bureaucracies which characterise so many public sector organisations for most of this century, to shift to a new management culture which aims always to put customers' needs first. Tom Ling's case study of the Benefits Agency (Chapter 3) illuminates the difficulties in applying the concept of the customer to benefit claimants. A customer is someone who is supposed to call the shots, who exercises his choice to get what really matches his expectations. And yet claimants traditionally have a dependency relationship with the state. What emerges is that the application of the concept of customer has to be handled carefully. A commercialised picture of the customer and the suppositions which go with it can lead to citizens' legitimate concerns being marginalised.

Many commentators on the introduction of Citizen's Charters have observed that the Government's approach to date has been more akin to charters on customer rights than to citizenship development. John Gyford, for example, notes (*see* Chapter 4) that the language of customers and consumerism does not always sit comfortably with that of citizenship, and he goes on to explain that if the state is to develop a better relationship with its citizens, then it must keep consumerist ideas to one side, and concentrate on those elements of the marketing approach which can be fruitfully cultivated in the public sector.

Another way of looking at the issue of formulating a customer focus which is suitable for the public sector is to examine its application, with a specific service example. Education is where the debate concerning the introduction of market forces into the public sector has been particularly intense in recent years. Mike Clayden gives a practitioner's view (in Chapter 5) on how in Islington they have developed a service culture which genuinely puts the needs of those they exist to serve — parents, pupils, governors, teachers, headteachers — at the centre of their service planning.

---

1   The award citation stated: 'It is unusual to come across an organisation like Braintree Council which has such a holistic approach to customer service, sustained over many years. Everything which the Council does is driven by 'customer' or resident need, right down to the organisational structure, methods of working and employment policies. In many respects the council outstrips most of the private sector.'

One of the most important management disciplines to bridge the gap between what a provider thinks and what the customer thinks is that of market research. Many in the public sector still fall into the trap of dismissing market research as superficial, when in fact it is a highly sophisticated tool which can be used to understand the feelings and opinions of those the public sector exists to serve. Brian Gosschalk and Warren Hatter set out in Chapter 6 how market research can help public sector managers sharpen their customer focus.

■ THE THREATS AND OPPORTUNITIES OF COMPETITION

At this point we may pick up once again the question of motivation. The leading-edge public sector bodies will always excel in meeting the needs of their customers. Informed by high-calibre advisors, led by inspiring leaders, they naturally serve their customers well. But what about the majority of public sector bodies which are not fired up by inspiring leaders, which have no one on their establishment who can tell the difference between a marketing strategy and an advertising campaign? How are they going to be motivated to adopt a marketing approach in their management thinking?

This is where competition really should come in. For those who are committed to putting their customers first in any event, competition could at best be a minor diversion, and at worst a source of serious disruption. This is not an excuse for the public sector, as it applies equally to the private sector. One needs only think of the Betamax video format which by all accounts was an extremely high-quality product, but it lost out — as did millions of potential users — because it failed to deal with the competition in the race to secure distributors.

But for those who are far from marketing-orientated, competition may be the only stimulus which can trigger a change in management culture. The introduction of competition into the public sector has certainly shaken up quite a few established hierarchies, and facilitated the development of the marketing approach in many organisations which would hitherto barely tolerate such managerial 'radicalism'. Yet the danger which competition poses to those who are already customer-driven, is also a threat to those who are just beginning to re-think their management strategies.

The introduction of competitive mechanisms into the National Health Service provides a clear example of how market forces can stimulate positive change, and yet undermine service cultures which are absolutely necessary for quality services for customers to be maintained. David Fillingham gives us an in-depth analysis (in Chapter 7) of the threats and opportunities which have been brought in by the internal market within the NHS. Whilst a partnership approach between the key players in the market can generate substantial benefits for all citizens, any naive, short-sighted approach to competition can cause everyone to lose out in the end.

It is difficult to say if the competition which has been brought into the public sector to date has been beneficial or harmful overall. Kieron Walsh gives a general summary of the more notable effects (Chapter 8), and concludes that whilst there have been financial savings on the contracting-out side (which may or may not be outweighed by the increase in costs on the client side), market mechanisms can undermine public accountabilities — as when client departments shift the blame for mistakes onto outside contractors or arms-length agencies — and breed a set of commercial values which may conflict with the spirit of public service.

One particular aspect of the problem of dealing with competitive pressures whilst having to retain the distinctive features of a public service is looked at closely by Serena Simmons and Elizabeth Ransom (in Chapter 9). They point out that it is ironic that just when many private sector organisations are beginning to appreciate the need to look beyond their financial balance sheets and plan for their wider social responsibilities, some public sector bodies unfamiliar with operating in a more competitive environment should assume that being efficient is about subordinating everything else to financial targets.

Just as the concept of customer can mislead one into perceiving citizens in a narrow consumerist mode — i.e. you look after them so long as they are more likely to pay you — the notion of being more business-like can lead to the trap of using a profit-at-all-social-costs paradigm which many leading business organisations already reject.

It is clear that much of the public rhetoric about the merits of competition actually misses the point. Competition does have an important role in terms of stimulating responsiveness, innovation, and the development of a marketing approach to management. But it can only fulfil this role if the objectives concerned are built into any process of introducing competition into the public sector. The problem comes when instead of using competitive conditions strategically to improve the customer focus of public sector bodies, competition is brought in as an ideological magic wand to put an end to inefficient practices and reduce public sector borrowing. Such an approach can be described as 'the 3-D approach', namely:

- Distracting

- Distorting

- Dangerous

Distracting: One of the main advantages of having a close working relationship between policy strategists and service deliverers is that the experience the latter gain from dealing with the users of the services can be constantly fed back to those concerned with developing service strategies. To put an artificial barrier between the two in the name of competition can distract both parties from sustaining the dialogue which is vital to customer responsiveness.

Distorting: So far most of the compulsory competitive mechanisms which have been introduced have placed the emphasis solely on cost savings. This is analogous to requiring a shopper to specify what he wants to buy before he goes into a shop, and to restrict him to buying what is cheapest in his specified category when he does go into the shop. It overlooks completely that an essential part of 'shopping around', for an individual shopper or for an organisation, is precisely to find out what is on offer and compare the different elements in assessing their overall value. To forbid a supplier to offer any benefits other than cheapness in order to influence a purchasing decision, is to distort grossly what effective purchasing is about. Such distortions would in turn mean that the real customers of public service would lose out, not because those responsible for service delivery have not come up with better product features, but because those who happen to be in the commissioning position are not allowed to take them into account.

Dangerous: Above all, ill-conceived competitive conditions can undermine the public service ethos. Public servants in this country take considerable pride in carrying on a tradition which places the needs of the public at the heart of their work. Of course it is important to root out any wasteful practices. But wherever there is a pressing need, the response has always been to meet that need as the highest priority. Artificial competitive conditions can, however, shift management thinking towards meeting short-term financial targets as opposed to meeting real human needs. In the name of looking after the cost centres, some operations to alleviate patients' pain are known to have been delayed. This need not be the result of making the public sector more competitive, but so long as those who are charged with introducing more competition into the public sector lack the sensitivity and sophistication to make the process genuinely beneficial to the customers of public service, it remains one of its most dangerous consequences.

One way to avoid misapplying competition is to target it on only those areas where the customer focus would not otherwise develop. The principles which the Government has adopted for incorporation into the Citizen's Charter are in fact excellent principles for guiding public sector management. The Charter Mark scheme, even if it is in its infancy, provides considerable potential for serving as a common yardstick for evaluating public sector bodies' performance. A systematic re-examination of the use of customer surveys combined with improvements to the Performance Indicators monitoring by the Audit Commission could yet lead to a process whereby customer-driven public sector organisations would be given due recognition and encouragement to carry on with their good work, and only those which fail to meet the required standards would be subject to the appropriate competitive pressures. Such a process would call for a sound understanding of marketing ideas, and a real appreciation of how they can be applied to the public sector. It may take time to develop, but it is certainly not impossible.

In the meantime, for public sector organisations which are being subject to competition, the challenge is to look beyond the financial figures which dominate the quasi-commercial process, and build an approach which places enhanced customer satisfaction at its core. For example, Guy Hollis and Janet Baker set out (in Chapter 10) how more effective preparations for market testing can be undertaken.

■ MARKETING IN ACTION

The competitive environment which is developing for the public sector may not be ideal in terms of stimulating better services for the customers of public sector bodies. But the opportunities generated by the emergence of such an environment should nonetheless be seized upon. What it undeniably supports is a management culture receptive to the marketing approach. Everyone working in the public sector should seek to learn about marketing practices which can be applied to improving the development and delivery of public services.

In Chapter 11, Miles Young provides an exposition of how direct marketing can be used to enable public sector organisations to develop closer relationships with their customers. The discipline of direct marketing involves the systematic identification of potential and actual customers who can then be brought into a two-way communications process. This means that the organisations concerned can get information out to the relevant groups and individuals much more effectively. Equally these groups and individuals would be encouraged and given the mechanism to pass their views back to those organisations.

Advertising, on the other hand, is appropriate for communications where one-to-one relationship is either difficult to identify or unnecessary. For example, an invitation to the public to express an interest in a particular issue would be difficult to target precisely because it is not yet clear who has an interest in the matter. Effective advertising in such cases would make the difference between securing public interest and reinforcing public apathy. Similarly, the attempt to recruit high-quality managers to join a public sector body needs to reach a large number of potential candidates who would be difficult if not impossible to identify individually. The subject of how to achieve more effective advertising is discussed by Gene Wonnacott in Chapter 12.

The benefits of seeing direct marketing, advertising, and other marketing tools in action include not only better results when one comes to apply them oneself, but the avoidance of bad applications. As with all management tools, whilst ignorance alone leads to missed opportunities, ignorance coupled with enthusiasm can lead to extremely costly mistakes. One area where marketing has featured strongly in the public domain, but where its deployment has been much questioned, is that of competition between the political parties for votes. Dominic Wring and Nicholas O'Shaughnessy (in Chapter 13) examine the role marketing has played in electoral campaigns, and make a number of observations which will be of interest to not only those who are keen to find out what lessons can be learnt in terms of improving future campaigning efforts, but to anyone concerned with how marketing can influence public perception of what matters in the running of the public sector.

In Chapter 14, James Kay provides us with a case study of Healthwise, a Regional Health Information Service which has been highly successful in achieving its objectives by utilising a variety of marketing techniques. Healthwise exists to help public health bodies get vital information across to the public, and to encourage individuals in different health risk categories to find out more about what they ought to know. Healthwise's experience shows that a professional marketing approach can raise service take-up substantially.

In a different field, the work of The Cambridgeshire Unit, a private–public sector joint venture to promote economic development in Cambridgeshire, provides an example of how marketing strategies can be developed to add value in a highly competitive environment. As Keith Haarhoff explains (in Chapter 15), The Cambridgeshire Unit has to establish a niche in the market. No public sector body has an automatic right to operate. If what it is supposed to offer is already adequately provided by others in the market, it has to question seriously its own position. On the other hand, once it is established that there is a gap which the private sector on its own is not covering, the resources of the public sector could be channelled into filling that gap.

Such an exposure to market forces clearly does not entail that public sector bodies should attempt to push out the competitors from the scene. On the contrary, it shows that by recognising the strengths of the competition and by working with them, public bodies can add new value which neither the private nor the public sector on its own can achieve. This is not to suggest that customers should lose out as a result of potential competitors co-operating rather than fighting against one another, because if the net result of the co-operation is not satisfactory, it would still leave a gap for new players to enter the market.

■ THE WAY FORWARD

All organisations should constantly strive to improve their performance. Organisations in the public sector are no different. By focusing on the needs of the customers, by establishing a real dialogue with those customers in determining how services can be improved for them, public sector bodies can give the public better services.

However, as this introductory chapter has shown, and as the contributions in the rest of this book will clearly amplify, there are three fundamental issues which politicians, managers, and citizens alike must take on board in any deliberations about how the public sector should be managed.

First, a purely consumerist conception of 'customer' is not only inadequate, but potentially highly misleading. The customers of public services are not just those who directly use the services on offer, but everyone who has a stake in the political institutions of this country — in other words, the citizens whose collective political rights provide the ultimate democratic basis of all public sector bodies. The customer focus should be developed in relation to what informed citizens think about the needs of, not just themselves, but of their communities. And they can only have informed views if public sector bodies at all levels manage to keep them informed.

Secondly, there should be a recognition that competition is required in certain conditions as a necessary stimulus to the development of the customer focus in public sector management. Equally there needs to be a recognition that competition can only provide such a stimulus, and not end up being counter-productive, if it is structured with the specific objective of improving customer responsiveness and raising service quality. Competition should not be praised or vilified on simplistic ideological grounds. It can be a powerful mechanism to break down outmoded hierarchies and open up organisations to more customer-focused management. Those responsible for introducing competitive conditions into the public sector should check at every step if their proposals would be likely to achieve the relevant goals in practice.

Finally, marketing is much more than publicity. It is a highly sophisticated management discipline about which most practitioners in the public sector still know all too little. It is not a question of whether or not to use marketing, but how to use it to give our customers the services they really require. There is much to be learnt from the marketing specialists. Provided the technical lessons are fitted into a strategic vision in tune with the ethos of public service, the public sector will be strengthened by the wider adoption of the marketing approach, and citizens will benefit from improving public services.

PART B
The Customer Focus

Chapter 2

BUILDING A CUSTOMER-DRIVEN CULTURE

by Charles Daybell

■ THE SEARCH FOR FOCUS

This is not intended to be a management guide to developing a customer-driven culture. Rather it sets out to chart how one authority, Braintree District Council, moved along a particular route during the decade 1983–93 trying to establish a new way of empowering people in order to deliver quality services to its customers. In so doing it may offer insight or guidance to other public sector organisations.

Some aspects are universal — there are basic management principles that should be followed if one is to be successful whatever business one is in, be it the public or the private sector. Other aspects, however, and this is what makes comparisons difficult and management more interesting, relate to the particular culture that was developed in Braintree. Other organisations need to find their own way in developing their cultures and values as these have to be particular to their respective style and ethos.

It seems to me that local government has been trying to renew or create a new philosophical and conceptual framework over the past decade — searching for a focus or an identity — something that councillors and staff could relate to and that would allow them to develop an understanding of the ethos of public service.

A public sector business needs to do five basic things:

First, to deliver what its citizens need or desire within a financially responsible framework.

Secondly, to create a unique identity for itself. It is no longer good enough to refer to the 'goodness' of public services when services are in competition with the private sector or from private contractors. Even where the service is contracted the authority still needs to understand its role and its identification with its public.

Thirdly, to recognise a characteristic of local government — all of its services are provided by people for people often in a one-to-one relationship with its citizens, or, in this context, its customers. Fourthly, to operate ethically, fairly and with integrity. Local governments are responsible bodies and must operate to the highest standards under public scrutiny.

Fifthly, to operate in a business-like manner within a democratic framework.

I shall not deal with these five aspects equally in this article. Some are covered elsewhere and space precludes all but a general comment. They provide a framework to the development of a management culture in Braintree. To understand the development of the management culture one also needs to consider those events during the last two decades which have influenced or driven changes. Changes are generated by the principal forces — external forces or internal forces, and the interaction between the two. Four events have been seminal in my own development.

The first of these is, I am sure, significant for a number of local government managers who started in the late 1960s and early 1970s. The move towards public participation in town planning and housing improvement areas initiated a new approach to the relationship between the public and local government. For idealistic and newly qualified professionals local government would never be the same again. From then on contributions from and involvement of the public became part of the public sector culture.

The second influence, for this writer, was local government reorganisation in 1973/74 which created District Councils with wider and substantial powers (principally Housing and Planning, but unfortunately not Social Services), and which stressed the need for corporate management and forward-planning systems for local authority business.

The third influence was the Audit Commission which made people think about the management of local authorities. It helped focus management. I do not wish to dwell on the three 'E's because in part they became a distraction and in my opinion moved many local authorities away from understanding or considering the importance of their public and their customers. It was assumed by the Commission initially and by central government, that the public wanted cheapness and economy. In my view the public wanted/wants effectiveness and quality assurance, but the importance of the Audit Commission cannot be underestimated.

The fourth influence were the writers and commentators who made management exciting again; who showed what could be done and encouraged people to share their experience. I, like many others, owe Professor John Stewart a lot. He encouraged ideas and demanded justification. Other writers who opened up new avenues, like Tom Peters, Charles Handy and Peter Drucker, consolidated my thinking on service quality, change management, empowering people and a 'can do' approach.

If you were willing to listen, read, experiment, the 1980s were exciting times. There were a number of newly appointed Chief Executives and Leaders who were willing to experiment and put new ideas into practice and who were crucially supported by Michael Clarke, Gerry Stoker, Mark Sheldrake and others.

These were the main influences. But pursuing any one of them exclusively was not going to lead anywhere. Pressing ahead with public involvement was pointless if management delivery and effectiveness were poor. Preparing vast corporate plans without involving the public would be, and was, wasteful of resources and achieved little except to discredit corporate planning. Pursuing economy and efficiencies without understanding the impact of such policies does little to make citizens and customers relate to local government. Introducing 'flavours of the month' from management gurus without understanding management basics creates instability and changes which are unsustainable over time.

I saw my role and target to develop the potential within the local government in Braintree and help create a focus for the people in the community in an integrated way. It required the development of new values for local government which could be readily understood by the public and be owned by the people who worked for the Council.

The next sections will chart how this approach was put into practice and how it developed. But like in all change mechanisms certain triggers were required to start the process off.

■ THE BRAINTREE EXPERIENCE

The three triggers that set Braintree on its way were initially straightforward. Firstly members, who were used to a high standard of performance, wanted to influence events rather than merely react.

Secondly a local economic crisis resulting principally from the abrupt closure of all of the Courtaulds factories in the District with the loss of some 4,000 jobs in the early 1980s.

Thirdly the appointment of a new Chief Executive to act as the agent of change and who was asked to help turn the local economy around.

Thus in autumn 1983 when I arrived, there were high expectations, a problem that demanded a response and a climate in which changes were expected, the only parameter being that the Council did not have cash to throw at problems. Many newly appointed Chief Executives will recognise a familiar scenario.

I believed the only way to tackle the economic problem was to take a holistic/corporate approach and to ensure that the management input would be relevant to the other changes which would inevitably follow. Often one of the first responses managers in local government make to an issue is either to seek structural change and/or to suggest new expenditure programmes. It seemed to me however that creating the conditions for local economic growth required a fundamental change in attitude — what could the Local Authority and every single employee *do* to make business and investment come to, or stay in Braintree. It would be pointless the Council saying it supported expansion if a potential investor was put off for example by the attitude of a planning officer, or by a health officer. Everyone in the organisation had to understand the issues and what their role was in promoting proper economic development. The approach had to be corporate and integrated — every facet, every service had to be examined to see what contribution it could make.

Employees were encouraged to perceive the issue from an external or customer aspect. How would they expect to be treated if they were on the other side of the counter?

The Corporate Economic Development Strategy evolved a slogan 'Braintree Means Business'. It had a number of component parts, but the critical elements concerned changing the management culture of the Council through the statement of Core Values.

Thus in 1984 the Council adopted the following management Core Values under Braintree Means Business:

- we are customer-orientated
- we believe in quality
- we are responsive and responsible
- we believe in the abilities of individuals
- we are action-orientated.

We found the staff readily related to these values as they concerned matters of direct interest to their jobs. We spent a considerable time in discussion and inculcating the values into the organisation. They were, and are seen, as primarily management values designed to improve service delivery through people. It also became clear very quickly that the campaign was also appropriate to the running of the whole Council. It became a seamless progression from core values directed at an economic strategy to core values reflecting the business approach across all of the Council's services and activities.

The journey had begun!

■ MANAGING CHANGE

By the end of 1984 the Council had embarked on a process with a clear commitment to a fundamental cultural change based around the principles of customer service — people and quality. They were not pious platitudes. Action programmes, training priorities, internal communications and budgets were tied into the process to ensure that the changes would be part of the organisation. Successes had to be achieved in terms of economic investment and in helping local businesses and start-ups. Development schemes had to be implemented and the pace of the Council had to increase. Regrettably there would be some casualties arising from the increased pace and requirements, but the staff responded to the greater urgency and purpose and to the openness and partnership which became the Braintree style of management.

I made it clear that a fundamental requirement would be the need for integration in pursuing a total management approach. From 1985 we began to integrate our policies and activities to reinforce the core values and principles. This was reinforced by a very simple objective — Braintree Council had to become the best Council in the country for its staff and for its customers.

A crucial element was the need to define and redefine accountabilities and to develop peoples' abilities. Formal performance appraisal systems were introduced for senior management in 1985 and all staff were brought into the system — which was geared around target setting, personal development plans and counselling — by 1988. (Performance-related pay systems for management and staff subsequently followed in 1986 and 1989 respectively.)

In parallel, the Council committed itself to putting 2 per cent of the payroll budget into training and development. That level of resource has been maintained despite financial pressures. The training function was completely reorganised with key staff appointed to deliver effective programmes geared to fulfilling the core values and the personal development programmes. Customer care training has always had the highest priority.

Fundamental to this approach was the requirement that we had a 'one-employee' policy. No-one should, in my view, be treated differently from another person in any aspect. The Council agreed to harmonise conditions for all employees, to deal positively with discrimination, to act responsibly towards its people and to aim to fulfil everyone's potential. There was a commitment to openness and partnership throughout the organisation.

Internal communications were overhauled and simplified. Regular briefings for all staff, a regular internal newsletter together with departmental newsletters were introduced. I made it a matter of principle that I should take an active part in the induction of all new staff and undertook regular briefings of all staff on major issues facing the Council. We commenced the process of simplifying the management structure by reducing tiers. By 1993 we had effectively reduced the number of tiers to four — Directors–Team Leaders–Technical Support–Administrative Support — and had continued to extend authority downwards to the front-end staff who are nearest to the customers.

All of these changes were subject to much consultation, involvement, monitoring and review with staff and their representatives. People in the organisation are the ones who develop the business and the systems that support the business and they must be involved.

Developing innovation, systems and new ways of working were encouraged by both formal and informal means. There were a number of objectives — to encourage people to understand, accept and enjoy continuous change — to develop better ways of serving customers and to develop better ways of working together. Evolutionary and continuous change probably characterised Braintree more than any other Local Authority during the 1980s.

Finally, within the process of integration we established a process of continuously involving our customers in the development and delivery of services. General and specific service surveys were introduced — many naive at first, but developing into sophisticated customer panels in the 1990s. New reception areas, one-stop shops for development, a regular Council newspaper, better designed and simple plain-English leaflets were introduced. The Council set up what was, and still probably is, the best customer complaints system in the United Kingdom with a clear process for complaints and effective reporting systems to senior management and members. Complaints were encouraged and given priority to ensure that customers develop confidence in the Council. The complaints system had three main aims; to help the Council become closer to our customer by 'active listening' to complaints; to make sure the Council provides more responsive services and management, and is seen to do so; to act as one form of monitoring for quality control purposes.

Marketing and promotion was set up to be an integral part of our customer focus. That is why, for instance, not only did we set a target of 60 per cent average turnout for District Council elections but also marketed and promoted the election process. The target for District elections was met in 1991 in two large wards with an overall average for the Council of 52 per cent. This represents between 5 per cent and 10 per cent better performance than comparable Councils. Marketing was integrated into our corporate management strategy because it has not only to consider the needs of our customers but also to communicate effectively the benefits of services to our customers.

■ SEEKING VALIDATION

Can cultural change be validated? Does it actually affect the delivery of services to customers or is it all a safe 'feel-good' factor incapable of measurement? Private sector businesses survive by performance and profit. The better performers bring added value through quality and customer service. Local government can only prosper if it is delivering, either directly or by using others, its services and functions in an effective and guaranteed manner. I therefore believe it is essential that the programmes, policies and outcomes involving customers and cultural change are capable of being measured and validated if possible by independent external bodies and by customers. That is why Braintree deliberately chose to subscribe to or participate in certain competitions, or invited external observers in order to enable us to validate the processes and changes being introduced.

Customer surveys have already been mentioned. I am firmly committed to asking people directly what they think about the way the Council services are delivered. Regular surveys provide reliable data and perceptions about services. They are an essential tool of political and of professional management especially where results are less than expected!

Bench-marking for our employee development programmes through assessment of results following training/education programmes was undertaken. The Council was the first District to commit itself to the requirements of Opportunity 2000. It was a pilot authority for the Investor in People award in 1991 and was the subject of a study by Edgar Wille and Chris Conway of the Ashridge Management Research Group. They discovered that

> there is an even wider sense in which Braintree as a District may be considered a learning organisation. Not only is work a learning and growing experience for the employees, but there is a sense of growth, improvement and learning about the whole business of Braintree. The Council members, the Council employees and the 'customers' served by the Council are part of one great partnership. And this is made explicit by the care with which communications are attended to by the Council.
>
> This is illustrated by what this study has described of the culture, mission, vision, service attitudes and business approach of Braintree. The authority is the enabler of wealth creation and the facilitator of quality of life development. It lies at the centre of a web of relationships between many of the elements which go to make up the community. It does not govern; it provides an environment conducive to such growth.
>
> Total population development and total business development provide the context in which there can be total employee development for those who work for the Council, or rather are employed to serve the population. The things which are done to serve the people who live in Braintree District and their impact on the populace, reinforce the learning of the employees as they strive to provide a professional service.
>
> The internal effort and the external response are independent, yet related means of employee growth and they sustain and feed each other. This is why much of this case study is taken up with the culture and philosophy of running the district, rather than restricting ourselves simply to what is conventionally thought of when we discuss training and development. The vision for the district is the basis of the mission of the employees.

(Wille, 1992).

The Council received the Investor in People award from the Secretary of State for Employment, David Hunt, at the beginning of 1993.

Performance Indicators and targets were set up initially in 1984 together with comparative testing against other local authorities. Committees were required to assess regularly the overall performance against the targets set at the start of the financial year.

Having used customer charters and contracts for some years we supported the concepts and ideals of the Citizen's Charter and were successful with two of our major services — Housing in 1992 and Planning in 1993. I do feel however that allowing individual services to be nominated rather undermines the value of the awards. It would seem to me that customers might be confused if one service got an award whilst another service within the same organisation was perceived by the public as being poor. Organisations should be judged corporately in the public sector and our submissions always put the individual service within the context of our management approach.

After being included by INLOGOV and the Local Government Management Board in the list of sixteen best managed Councils compiled by Local Authority Chief Executives, Braintree was selected to represent the United Kingdom in the prestigious Bertelsmann competition with ten other local authorities from around the world in October 1993. We made an impressive contribution, being particularly strong on quality, on developing and empowering people and for the customer culture which was seen as going right across the Council's services. British local authorities can compete on the world stage, but the fact that we raise so little of our finances locally compared with elsewhere does not make our system a model which other countries wish to emulate.

Finally in the context of validation I wish to refer to Quality and Quality Assurance. Quality was one of the core values from 1984, and we were probably the first Local Authority to express such a value. I felt and feel strongly today that the public sector should be pursuing quality with ruthlessness. Our public expect quality — not high cost, but services that always meet agreed performance standards. Clearly quality validation is an emotive issue since there is a strong view that services, particularly local government services, cannot be measured and in any event it will be expensive, time-consuming, etc. etc.

I fundamentally disagree. All processes can be measured, as can outputs and inputs even if inexactly. Their relevance is in engendering greater confidence in our customers and in the staff of local government.

We chose a process through the British Standard Institute to an international standard BS5750/ISO 9000 knowing that the outcome would only be a marker on the journey towards total quality. Within a period of under two years the Council had achieved the registration of all 70 services and expects to achieve Company-wide registration in 1994. In 1993 the Council also won the first Local Government Quality Award sponsored by P.A. Management Consultants and Solace (Society of Local Authority Chief Executives). Those awards recognise the steps the Council has taken to commit itself to the provision of services to guaranteed standards. The favourable response from the public and the involvement and enthusiasm of the departmental quality teams have given the Council a sound basis for the route to total quality management.

■ BRINGING IT TOGETHER

Validation and bench-marking are essential elements of performance management. The integration of policies and strategies is of equal importance if services are to be delivered corporately. One of the key tasks of a Chief Executive is to ensure that there is co-ordination and that the values of the organisation are reflected and maintained in the operations of the local authority.

Whilst we had been developing corporate strategies since the early 1980s there was still a gap between thinking and doing and between political and professional objectives. A mechanism was established using 2nd-tier officers and senior members, the Policy Action Group, whose task was to provide a corporate strategy and to act as a think-tank. Their first document — The Way Forward — provided a framework for integrating policies and this was subsequently developed through workshops, including residential workshops for Chairmen and Vice-Chairmen (drawn from all political parties). The refinement of the approach in 1992/93 incorporated a significant element of customer and external organisational input into the strategy.

Rigorous processes of planning control and review

The Council's overall direction is guided by the corporate strategy. The current strategy, approved in 1991, communicates in simple form:

- the Council's overall Statement of Purpose
- the Council's Vision of the District in the year 2000

Braintree's mission and vision of the future

Braintree has a simple statement of purpose, as a focus for the organisation. This sets out both the basic assumptions of the Council and the principles which guide the way we operate. The culture, the quality concern, the customer care, people development all flow from it. It states that the Council will:

- secure the best possible conditions for all who live in our district to lead a high quality of life
- focus on our customers and provide the quality services they require
- ensure all our staff are given opportunities for development, through training, appraisal, respect and support
- operate in a business-like manner with clear accountabilities, and ensure that targets are met

Braintree Council also has a Vision Statement, to act as an outward focus for the future direction of the Council.

That vision is of a District which:

1. is prosperous, clean, and socially balanced
2. meets the basic needs of all in our community for affordable housing and a range of housing choice, for worthwhile employment and for security, health and welfare services and personal mobility
3. retains, respects and enhances its attractive environment, particularly its countryside, villages, historic buildings and conservation areas
4. whilst retaining its traditional character provides a range of modern industry on quality business parks, encourages initiative and enterprise as well as quality shopping, arts, leisure, education and welfare facilities
5. has thriving town centres at Braintree, Witham and Halstead. Town centres which are safe, convenient, accessible and attractive to shoppers and those who live and work there
6. meets the demand for efficient movement of road traffic, but not at the expense of safety and environmental conditions (particularly in our towns and villages) or the neglect of public transport

7. meets the particular leisure, welfare and housing needs of the young and the elderly
8. exhibits a real pride and respect on the part of all sections of the community, public and private, in its surroundings, with clean and tidy streets, parks and open spaces and property that is well-maintained

Strategic objectives

Together, the Mission and Vision Statements provide the overall context for future Council action. That action is set out in a series of twelve strategic objectives which covered:

Democracy	Economic development	Housing
Customers' interests	Skills development	Leisure
Quality	Environment	Transport
Care of the disadvantaged	Health	Management

In leaflet format, these provide guidance to committees, councillors and managers, Council customers and others as to:

● the future scope and direction of the Council's activities
● the values and expectations of the organisation
● the framework for future policy and operation decisions

The Strategy also clarifies the corporate culture, management and staff development, improving systems and resource allocation, links with outside organisations, and stressing the need to fit the Council's structure to its strategy. It provides the framework for the Council's annual budget, for the business systems and committee annual plans and targets. It is the key to the performance management systems.

CORPORATE STRATEGY
Mission/vision
Corporate strategy
Service strategies
[HIPS, Local plan, Recreation, Manpower etc.]
Committee annual plans
Service/business plans
Committee targets
Individual targets/performance appraisal

Corporate business system

Priorities are translated into action through the corporate business system. This is an annual cycle which incorporates:

- An Annual Priorities Report setting out key areas for action across the Council over the following year, and setting guidelines concerning the overall budget
- Committee Annual Plans, which are annual statements of each Committee's intentions to achieve
  (i) the objectives set out in the Annual Priorities Report, and
  (ii) any service strategies and business plan priorities within the Committee's responsibilities.
- The annual budget decisions
- Committee targets to achieve the intentions set out in the Annual Priorities Report and Committee Annual Plans
- Committee quarterly monitoring of targets and performance
- annual review of achievements and a programme of service reviews to ensure that the Council is delivering effective services which meet its priorities and which represent value for money.

Let us look in more detail at the strategic objectives in respect of customers and customers' interests. These are:

To provide customers with adequate information and advice, and provide full opportunities for comment, complaint and redress.

To identify customer needs and expectations and develop policies and services which recognise and meet those needs.

Customer care is given top priority in the Council's activities and guides the approach to service development, internal organisation/systems, training and staff development.

Braintree's Citizen's Charter

The Council's Charter — Your Guarantee of Quality — is a major document setting out the Council's relationship with the people of the district, and outlining the essential standards of quality which we guarantee. It includes such commitments as:

- We believe in services which are delivered in a professional and efficient manner, and in being reliable and friendly towards our customers. Our employees are trained to be competent and professional in their work and to show that we are caring and trustworthy.
- The Council will listen to the views of people living in the district and will offer opportunities for their views to be put in public.
- The Council will continue to bring discussion and debate of local issues to the places affected by these decisions. Committee meetings and opportunities for consultation will be brought to your local towns so that you can choose to take part if you wish.

Braintree's Charter is widely publicised. Charter leaflets are available at all the Council's outlets, and a simpler version was incorporated in the Council's newspaper — *The Reporter* — delivered free to every household in the District.

Two key groups of customers have a separate Charter: industrial/commercial tenants and council house tenants.

The Tenants' Charter is written in plain English and sets out general tenancy conditions and provides other useful information for tenants, embracing all the housing services offered, including housing advice, the Carecall elderly persons' alarm system, etc. It specifically incorporates advice on:

- the detailed service standards being offered (how long repairs will take etc.)
- what rights the tenant has if standards are not met
- how to go about making suggestions and complaints.

The Tenants' Charter is regularly updated and delivered to existing tenants and handed to all new tenants as part of the 'signing up' procedure for the house. A 'Welcome to your new home' pack as part of the customer focus strategy is under development. This will provide useful information to new occupiers, will include the Tenants' Charter, and will be followed up with a 'Welcome to your new home' card.

Customer contracts

In addition to these major corporate documents, detailed standards for selected services are set out in individual customer contracts. In a simple leaflet, these explain:

- relevant customer information about the service provided
- the precise standards our customers can expect
- what to do if things go wrong

Following a successful experiment with a small number of customer contracts, it is intended to cover all appropriate services that the Council delivers.

Market research and other forms of 'active listening'

The Council actively carries out market research to learn directly from our customers. This takes the form of different types of questionnaires, customer satisfaction cards, test marketing, public forums, customer panels, exhibitions, etc:

The Council's Customer Survey Card is available at all the Council's outlets, and invites immediate feedback on the service customers have just received in their dealings with the Council.

The Customer First Suggestion Scheme invites our customers to suggest ways in which the Council can provide better services. Every suggestion the Council receives is seen personally by the Chief Executive, who replies direct.

The Council's Question Time initiative offers citizens an open invitation to ask a question, or make a statement, at the Area Committee meetings, on any matter of Council business or local concern. The aim is to involve the public in Council meetings, and open up decision-making to more popular scrutiny. For this reason, Area Committees meet at convenient locations for the individual communities they serve.

From sources such as these, there now exists a considerable body of information about our customers' attitudes to the Council's policies and performance, which is being added to continually.

Communication with our customers

The Council is committed to providing a full range of informatic in plain English about the Council's activities.

The Council circulates an A to Z of Council services. This brocht — *The Quality of Life Catalogue* — sets out the main contacts from 1 customer's point of view, with sections on Your Health, Your Leis Time, Your Home, etc. This is supplemented by the quarte newspaper — *The Reporter* — which provides topical informatior Council services, events and initiatives.

Courteous and efficient staff

Braintree Council is obsessed with customer care:

- At induction sessions, which take place for all staff, the Chief Executive reinforces the Council's commitment to customers and quality.
- A programme of customer care training is available to all staff. Core training in customer care (telephone answering, etc.) is attended by all staff, with thorough training offered to front-line staff in detailed aspects of customer care, such as handling difficult customers.
- Except in particularly sensitive cases, staff are encouraged to identify themselves personally in letters and on the telephone. Name badges are worn by all staff.
- Uniforms are provided for receptionists and front-line staff, including skilled and operational staff.

Management for performance in a customer-driven culture requires a co-ordinated and comprehensive approach. It is no good being excellent in one area if the customers are let down elsewhere. In Braintree, over a decade we developed a 'Total Management Approach' which ties together all of the threads which create a quality organisation. Our experience has shown that unless a corporate strategy reinforces the primacy of quality and customer care, unless there is a firm political commitment, and unless the processes and structure are in place to translate these good intentions into action, much of the effort will be dissipated or wrongly directed.

■ LESSONS

Good organisations are characterised by their ability to learn from experience and to evolve continuously, and to refine and improve the manner in which they work. There are no set rules, but senior managers need to give themselves time to reflect on what is happening, and clearly need to ensure that there are adequate formal and informal listening arrangements.

It requires a commitment from managers to ensure there is an 'open' style of communications and essentially to ensure that they live the culture of the organisation. As Tom Peters has said: "It's not that staff don't take any notice of what the manager does, it's that they do!" (Peters and Waterman, 1982).

It is about leadership and giving people a sense of direction and purpose. Essentially it is about the seven P's.

Purpose

People need to know where an organisation is going, what its goals and objectives are and what is expected of them.

Performance

All organisations are here to perform, to achieve results. It is the raison d'être of all organisations to achieve the objectives laid down by, in local government's case, the elected members.

Pride

If you know where you are going and achieve targets people will take pride in an organisation. It is a cultural issue and one that is much neglected in Local Government. Highly motivated people can achieve far more, and one of the key, if not the key role of senior management and indeed members, is to ensure that people are proud of what they do and what the organisation achieves.

Perseverance

Change cannot happen overnight. Cultural change to create a customer-driven organisation does not happen instantly. Too many managers believe if they sloganise the office a magical change will appear — note the influx of 'The Customer is King' notices that appear.

You have to work and work at creating and sustaining value changes. There is no end point, no peak to say you have achieved the state of management bliss. Managing a change which has been described as a journey with no end, requires particular skills and perseverance.

Partnership

No-one is going to change local government practice on their own. It requires the involvement of many people both inside and outside the authority. Partnership describes a condition in which everyone has a stake — customers/citizens, members, staff, unions, businesses and government. It requires everyone to have a commitment to making partnership work.

Participation

Equally participation is about creating a stake in the business and owning/sharing the values and the culture. More fundamentally it is about empowering *all* people to take charge of their part of the business and allowing them to fulfil their potential as far as is possible. You must not short-change the people in your business.

People

Last but most important, local government and business is about people. Everything we do requires an individual or teams of individuals to do it. The public sector and service businesses are essentially 'people' driven with services usually being delivered on a one-to-one basis to customers. It is not about the biggest/fastest computer or the largest refuse freighter. They all require people to operate them. A customer culture is about people and how well they are trained, motivated and led on a continuous basis. The essential success of Braintree is how we trained the people who worked for the Council.

The philosophy is best described by Akio Morita, the Chairman of Sony Corporation:

> 'No theory, or plan, or government policy will make a business a success;
> that can only be done by People'.

■ THE FUTURE

Can cultural and value-driven organisations survive the pressures and instability inherent in the local governments of the United Kingdom?

It is an issue of great concern since those pressures are increasing and many of them are directed at the very nature of local government. Functional changes, compulsory competitive tendering, local government review, and reduced financial accountabilities might suggest local authorities and managers should batten down the hatches and switch on the automatic pilot — the 'why bother' syndrome.

In my view the opposite should apply. It is even more necessary now to gain customer and citizen support for local government. Not just because local democracy is at stake but to ensure that our customers get the quality and range of services they require. In the same way that it is a maxim of marketing not to reduce advertising when times are tough it is, in my view, even more essential for local authorities to address the concerns of its customers and to become even more responsive and to deliver quality services when times are tough. You neglect your people and your customers at your peril and voting percentages in Local Government elections show how far Local Government has neglected its voters.

Clearly I can be accused of idealism since, for many, the 'decline' of local government is due to the way central government influences and interferes with local government. I am realistic enough to know that local government will not flourish whilst central government holds it generally in disdain and wants to prescribe and prohibit behaviour. But putting the blame totally on one side only will not change things. I have called elsewhere for a new approach from central government and for a proper definition of roles. To ensure that there is effective dialogue and partnership with central government requires a commitment from local government too. That commitment must be to ensure the better management of people and a greater commitment from managers towards the values of a customer culture, quality, together with the Citizen's Charter principles.

■ REFLECTIONS

I have described how a customer-driven organisation can be effective and successful but being successful does not, in the UK, always bring credit. For instance all of our local government legislation assumes the worst and the acts and circulars are framed to restrict or stop actions. A huge amount of creative energy has been put in by local authorities to circumvent that legislation; energy which could have been more productively used in developing better customer services. Often where innovations have been implemented successfully they have been carried out by bloody-minded and determined people who have not been prepared to accept prescriptive legislation.

Successes ought to be imitated, applauded and rewarded. Central government needs to trust local authorities and should be aiming to give them freedom to operate within a defined and agreed partnership. The strong message we gained from the Bertelsmann Prize was that such trust operates elsewhere in the world. Given that trust and freedom there would be a renaissance in local government — a flowering of the huge potential that exists, probably less central government expenditure and more accountability to its citizens.

If we do not make these changes why should any local authority want to achieve excellence? Indeed why do we need League Tables if there is no reward or promotion for the best authorities and no real sanction against the mediocre? Why should any local authority aim to be good, or different or entrepreneurial or innovative when they can still get their grants and tax income no matter how well they perform?

The issues I have raised concern the purpose, identity and performance of local government. By creating a customer- and quality-driven culture I expected there would be higher levels of involvement, motivation and performance together with increased customer support. What the Council and the Community received was beyond my expectations. The commitment by the staff at Braintree was extraordinary and to see people producing high quality work and to see people develop has been a privilege for me. The awards the Council has achieved are theirs and there is nothing that their highly motivated people cannot achieve.

As Edgar Wille and Chris Conway pointed out:

We might not immediately associate total quality management with the running of a large local authority in Essex (UK), but as Chris Conway and I interviewed employees, ranging from the chief executive to a refuse collector, we found the question of quality paramount.

The District slogan is 'Braintree Means Business', and when we went to see how they were doing, we found that everyone we spoke to who worked for the Council had the same general idea. They all spoke of the 'customers'. Everyone we met — telephone operator, chief executive, refuse collector, receptionist, personnel director, group accountant, swimming pool manager, planner, environmental health manager — shared the same approach.

For the past few years, Braintree has been at the forefront of management in the public sector. Our approach is based on a belief that local authority staff, given support, development and motivation, can achieve extraordinary results. The performance and high standards achieved, the partnership between the Council and the community, and the partnership between members and staff, provide an indication of what could be achieved by all public sector organisations if they are prepared to change and to embrace a total management approach.

■ REFERENCES

PETERS, T. and WATERMAN, R. H. (1982) *In Search of Excellence*, New York, Harper & Row.
WILLE, E. (1992) *Quality: Achieving Excellence*, London, Century Business.

Author's acknowledgement

There are many members of staff at Braintree District who have made the journey successful, but I would particularly mention Rob Atkins. My thanks also go to John Stewart, Michael Clarke, Mark Sheldrake, Gerry Stoker, John Bennington, Roger Paine and John Downs for their support and encouragement. Special thanks also to Hilary Cropper from FI Group plc and Alex Orr from Expamet plc who helped me learn how to motivate and develop people.

Chapter 3

CASE STUDY: THE BENEFITS AGENCY — CLAIMANTS AS CUSTOMERS

by Tom Ling

■ THE PURPOSE OF THIS CHAPTER

In this chapter we have the opportunity to explore the issues surrounding the customer focus in the public sector with the help of a case study. Case studies are useful because, by drawing upon one agency or sequence of events, we gain a sharper sense of how wider processes and relationships produce specific consequences. Case studies are not usually selected simply because they are 'typical' in some straightforward sense. Rather, their value lies in their capacity to enrich our understanding in some important respect. In this sense, the Benefits Agency is a useful case study because it lies at the intersection of key aspects of the customer focus such as how 'the customer' is defined, what the parameters are within which customer choice operates, and how Charters might shape customer choice. These questions, in turn, prompt a consideration of how the dynamic of change may alter the whole project of which the customer focus is a central part.

This chapter starts with a consideration of the origins and context of the customer focus before locating the emergence of the Benefits Agency within this context. We then consider the consequences of the customer focus for the Benefits Agency and discuss how this might produce tensions between the 'citizen' and the 'customer' and how a redefined view of 'the customer' might address these tensions. Finally and briefly, on the basis of the arguments presented, we consider the prospects for the customer focus in the final years of this century.

◼ THE ORIGINS AND CONTEXT OF THE CUSTOMER FOCUS

The origins of the customer focus in public sector management are diverse and complex. To some extent, these often conflicting origins are reflected in the expectations which surround the customer focus today. Reflecting on these origins prompts two thoughts; the first is that not all of these expectations can be simultaneously satisfied, and the second is that the 'customer focus' may be inherently unstable. In this section we examine some of the most important origins of the customer focus before going on to examine the Benefits Agency in this light. These origins are considered below under the three headings of:

- the revival of market-based thinking

- concern with controlling the professionals and the old Establishment

- concern with controlling public expenditure

The revival of market-based thinking

This is not the place to attempt a wholesale consideration of the revival in the 1970s of certain nineteenth-century liberal arguments concerning the efficacy of the market and the reorientation of these arguments towards the problems of the late twentieth century. However, certain aspects of these ideas contributed to the emphasis on the customer focus which we find in the 1990s.

The conception of 'the customer' which this entailed has had a significant impact on the implementation of the customer focus. At the heart of this approach is a focus on the primacy of the rational, choosing individuals who both understand and express their needs, and can calculate the best way to maximise their own need-satisfaction (*see* Buchanan, 1968; Friedman, 1980; and Hayek, 1986). This is in contrast to both traditional conservative and more reformist claims which suggest that as individuals we tend to have shifting preferences, one-sided conceptions of our own interests and needs, and that we tend to clarify and develop these conceptions through our interactions with others rather than through a process of introverted calculation. It is likely that when in contact with different public services individuals conform more to one model than to the other; but it is a central part of the argument of this chapter that a customer focus which systematically adopts only the former model of the customer tends to deny access to significant sections of society.

The focus upon this sort of individualism had two important consequences for public sector managers. The first is to be found in the public choice critique of public sector bureaucracies (*see* Niskanen, 1971; and Mitchell, 1988). According to this approach, if we assume that individuals are self-motivated and rational we should not assume that the moment they become employed by a public agency they suddenly become altruistic and dedicated only to the greater public good. Therefore, managers within public agencies will seek to maximise their own self-interests, and this will manifest itself by managers seeking to maximise both the budget under their control and the size of the staff group working under them. The only way to impose a discipline upon public sector managers, therefore, is to expose them to market forces and to competition.

This critique of public sector bureaucracy dovetails neatly with the other feature of free-market individualism; its emphasis upon the market as a co-ordinating mechanism superior in several respects to bureaucratic mechanisms (this is an argument which in Britain is especially associated with Hayek). According to this view, markets allow for a diversity of needs to be satisfied in a way which maximises the level of need satisfaction in society. Bureaucracies could never hope systematically to emulate such diversity of provision and to match it to the diversity of needs because they lack the necessary information. Therefore, the preferred alternative to the public bureaucracy is the market.

Bringing these arguments together had immediate consequences for the way in which public sector management was talked about and assessed in the 1980s. Broadly, there were two different outcomes. The first was to sell public assets into private hands which (it was hoped) would be more responsive to market mechanisms. The second was to introduce changes designed to make public sector managers behave as if they were in a market environment. These mechanisms include the use of internal markets and contract-like relationships operating within public organisations and between different public sector cost centres.

In the first instance, getting public sector managers to behave more like private sector managers involved the importation of ideas and personnel from the private sector to reshape the membership and calculations of crucial agencies within the public sector. Sir Roy Griffiths, for example, was brought in from the retailing sector to produce a report on the Health Service in which it was stated that, despite some differences, 'The clear similarities between NHS management and business management are much more important' (DHSS, 1983). Similarly, Sir Derek Rayner was brought in to conduct reviews of the working practices of public sector managers which were judged largely against the criteria of the private sector. At the forefront of trying to generalise and stabilise these changes throughout the public sector was the Audit Commission. Common to these techniques was an emphasis on decentralising budgets; the construction of contract-like relationships within the public sector (including the responses to compulsory competitive tendering); a concern to establish clear objectives and to assess performance against indicators based on these objectives; and to link performance (defined in relation to the performance indicators) to reward.

This strategy was not without its successes but significant problems quickly emerged. The use of performance indicators and contract-like relationships as a sort of government by remote control (as opposed to 'hands-on' line management) led to the need to construct targets and objectives which could then be monitored and managed. In terms of contract compliance and performance indicators, ambiguity is reduced where clear-cut, quantitative measures are used, and this was, indeed, the preferred option in most parts of the public sector. However, such clear-cut quantitative measures often failed to capture the complex purposes of policies. Thus targets and the intentions of policy-makers on occasions came adrift. A spectacular example of this came in 1993 when the Child Support Agency was given cash targets of the amounts to be saved by the Treasury as a result of compelling absent fathers to pay more towards the up-keep of their children. The result was that the Agency prioritised its pursuit of the most accessible fathers (usually the ones who were already making contributions) and not the errant fathers whom (apparently) the Government had in mind when it launched the Agency.

It was partly in response to this situation that, towards the end of the 1980s there emerged an increasing emphasis upon the customer focus in particular and quality in general. 'Quality' was an attempt to address the problems created by depending upon quantitative indices of management success. In the sense used here it relates to the establishment of pre-set criteria against which performance will be monitored, measured and rewarded. However, as Pollitt (1993a) has demonstrated in relation to differing constructions of 'quality' in the NHS, there are considerable conflicts amongst managers, doctors, patients, and nurses over how 'quality' is defined. Indeed, in an influential approach proposed by Robert Maxwell of the Kings Fund, the diversity of elements which shaped quality is emphasised, even celebrated (see Maxwell, 1984, 1992). As implemented in East Anglia, the approach to quality embraces six dimensions; effectiveness, acceptability, efficiency, access, equity and relevance. It is accepted from the outset that there will be conflicts and trade-offs amongst these. Furthermore, under the terms of The Priorities and Planning Guidance for 1994/95 issued under cover of EL(93)54, all NHS Authorities and Trusts are required to 'demonstrate an organisation-wide approach to quality'. It is in relation to such conflicts that we should locate the 'customer focus'. The customer focus, in part, is an attempt to relate the definition of quality to the experience of the customer and thus to direct provision towards their diverse choices.

However, the subtleties and complexities involved in defining quality cannot be resolved with reference to 'the customer' in this way. There are at least three problems with trying to use a free-market conception of the customer in this way. The first is that it is not always clear who 'the customer' is. In higher education, for example, when a University offers a BSc in nursing which is partly funded by Health Authority money, is 'the customer' the individual student, the Health Authority, the Higher Education Funding Council, the wider public (who, through their taxes, pay for the course and who provide the future patients of the trained nurses and therefore have a particular interest in the quality of their education), or is it in some sense the Government? A similar problem arises in the process of care assessment where both informal carers and those in need of care are in some sense customers but with different needs. It is in the nature of many publicly provided goods that 'the customer' is elusive.

The second problem arises when a 'customer focus' leads to a lack of co-ordination between public agencies and even to inter-agency rivalry and this, in turn, leads to manifest inefficiencies. For example, the Audit Commission (1989) noted that a market-led training system made it difficult to plan a coherent strategy for meeting future training needs in a changing labour market. This can become even more of a problem where decentralised budgets lead to agencies externalising their costs onto other agencies wherever possible (although if money follows the customer this should not happen so frequently).

A third problem arises from the conception of 'the customer' embodied in free-market thinking. We have already noted the difficulty associated with identifying who the customer is in any given situation. But in addition, it is only by investing the term with a generous degree of vagueness that it becomes possible to use the term 'customer' equally to describe individuals buying apples at the corner shop, buying services from a monopolistic private sector provider, being bought services by a local authority from a choice of competitive providers, and being provided with a service by a monopolistic public sector agency.

This is not to say that the customer focus should not be pursued. However, we should recognise that there are problems associated with it and, to sum up the argument so far, three have been suggested. The first is that it is vague and inconsistent. Indeed, the widespread support for it may reflect the fact that different meanings can be read into it. The second is that there are few unproblematic customers of the sort implied by free-market thinking. The third is that there is no guarantee that social efficiency will be maximised. One is reminded of the story of the doctor whose patients liked him greatly but who died young.

So far, we have discussed the origins of customer focus as if they were largely, or even exclusively, about technical efficiency. This, however, is not always supported by the evidence. The origins of the dynamic which was to lead to the customer focus lie not only in technical concerns of efficiency but also in the concern with the extent to which professionals and Establishment bureaucrats had appropriated to themselves power over policy-making and the allocation of resources.

Concern with controlling the professionals and the old Establishment

From the 1960s onwards, politicians from all sides and sections of the Conservative Party (in particular) were becoming increasingly concerned about how to control the public sector. This concern about the inability of the central state to control the rest of the state system was reflected in official statements at least as far back as the early 1970s (HMSO, 1970; HMSO, 1971). But it was also apparent in the growing concern about the alleged uncontrollability of public sector professionals. Indeed, the whole point about being a professional is that one is accountable to a professional body rather than to the government of the day. There is little doubt that within the state, professional interests exerted a considerable influence over policy formulation and implementation (Dunleavy, 1981). Concern about this was expressed by the marxist left and other radicals but politically it was the Conservative Party which aligned itself most clearly with 'the people' against the old self-interested state as part of its more populist approach following Mrs Thatcher's elevation to the leadership of the Party (see Hall and Jacques (eds), 1983). This concern, especially under Mrs Thatcher's premiership, was extended to the old-style public school-Oxbridge senior civil servant, reflecting what appears to be Mrs Thatcher's personal distaste for this sort of Establishment figure (*see* Hennessy, 1989, pp. 632–3).

Therefore, *as part* of the attempt to regain control over the public sector it became necessary to challenge the power which professionals had secured over policy-making, policy implementation and, in general, the allocation of public resources. In this sense, public *administrators* were to become public sector *managers* with an extended brief which was eventually to include the possibility of the right to manage the professionals (the implications of this are dealt with extensively in Clarke *et al.* (eds), 1993). At the same time, and as a necessary part of this process, the recipients of welfare were to change from being *clients* (or patients, or claimants, etc.) and become *customers*. Under the emerging regime the purpose of public sector managers was to go beyond their pre-1979 brief of ensuring probity and natural justice to a new brief which was concerned with allocative and productive efficiency. The extent to which they have been able to do this has depended, amongst other things, on the extent to which professionals have been able to defend their power base.

Whether this formed part of a pre-arranged strategy or whether it simply emerged as an outcome of the politics of the 1980s is unclear. In any case, the process remains incomplete. In cases such as the Health Service, the Griffiths Report (DHSS, 1983) stopped short of giving managers power over doctors and even the reforms following *Working for Patients* (HMSO, 1989) did not fully consolidate the power of management. Elsewhere, the degree of autonomy of professionals and semi-professionals has been more effectively reduced, as in the case of social workers.

The attempt to replace professional judgement with a more accountable and rationalised managerial system was always going to be more difficult in some public services than others. It is likely that the problems of control which led to the attempt to bring professionals under stronger managerial direction will not disappear as the power of professionals is weakened; the problems will be displaced to reappear in a different guise at the heart of the customer focus.

Concern with controlling public expenditure

The third element shaping the customer focus is the objective of controlling public expenditure. From the earliest attempts to construct a new managerialism for the public sector through to the development of the 'customer focus' more recently, reforms have been associated with the objective of saving money (or, at least, containing any increases in expenditure). Downward pressure upon public sector expenditure is not an inevitable feature of the customer focus but the consequence of this close association has led public sector managers to adopt narrower conceptions of the customer than, perhaps, they would often like. The range of choices available to the customer has therefore been narrow and, as is argued below, where the choice of exit (i.e. refusing to buy a service) is not a real option and the exercise of voice (i.e. being able to influence the nature of the services provided) is constrained by expenditure limits, the radicalism of the customer focus will be limited.

Adding to this pressure has been the cost of establishing and then managing new financial and management systems such as the internal market in the NHS, CCT in local government, or the purchaser/provider split in community care. These not only increase overall costs but remove resources from the point of service delivery and lead to the possibility of yet further tension between service deliverers and managers. The 'customer focus' involves a commitment to ensuring the widespread provision of information regarding the availability of services, equal access to these services, providing mechanisms for the public's voices to be heard, and the creation of a meaningful complaints procedure. If these commitments are to succeed the machinery needed to make them work will be expensive to operate, and these costs may be hard to defend in the context of, say, a local authority budget-setting meeting.

■ THE ARGUMENT SO FAR

This brief consideration of the context of the customer focus in the public sector demonstrates that it is not without its tensions, ambiguities and contradictions. At the risk of over-simplifying, it may be said to form part of the third of three waves of management fashion since the 1960s. In the first, public sector administrators were more concerned with probity, financial accountability and administering a public sector in which professionals exercised substantial (some would say overwhelming) influence. This style of management was widely perceived to be breaking down in the 1970s, and in the 1980s the Conservative governments proposed their own blend of free-market arguments combined with a determination to get a grip on both expenditure and the activities of professionals and the old Establishment bureaucrats. For a variety of reasons, this system was perceived to be incapable of meeting all of the policy objectives of the 1980s (*see* Pollitt, 1993b) and by the beginning of the 1990s, the customer focus in particular and quality in general, had emerged as touchstones of public sector management. In order to explore at least some of these issues further, we are now going to examine the case of the Benefits Agency.

■ *NEXT STEPS* AND THE BENEFITS AGENCY

The processes outlined above had particular nuances and distinctive qualities in the case of social security. In the first place, there was no well-organised and powerful professional body to overcome. For this reason it was possible to develop some of the systems of financial and managerial controls earlier and more quickly than was the case in, say health. Secondly, social security was not only the responsibility of a central government department but it was also directly administered by that department (unlike those services which are administered locally). Thirdly, whilst there were, by the 1990s, some twenty million people in receipt of some form of transfer payment through the social security system, they were poorly organised and did not represent a coherent group with a strong perception of shared interests. For all three of these reasons developments in social security policy ought, other things being equal, to represent a relatively unalloyed manifestation of Government intentions; it is managed directly by the central government, there are no powerful professional organisations controlling the delivery of services, and pressure and interest groups are poorly organised. The dates relevant to the emergence of the customer focus in the Benefits Agency are briefly outlined in Figure 3.1 (the significance of these events are dealt with in the following sections).

1982   DHSS publish the Operational Strategy
1988   Implementation of the Operational Strategy begins
1988   DHSS publishes *The Business of Service* a report which is highly critical of the existing management of benefits
1988   Publication of the *Next Steps* report
1991   Benefits Agency is launched
1991   Official launch of the Citizens' Charter by the Prime Minister
1992   Benefits Agency publishes its own *Customer Charter*

Figure 3.1

It is not surprising that central governments were anxious to get a grip on social security expenditure. By the 1990s it accounted for 30.4 per cent of all UK public expenditure, that is, £58.6 billion or 9.8 per cent of GDP. Over 60,000 staff delivered benefits through an administrative system which cost some £2 billion to run (Benefits Agency, 1992). From the Conservative Party coming to power in 1979 to 1991/92 real expenditure on social security rose by 44 per cent. Bradshaw (1991) estimates an increase of £8.3 billion by the end of the 1990s assuming no policy changes and 5 per cent unemployment. Therefore we can safely assume that downward pressure on these increases will be applied wherever possible. It would be a mistake, however, to regard the changes in the management of social security (and the customer focus in particular) as simply 'window dressing' designed to divert attention from cuts in entitlements.

As early as 1982 the Department of Health and Social Security outlined its Operational Strategy which was to involve the computerisation of the administration of social security (DHSS, 1982). The statement outlined three main objectives: to improve efficiency and reduce costs, to improve the quality of service to the public, and to improve the working experience of social security staff. Thus the customer focus (although not in name) was already there in the early 1980s. Implementation of the Operational Strategy was not begun until April 1988 but by this time events were unfolding rapidly which affected the administration of social security, and in the same year the DHSS produced *The Business of Service*, a highly critical report on social security administration (DHSS, 1988).

The publication of this report (and the language used) suggests a number of important points. The first is that, under the impact of Griffiths, Rayner, and the other initiatives in public sector management, there had been a shift in the culture of report writing in the public sector. Far from any criticisms being hedged around, it had become acceptable (indeed, almost obligatory) to criticise existing management practice. The second point is that the language of the criticisms (even more clearly than the 1982 Report) is one of a 'customer focus'. The criticisms concentrated on the length of times claimants had to wait to have their claims processed, or to wait for an interview in the office, or how often payments were inaccurate, and so forth. The extent to which thinking in the Department of Social Security had evolved is shown by their general support for the 'whole person' concept (according to which the various social security entitlements of each customer should be dealt with in one place and at one time) (*see* Adler and Sainsbury, 1990). Whilst the customer focus is often linked to Charters (and thus to John Major) it is clear that the thinking in many areas of public management were already moving in this direction. The third point is that the criticisms dovetailed with the thinking going on in the Treasury which culminated in the production of the *Next Steps* report, also in 1988 (Efficiency Unit, 1988).

The *Next Steps* report recognised that the devolving downwards of non-strategic decisions within the civil service under the Financial Management Initiative had failed to produce the expected transformations in efficiency. In part, it was argued, this was because the old departmental structure kept drawing the central government into non-strategic decision-taking. In consequence, the report argued, the civil service should be broken up into separate agencies, each of which would be run by a chief executive who would be given his or her strategic orientation by the Framework Agreement between the agency and the central department. In this way all non-strategic decisions would be the responsibility of the chief executive (although quite where this leaves the constitutional convention of ministerial responsibility is uncertain). The civil service would thus be reduced to a strategic core responsible for drawing up Framework Agreements, monitoring their achievement, and (in collaboration with the Agency) devising policies for the future.

In this way the ethos of a unitary civil service within which civil servants had job security for life, a clear career pattern, and an interest in probity and a close attention to following rule-governed processes is challenged by the ethos of managers moving in and out of agencies (and the public sector as a whole), following opportunistic career patterns, and having an interest in outcomes and not processes (usefully summarised in Kelly, 1991, p. 182; *see also* Ling, 1993). To the extent that the old ethos has been overwhelmed, the traditional British Establishment has been weakened.

For the administration of social security, the immediate consequence of *Next Steps* was the creation of five separate agencies as outlined in Figure 3.2.

Department of Social Security Headquarters

BENEFITS AGENCY	CONTRIBUTIONS AGENCY	IT SERVICES AGENCY	RESETTLEMENT AGENCY	CHILD SUPPORT AGENCY
Launch: April 1991	Launch: April 1991	Launch: April 1990	Launch: May 1989	Launch: April 1993

Source: HMSO 1991a, p. 35.

Figure 3.2 The organisation of the Department of Social Security

■ THE IMPACT OF AGENCY STATUS ON THE CUSTOMER FOCUS IN SOCIAL SECURITY

The resources committed to the customer focus in the Benefits Agency by 1992 were considerable. In April 1991 a 'Have Your Say' leaflet was designed to facilitate customer feedback. From that time, the Chief Executive of the Agency has held six-monthly meetings with the National Association of Citizens Advice Bureaux, and six-monthly meetings with the British Association of Social Workers. The Agency liaises with the Commission for Racial Equality, and claims to have established 'good working relationships' with the Royal National Institute for the Blind, Child Poverty Action Group, Campaign for the Homeless and Roofless, Age Concern and the National Council for One-Parent Families (*see* Benefits Agency, 1992, p. 11). In addition, all Units had appointed Customer Service Managers and in January 1992 its own Customer Charter was launched. Corporate dress and name badges were introduced and facilities used by the public improved. In addition, a 'high-level' target for 1991/92 was to ensure that 85 per cent of BA customers were satisfied with the service they received (*see* Benefits Agency, 1992).

Two parts of the Framework Agreement establishing the objectives of the Benefits Agency were particularly relevant to encouraging this approach. The first is the achievement of progress towards the implementation of the Operational Strategy and the second is the achievement of customer satisfaction. Let us look at these in turn.

The Operational Strategy is relevant to the customer focus because one of its stated purposes is the improvement of the quality of service to the public (DHSS, 1982, p. 1). However, as we have already suggested, within the phrase 'quality of service' there is room for conflict and differences in emphasis. As Adler (1992) has shown, at least three differing interpretations are available. It might mean the cost-effectiveness of the service, it might mean 'quality' in the particular sense of a professional–client relationship with power remaining with a paternalistic agency, or it might mean the clear articulation of legally binding rights and ready forms of redress where these rights are not met. These tensions are well recognised amongst those responsible for the operation of the system. In 1991 the Chief Adjudication Officer noted 'the tension between good adjudication and the need to clear claims quickly', adding that these tensions were 'still evident' (HMSO, 1991b, p.5). As things turned out, according to Adler, 'the interests of the government were put first, those of the staff next and those of claimants last' (Adler, 1992, p.4).

The consequence of this 'ranking' of conflicting interests is that administrative savings tended to be prioritised over the quality of service whilst the 'quality of service' was itself given a narrow meaning. For example, the Benefits Agency commits itself to being courteous, fair, confidential, private and accessible. It sets clearance time targets for payments, and it promises to consult with the representatives of ethnic minorities and disabled people. These are all highly desirable. But quality might also concern other issues such as take-up rates, for example. Some of the most vulnerable groups are likely to have low take-up rates for certain benefits. Equally, the appeals procedure has to go through the Benefits Agency and many less assertive claimants (or customers) might find this difficult. Some have suggested the need to provide other agencies to whom claimants could go for support (*see* Randall, 1992). These could be new agencies (such as a Benefits ombudsman) or empowered existing agencies (such as local authorities). These would project a sense of advocacy on behalf of the claimant which the Benefits Agency itself could not achieve. Indeed, one could imagine a 'mixed economy of advocacy' in which a variety of supports would be available to those who had grievances against public agencies, leaving the customers free to choose the form of advocacy which they felt to be most appropriate. The performance indicators needed to measure this sort of target would be different from the existing ones.

This raises the fundamental question of the extent to which a full embracing of a customer focus is achievable within the *Next Steps* structure (or, indeed other such quasi-contractual relationships). To this question there are two plausible answers. The first is that the way in which *Next Steps* has been set up undermines the customer focus in significant ways. The second is a more guarded claim that at least some of the fundamental objectives of the customer focus can be achieved by the more complete application of some of the principles underlying the *Next Steps* Report. In other words, it would be necessary to give the *Next Steps* structure a more radical form. These claims are explored in the following paragraphs.

The first claim is also relevant to every public agency which is responsible to a 'core' for delivering a service. (In this sense the 'core' is the department which sets the budget and lays down the contract-like requirements to be adhered to by the service provider.) If the core does not reorganise then it is unlikely to be able to make the system work effectively on the grounds that the organisation and ethos required to make an old-style departmental structure work are different from those associated with quality assurance, monitoring, establishing targets and so forth. Metcalfe and Richards (1990, p.235) are among many observers who detect a significant failing in the core government departments in this respect. More serious than this, however, is the fact that if the tensions and conflicts inherent within the Operational Strategy are not expressly addressed, and in a way which produces a commitment to a clearly defined customer focus, then the customer focus will tend to be compromised in favour of economy or managerial ease. It is an unfortunate feature of the current debate over the impact of the Citizen's Charter that it has drawn attention towards the agencies which are responsible for delivering the service when at least as much attention should be directed towards the core.

The failure to reorganise the core has led some to argue that the customer focus will make little difference. According to this view, it is convenient for central government to insist on the primacy of the customer focus, to blame local delivery agencies when this is not achieved, whilst failing to provide the resources which delivery agencies require. Below, I wish to argue that for better and for worse, the customer focus is not a sham. But for the moment I wish to argue that it is possible to develop further the customer focus only within a particular set of political conditions.

The limits to the customer focus in the Benefits Agency are only in part due to constrained resources. They are also due to accepting a particular conception of 'the customer' which draws heavily on the free-market theory outlined at the start of this chapter. According to this conception of the customer, it is sufficient to make information freely available to individual consumers for them to make the necessary calculations to act in their own best interests. As a result of these individual actions, something approaching the greatest good for the greatest number (or the 'public interest') will be secured. In relation to benefits, there are at least two problems with this argument.

The first is that we know that not all of the Benefits Agency's customers are such fully empowered individuals waiting to assert their right to know and their right to benefit. Amongst the most needy there are many who are not even aware of their rights to benefit. There are even more who would be unwilling to use the Claimants' Charter to assert their right to appeal. For such people alternative mechanisms are necessary if they are to be genuinely empowered. A system based upon the equal rights of all to assert their rights is highly desirable but it will always benefit those most capable of asserting themselves within that system. Public sector managers with a responsibility for the customer focus cannot avoid addressing the questions posed by the free-market conception of individual action

The second problem is that by individuating claimants into rightful separate customers, collective responses to social problems are undermined. Without in any sense wishing to favour collective rights over individual rights, I should like to consider the case for the co-evolution of collectively and individually guaranteed rights to benefit without an exclusive dependency on either.

■ CLAIMANTS: CUSTOMERS OR CITIZENS?

A key document from the Benefits Agency, outlining its commitment to the customer focus, is its Customer Charter, first published early in 1992. This follows on from the official launch of the Citizen's Charter in July 1991 in which the Prime Minister announced 'I want the Citizen's Charter to be one of the central themes in public life in the 1990s' (Prime Minister, 1991, p.2). The senior management of the Benefits Agency has embraced Charterism with enthusiasm and in 1992 the Benefits Agency submitted three applications for Charter Mark awards and was successful with two. More recently, in February 1993, the Charter Mark scheme was relaunched to give an additional impetus (it was hoped) to the initiative. The intention behind this was to encourage more public organisations to apply for a Charter Mark award and thereby generalise good practice throughout the public sector. (Interestingly, some managers in the public sector have more recently begun to apply for the British Standards Institute 'quality' Kitemark, BS5750, but whether or not these two schemes will come into competition in the future is hard to predict.)

The Charter Mark Scheme *Guide for Applicants* (Cabinet Office, 1993), gives a clear indication of what is being hoped for. It lists nine criteria which might be summarised as:

1. Setting and monitoring explicit standards and publishing outcomes.
2. Providing full and accurate information about how services are run, what they cost, how well they perform and who is in charge.
3. Consulting the public before establishing priorities and standards and providing choice wherever practicable.
4. Being courteous and helpful.
5. Having well-publicised and accessible complaints procedures.
6. Providing value for money.
7. Providing customer satisfaction.
8. Providing measurable improvements on previous standards.
9. Providing innovative improvements at no additional cost to the tax-payer or consumer.

It is worth stressing here that each of these is concerned with constituting and satisfying the sovereign consumer. Indeed, 'quality' throughout the public sector is increasingly defined in these terms and the Charter Mark award scheme is a deliberate attempt to encourage this trend. This further encourages already well-developed trends in this direction in the Benefits Agency. What are the consequences of so orientating the public sector and what might limit the extent of such a reorientation?

The first consequence is that by pulling accountability downwards and entrenching this accountability within decentralised agencies, the existing constitutional arrangements come under stress. The current doctrine is that the Minister is responsible to Parliament for everything that happens in his or her department. However limited this form of scrutiny may be in practice, it provides a crucial constitutional mechanism through which the legislature controls the executive. On the other hand, the Framework Agreement makes the Chief Executive responsible for the affairs of his or her Agency (within the terms of the Agreement) and already, on matters which are deemed to be non-strategic, MPs are referred directly to the Chief Executive. This has been recognised both in Committee (see HC, 1991, p.xxiii) and by individual MPs (Kaufman, 1992). Other experienced observers appear to believe that what has happened is not possible within the terms of existing constitutional arrangements (Pliatzky, 1992). At some stage there would need to be a radical reformulation of the doctrine of ministerial responsibility, and whilst many would want to see the existing arrangements scrapped, few agree on what they should be changed to.

The second problem is a political one. It can be argued that the best defence of citizens' interests lies not only in individual rights of the sort embodied in the Benefits Agency's Customer Charter but in the vibrancy of organisations in civil society which can provide a bulwark against state power. According to this perspective, the formal and legal rights of individuals have, historically, never proved to be a sufficient defence against the growth of state power. Therefore, it is argued, the capacity of a 'consumerist' state to erode more collective and participatory forms of political action and to replace these with an individuated and formal mode of action, is the capacity to erode the very institutional basis for a successful democracy. Shell (1993) asks 'is not real citizenship stronger stuff than this?' and concludes that 'a fraudulent concept of citizenship is being peddled'.

This is an argument which needs to be treated with some care if we are to extract the kernel of good sense which it contains. It is not the case that organisations based in civil society have typically been characterised by their concern for the equal rights of all and the protection of individual rights. They are typically sectional and reinforce rather than challenge existing inequalities. Furthermore, it makes little sense to talk of the development of civil organisations independently of the development of the public sector. Groups do not form their identities in isolation from public bodies. Rather, they share the same history (albeit experiencing it differently). However, despite these criticisms, there remains an argument for believing that when rights are entrenched only in the public sector, they are not entrenched at all.

The third problem is of a slightly different sort again and this time it goes to the heart of free-market claims about efficiency. The customer focus is not expected, of itself, to ensure the efficiency of the whole of the public sector. Also, other things being equal, a customer focus will increase rather than decrease the likelihood of meeting social needs. However, in the particular institutional setting of the public sector in the 1990s there are senses in which it may work to undermine the capacity of the public sector to meet social needs. There are at least two common situations where this can arise.

For the first situation we might imagine circumstances in which a County Council decides to 'externalise' its training division in order to bring the service more closely into line with its customers. Every meeting which then takes place between the Council and the new agency will have to be costed and records kept. The same would be true of all meetings with other clients. Equally steps would have to be taken to consult with customers, to provide them with information, to publicise complaints procedures and to absorb customer preferences into the quality assurance process of the new agency. The Chief Executive of the agency would then have information and controls in place which would allow the organisation to match more closely its resources to social need, and this is of benefit to society. However, if the cost of operating this system exceeds the value of the benefits derived from improved targeting then there is a net loss to society.

A second problem arises because of the bounded nature of public organisations serving the public. A health authority is concerned with the 'customer' only in a particular range of contexts; it is the health of the 'customer' and not their housing or transport needs, for example, which are of concern. There is a particular culture within a health service, and there are particular techniques of care available. There are particular financial and quality targets which the agency must meet. All of these will shape the extent to which a health service agency operates with a bounded rationality. The customer focus can, in these circumstances, lead agencies to externalise costs onto other bodies or people. For example, by sending a patient to a hospital some distance away a health authority purchaser might provide the best value for money in terms of health care. If the result is that the patient's family then spends more on transport when visiting the patient than was saved on health costs there is once again a net loss to society.

This is a particular example of a general problem of co-ordinating service provision across a range of semi-autonomous public and private agencies when each of these is bounded in its activities as an organisation. These problems multiply in the context of planning to meet anticipated social changes. The free-market response to this would be to suggest further reforms to make organisations unbounded but the onus must be on those proposing this to suggest what an organisation would look like which had no boundaries, culture, favoured technologies and so on. This is a conception of a deliberately 'chaotic' organisation whose fluidity and flux are made necessary by the fragmentation of the wider social world. Obviously, for the foreseeable future we shall have bounded organisations in the public sector and some degree of co-ordinating can be achieved (typically by the purchasers.) However, such co-ordinating must involve a cost, and sometimes a high one. In a context of decentralised cost centres and *Next Steps* agencies the customer focus poses as many problems for inter-agency co-operation as it provides solutions.

We can see from this that the question of whether or not we are becoming — or should already be — customers rather than citizens is multi-dimensional. The changes so far, however limited, have already posed constitutional questions which have yet to be answered and further progress down this road would compel a response. On the other hand, the doctrine of ministerial responsibility is widely seen to be inappropriate in the context of the 1990s — although what should replace it is argued over — and these problems, in themselves, should not present an insuperable barrier to the further development of the customer focus.

Politically, the most substantial criticism to be made of the customer focus is that it corrodes the civil basis for a vibrant democracy. This, however, is because of the particular way in which the customer-focused service has been structured. If one argues against the free-market conception of a utility-maximising consumer with a fairly fixed schedule of preferences and argues for a more open conception of the social individual then different conclusions follow. Choices made by individuals with regard to public services demonstrate constantly shifting priorities, internally incoherent demands, and a fluctuating set of attitudes towards identical services. That these should be fixed in surveys and opinion polls is no more self-evidently true than the argument that preferences should be established in a more collective and inter-active manner. Representative organisations should be encouraged to enter into the policy-making process as well as given a responsibility for stimulating an informed debate amongst their members. The customer focus, given the political will, can become the basis for strengthening civil organisations with the consequence that citizenship would be expanded to include a customer focus which was concerned *both* with the sorts of commitments established in the Benefits Agency's Customer Charter and with the entrenchment of these rights in a vibrant and assertive civil society. For the Benefits Agency this would involve taking further its existing commitments to consult with the representatives of ethnic minorities and disabled people, establishing more open forums within which 'customers' conceptions of qualities could be developed in discussion with both managers and other claimants, and relinquishing control over the appeals procedure to other, preferably democratically accountable, bodies. This could then give rise to a mixed economy of advocacy in which no single institutional mechanism for guaranteeing rights would be privileged over all others.

This version of the customer focus is compatible with social efficiency. We have seen the possibility that the customer focus, when combined with fragmented and bounded agencies, produces outcomes which are sub-optimal. This in itself does not constitute a case for abandoning the customer focus but it does pose questions about how agencies can be prevented from externalising costs and how inter-agency co-operation can be secured where the reward system works against it.

■ CONCLUSIONS: THE OUTLOOK FOR THE CUSTOMER FOCUS

This chapter has highlighted the dynamic of change in the management of the public sector using the example of the Benefits Agency as appropriate. It shows a rapid process of change throughout the 1980s as attempts were made to construct a distinctive approach to managing the state. Will the customer focus be swept away in an apparently endless process of public sector reform, or will it provide the basis for a period of consolidation? If it is the former, will there emerge in the public sector agencies capable of managing permanent institutionalised innovation or will the outcome be fragmentation and disillusionment? The Citizen's Charter is just one part of a wider and more deeply rooted customer focus, but will the political commitment given to it by John Major provide the basis for some stability?

Public sector management is currently at the intersection of powerful and conflicting forces. In this context the ambiguities in terms like 'quality', 'customer', 'market' and 'efficiency' are functional in that they allow for the simultaneous mobilisation of a variety of potentially conflicting interests. This is important because, as Pollitt has argued more widely '[M]anagerialism is the "acceptable face" of new right thinking concerning the state. It is an ingredient in the *pot pourri* which can attract support beyond the new right itself' (Pollitt, 1993a, p. 49). In my view, however, the feature of the new managerialism with which we have been most concerned here, the customer focus, is not in any simple sense firmly wedded to the new right. The customer focus is sufficiently diverse and contested to allow it to be linked to a variety of political positions. As much as being 'agents' of the new right, public sector managers are constrained by a variety of often incompatible expectations. Managers in the Benefits Agency are not dissimilar in this respect to managers elsewhere in the public sector.

We can therefore say with some certainty that the flux and volatility which have characterised public sector management will continue. If the dilemmas and conflicts associated with this flux cannot be resolved in the Benefits Agency then it is unlikely that they will be resolved elsewhere since, as we have argued, the Benefits Agency is more susceptible to pressure in this direction. However, whatever else happens, the customer focus is likely to play a part whatever the outcome but, like 'quality', the meaning which it is given will vary from one context to another.

Consequently, whether it is part of a strategic narrowing down of citizenship to mean little more than being a rightful consumer of public services, or whether it will involve the expansion of 'citizenship' to include legally based and institutionally supported rights of all customers, is still open to political argument.

■ REFERENCES

ADLER, M. (1992) 'Realising the Potential of the Operational Strategy', *Benefits*, April/May 1992.

ADLER, M. and SAINSBURY, R. (1990), *Putting the Whole Person Concept into Practice: Final Report (parts I and II)*, Department of Social Policy and Social Work, University of Edinburgh.

AUDIT COMMISSION (1989) *Urban Regeneration and Economic Development. The Local Authority Dimension*, London, HMSO.

BENEFITS AGENCY (1992) *Benefits Agency Annual Report 1991/1992*, Leeds, Benefits Agency.

BRADSHAW, J. (1991) 'Social Security Expenditure in the 1990s', *Public Money and Management*, vol 11, no 4, Winter 1991.

CABINET OFFICE (1993) *The Citizen's Charter Charter Mark Scheme 1993. Guide for Applicants*, London, Cabinet Office and Central Office of Information.

CLARKE, J., COCHRANE, A., and MCLAUGHLIN, E. (eds) (1993) *Managing Social Policy*, London, Sage.

DHSS (1982) *Social Security Operational Strategy: A Framework for the Future*, London, HMSO.

DHSS (1983) *NHS Management Inquiry* (The Griffiths Report), London, DHSS.

DHSS (1988) *The Business of Service, The Report of the Regional Organisation Scrutiny*, London, HMSO.

DUNLEAVY, P. (1981) *The Politics of Mass Housing in Britain: A Study of Corporate Power and Professional Influence in the Welfare State*, Oxford University Press, Oxford.

EFFICIENCY UNIT (1988) *Improving Management in Government: The Next Steps*, London, HMSO.

FRIEDMAN, M. and FRIEDMAN, R. (1980) *Free to Choose: a personal statement*, Harmondsworth, Penguin.

HC (1991) *Treasury and Civil Service Committee 7th Report 'The Next Step Initiative'*, House of Commons, Session 1990–91 496.

HMSO (1970) *The Reorganization of Central Government*, London, HMSO, Cmnd 4506.

HMSO (1971) *New Trends in Government*, Civil Service Department, London, HMSO.

HMSO (1989) *Working for Patients*, London, HMSO, CMM 555.

HMSO (1991a) *The Government's Expenditure Plans 1991–1992 to 1993–1994, Social Security*, London, HMSO, CMM 1514.

HMSO (1991b) *Annual Report of the CAO for 1990–91 on Adjudication Standards*, HMSO, London.

HALL, S. and JACQUES, M. (eds) (1983) *The Politics of Thatcherism*, Lawrence and Wishart, London.

HAYEK, F. (1986) *The Road to Serfdom*, London, Ark Paperbacks (first published in 1944).

HENNESSY, P. (1989) *Whitehall*, London, Secker and Warburg.

KAUFMAN, G. (1992) 'Privatising the Ministers', *The Guardian*, 7 December 1992.

KELLY, A. (1991) 'The "new" managerialism in the social services' in Carter, P., Jeffs, T. and Smith, M.K. (eds) *Social Work and Social Welfare Yearbook 3*, Milton Keynes, Open University Press.

LING, T. (1993) 'Whose Benefit? "Next Steps", the new managerialism and social security' in Clarke, J., Cochrane, A. and McLaughlin, E. (eds) *Managing Social Policy*, London, Sage.

MAXWELL, R. J. (1984) 'Quality assessment in Health', *British Medical Journal*, vol 288, 12 May 1984.

MAXWELL, R. J. (1992) 'Dimensions of quality revisited: from thought to action', *Health Care*, 1992: 1.

METCALFE, L. and RICHARDS, S. (1990) *Improving Public Management*, 2nd edn, London, Sage.

MITCHELL, W. C. (1988) *Government as it Is*, London, Institute of Economic Affairs.

NISKANEN, W. (1973) *Bureaucracy: Servant or Master?*, London, Institute of Economic Affairs.

PLIATZKY, L. (1992) 'Quangos and Agencies', *Public Administration*, vol 70, Winter 1992.

PRIME MINISTER (1991) *The Citizen's Charter: Raising the Standard*, London, HMSO, Cmnd 1599.

POLLITT, C. (1993a) *Managerialism and the Public Services*, Oxford, Blackwell.

POLLITT, C. (1993b) 'The struggle for quality: the case of the National Health Service', *Policy and Politics*, vol 21, no 3.

RANDALL, A. (1992) 'Service Planning — An agenda for the Benefits Agency', *Benefits*, April/May 1992.

SHELL, D. (1993) 'The British Constitution 1991–2', *Parliamentary Affairs*, 1993.

Chapter 4

CONSUMERISM AND CITIZENSHIP

by John Gyford

A major development in the public sector during and since the 1980s was a heightened concern over the relations between the providers and the users of public services. This concern was part of a broader re-evaluation of the post-1945 welfare state. As such it reflected shifting public and political perceptions of the vices and virtues of the twin pillars of bureaucracy and professionalism upon which the welfare state had relied for the delivery of its services. A more articulate and more assertive public was no longer prepared to accept that professional experts always knew best or to tolerate 'no' for an answer from the official on the other side of the desk. In the political arena the emergence of a strongly free-market New Right and of a New Left arguing for a more participatory democracy meant that established modes of service delivery came under increasing scrutiny from both ends of the political spectrum.

This was especially true in the case of local government, where services provided through professionalised bureaucracies were formally accountable to the public through the institutions of representative democracy incarnated in the form of elected local councillors. A sense that this formal accountability was in practice inadequate gave rise to a search for new approaches to the provider–user relationship. As a result there was an attempt to clarify the nature and role of the public for whom services were being provided; and there were attempts to reorganise the structures and procedures of service delivery. From these initiatives there emerged both a new language and new practices in the world of local authority services.

■ A NEW LANGUAGE AND NEW PRACTICES

One observer of recent trends in council service delivery noted that not only was there a considerable variety of terms being used to describe those who received the services — the public, customers, users, consumers and clients — but also that those terms appeared to be 'used interchangeably by many respondents with scant regard for nuances of meaning' (Hague, 1989, p. 16). Such a tendency is illustrated for example in one of the pioneering charter initiatives: York City Council's Citizen's Charter refers variously to citizens, residents, customers, user groups and people. There may of course be good presentational arguments for avoiding a monotonous repetition of a single term, whether it be citizens, consumers or whatever, in documents designed to be read by a general public not much concerned with semantic or conceptual niceties. Nevertheless the very fact of this interchangeable usage of terminology, and of the particular terms involved, serves to reflect three significant developments in local government in recent years. First, there has indeed been something of a change in the language in which the public are described; second, the change in language has been accompanied by related changes at the practical or operational level; and third, behind — or bound up with — the changes in language and practice there lie some important debates about underlying concepts and assumptions.

At the risk of oversimplification it appears that we are now in a period in which, within local government, a new language has challenged and supplemented, if not yet wholly replaced, an old language so far as describing the public is concerned. The classic terminology of the old language was that of the ratepayer, the voter, the client and the tenant. What was common to all those terms was that they carried or acquired a certain connotation of passivity. Ratepayers for example, despite (or perhaps because of?) the special protection afforded them by the legal notion of the council's 'fiduciary duty' to them, were regarded, not least by themselves, as in constant danger of being put upon by the producers and users of council services whose rate income they were spending: theirs was a state of victimhood. Voters were regarded mainly as notorious for their apathy and for their low turnout when the local elections came round. Even when they did vote they displayed their apathy towards local government by casting their vote on the basis of national issues rather than as a verdict on local council performance. As for the client and the tenant, these were terms very much bound up with their relations respectively with the professional and the landlord; they implied notions of dependency and patronage.

The new language in which the public is described is one which sees that public as being in various ways more demanding, more assertive, and more conscious of their rights. It is a language which reflects an active rather than a passive role and moreover one which emphasises the rights and interest of the public against the producers of those services which the public use. It is in particular the language of consumerism and citizenship.

Such a shift in language might be regarded as no more than a passing fashion or perhaps merely as new labels used to describe a relationship that is in practice little changed. Perhaps it may be no more than a series of rhetorical gestures, employed by local authorities eager to display that they too, at least to outward appearance, have cottoned on to the latest ploy in local government's battle to defend its continued right to have an effective role in the local community. Sometimes, certainly, even those who use the new language seem uncertain of the exact meaning or implication: 'who *are* our consumers?' or 'what do we *mean* by citizens?' are phrases that still crop up in local authority circles on occasion.

One important response to questions such as these is along the lines suggested by Stewart and his colleagues:

> . . . there are customers, clients, consumers and there are citizens. The public sector organisation can and should be concerned with a particular customer but has also other concerns. Consumerism is by itself no guarantee of the public interest.
>
> (Stewart and Ranson, 1988, pp. 13–14)

> Consumerism defined the public as consumers of public services. The Citizen's Charter goes further by seeing the citizen as a customer, since its emphasis is upon the individual in receipt of a service, rather than on the citizen as an active participant in government . . . the language of consumerism, with its emphasis on the customer, is inadequate to encompass the complexities of public action.
>
> (Stewart and Walsh, 1992, p. 514)

The distinction being drawn here is between the consumer as an individual concerned with his or her personal receipt and experience of a service and the citizen as someone participating in governmental affairs dealing with the broader public interest. The implications of this distinction will be explored at a later stage but for the present it can serve as a basis for a brief review of recent local authority initiatives which aim at responding to the public as consumer and citizen respectively and at moving beyond a new language to a new practice.

In addressing the needs of consumers, local government has come to recognise what have been described as 'the major principles of consumerism . . . those of choice, access, information, safety, representation and redress' (Smith, 1986, p. 3). The same principles have been reformulated as the 'seven pillars of consumer wisdom' by the director of the Consumers' Association, John Beishon:

- is there access to the goods and services needed and wanted, when and where consumers want them?

- is there a range of choice available?

- is there enough information readily available about the product or the service?

- can the consumer get adequate redress if things go wrong?

- is the product or service safe?

- is the market place or service provision fair across the community of consumers?

- and are consumers' interests represented where the decisions are made with equal power compared with the manufacturers, advertisers and producers?

(Beishon, 1989, p. 16)

It is possible to identify a number of new local authority practices in recent years which in varying ways respond to consumer needs in the areas specified above by Beishon and Smith. Thus Fenwick (1989) has identified seven main consumerist strategies currently being followed in local government. They are: direct collection of public views, through surveys for example; improved access to services, including decentralisation; improved access to information; the use of subjective performance indicators; active marketing and public relations; increased public participation and accountability; and changes in administrative and managerial style inspired by the notion of managerial 'excellence'. For a more specific list of such measures we may consult the 232 ideas produced by the staff of East Dorset District Council in 1989. They included a five-day target time for answering letters, name badges for staff, an Lplate badge for new staff, flowers and a tea and coffee machine in the reception area, case officer identification on all correspondence, toys for children in the reception area, evening opening one day a week, a public open day, home visits for the disabled and a book for visitors' comments. In much more general terms Walsh (1990, p. 25) has urged the importance of such factors as reliability, responsiveness, competence, access, courtesy, communication, credibility, security, understanding and knowledge, and many local authorities have attempted to address these aspects of service provision in the course of redesigning the relations between providers and consumers.

Other ventures designed to improve the lot of the service consumer have included for example, those introduced in York, Newcastle-upon-Tyne, Cambridge City, Cambridgeshire and Braintree. York City Council began the production of an annual Citizen's Charter in 1989 to tell local residents in advance what the council was hoping to achieve in its various services; it also introduced customer contracts for street cleaning, specifying to all residents in two areas of the city the frequency, type, cost and standard of sweeping they could expect and detailing how residents could follow up any apparent shortcoming. Other councils have linked the contract idea with the payment of compensation for failure to perform. Thus Newcastle-upon-Tyne City Council devised a compensation scheme for tenants whose repair deadlines were not met, whilst Cambridge City Council allows tenants in that situation to get the work done and then to charge the cost to the council. On a quite different tack other councils have been reviewing their own internal committee arrangements to see whether there is a better way of enabling elected members to focus on customer requirements rather than on the details of service administration. Cambridgeshire County Council, for example, abolished most subcommittees and reduced the role of main service committees. It created instead a number of service advisory groups working with client groups and public and voluntary bodies in particular service areas and also set up select panels to look at individual issues with the aid of outside as well as inside expertise. Finally, Braintree District Council has been setting up a series of Customer Panels to provide feedback on service performance for a variety of both internal and external services. The most recent initiative, in 1993, entails the creation of a panel to cover the planning and building control services, potentially involving such service users as builders, developers and local amenity societies.

New practices such as those recounted above may be regarded as being varyingly cosmetic and substantive in their nature. Ultimately, however, they all have a consumerist perspective in that they are concerned with the consumer experience of individual services rather than with the involvement of the public in matters of the broader public interest through participation in government as suggested by Stewart, Ranson and Walsh. Examples of initiatives in the latter field include those described below.

Middlesbrough District Council for example established eleven community councils between 1984 and 1986, each with the right to be consulted by the local authority before decisions are made relating to its area. The community councils hold open meetings chaired by a ward councillor at four-to six-weekly intervals and are themselves composed partly of elected residents and partly of representatives of local voluntary organisations. Although essentially consultative bodies they each have a very modest four-figure budget expendable on items within the council's overall powers and policy.

Having decentralised much, though not all, of its service delivery, on the basis of twenty-four neighbourhoods, each with its own neighbourhood office, Islington moved in 1986 towards the setting up of neighbourhood forums as the democratisation element in its decentralisation scheme. The forums were given the formal status of advisory committees of the council with terms of reference which included the following: to comment on planning and licensing applications; to draw up programmes for the spending of neighbourhood office budgets; to help integrate the local community; to act as a sounding board for local views; and to operate within an equal opportunities framework. The council produced a model constitution for the forums, though they could develop their own constitution subject to council approval. Membership of the forums was based on election, nomination by local organisations or a mixture of the two. In practice two forums opted for an elected body, six for representation from organisations and the remaining sixteen for a mixture of the two mechanisms. Whatever the mode chosen the approved constitutions required a minimum of two places on each forum to be reserved for each of five normally under-represented sections of the community — people under 21, elderly people, disabled people, women with caring responsibilities and people from ethnic minorities.

In the case of Glasgow the system of community councils provided for by the Local Government (Scotland) Act 1973, was put into effect in 1976–7 with rather more ambition than in some other Scottish authorities. Community councils in Scotland are to some degree similar to English parish councils. They were however created more recently than the parish councils of England, to serve as a grassroots counterweight to the enlarged authorities which emerged out of the Scottish local government reorganisation of the 1970s. Although their statutory powers are minimal in terms of service provision they are entitled to express the views of their local communities to the appropriate district and regional councils. They thus have, potentially, a key role in consultative terms, though experience suggests that on occasion they may find themselves at odds with other consultees such as local tenants' associations. The city of Glasgow now has 100 community councils with a membership that may consist both of those directly elected and of those nominated by local organisations: the lower age limit for both voting and membership is sixteen, and three per cent of the approximately 2000 community councillors in Glasgow are from this age group, which remains disenfranchised south of the border. The activities of the councils, which are grant-aided by the city council, have developed in a number of directions. From an initial concern with establishing or preserving local community identities through galas and festivals they have moved on to such activities as campaigning on local issues in order to influence the city council, the health authority, British Rail and other public bodies, the provision of certain welfare services such as lunch clubs for pensioners, and participation in the city council's area management committees. These area bodies, established in 1980, allowed for co-option of community council representatives from 1983 onwards, letting them join with district and regional councillors in monitoring local service provision, advising the central Policy and Resources Committee on local issues and controlling a six-figure area budget for environmental improvements and projects.

Duncan (1990, p. 15) suggests that the main lesson from Glasgow for other urban authorities which are proposing to increase local participation by infusing representative with direct democracy, is that establishing the decision-making structure in itself is insufficient. In order for grassroots or direct democracy to make a substantive contribution to decision-making, and to sustain this input, it is crucial that they have access to a support system, which can provide them with a wide range of services and information. In Glasgow's case the necessary support is provided by a Community Councils Resource Centre funded by the city council and staffed by the University of Strathclyde. The centre provides such facilities or resources as training, a library, stationery, photocopying, information both on substantive local issues (such as planning) and on questions of organisation and procedure and advice on new and proposed legislation.

The extent to which the community council scheme in Glasgow has depended for its success on some sort of 'infrastructure for citizenship' (Lister, 1990, p. 46) clearly differentiates it from such modest schemes as flowers in the reception areas or name badges for staff. It is at the very least more demanding in terms of resources. Can it however also be seen as different not merely in those terms but also in more fundamental ways? In so far as it is addressing 'the complexities of public action' to which Stewart and Walsh referred, rather than the individual receipt of particular services, it can be seen as an exercise in citizenship rather than consumerism. As we have suggested earlier, differences between citizenship and consumerism are more than purely rhetorical. The two terms are indeed both elements of the new language and the new practice of local authority relations with a more active and demanding public. They do however also open up some important questions about the political culture and structure within which those relations should develop.

Moreover any debate about consumerism and citizenship need not, and should not, be confined to the world of local government. It is a debate whose relevance extends beyond the public sector towards the voluntary and private sectors as well.

■ CONSUMERISM AND CITIZENSHIP COMPARED

One approach to the debate is to see citizenship and consumerism as basically competing and antagonistic ideas. In this light citizenship represents the belief that politics ought to be the ultimate arena of decision-making, whereas consumerism gives priority to the decision of the marketplace or of quasi-markets. This can be seen as broadly a left–right division of views. Thus Rustin (1985, p. 38) argues that 'A preference for political mechanisms over all others should . . . be a signal mark of socialist values' on the grounds that politics 'uniquely equalizes the formal powers of individuals in society in contrast to the greater inequality of resources which derives from the market'. Conversely, from the right-wing Institute of Economic Affairs, Harris and Seldon (1979, p. 68) applaud 'the sovereign consumer in competitive markets' and decry the 'choice-denying crudity of the ballot-box'. The notion that there are here two contending concepts of democracy receives support from Blunkett and Jackson (1987, p. 4). They identify 'a clash between political democracy and "economic democracy"' as the underlying issue in the local government conflicts of the 1980s and they argue for the defence and extension of political democracy as against the 'magic of the market place'.

The primary roles in these contending visions are of course those of the citizen and the consumer respectively. If the historic symbol of political democracy is the citizen debating in the Roman forum or the Greek agora, then the contemporary symbol of market democracy is the consumer making price comparisons in the indoor shopping mall. As those images suggest, debates amongst citizens within political democracy lead to collective decisions; comparison shopping by consumers in the market place leads to individual or personal decisions. Here again we see an element of a left–right dichotomy. It would be possible to stop at this point and simply conclude that citizenship and political democracy are the left-wing antitheses of the consumerism and market democracy of the right. There is however another way of formulating these relationships, namely that whilst allowing for the general biases just referred to there are also identifiable versions of both consumerism and citizenship which are respectively individualist and collectivist.

For those on the right, consumerism celebrates the role of the individual in the marketplace; the market allows consumers not only to express their existing preferences but also to discover new ones through sampling new goods and services provided at the risk of entrepreneurs. From this perspective the provider of goods and services is ultimately at the mercy of the consumer. This is perhaps merely a variation on the old saying that the 'customer is always right' but in either version the emphasis is very much on the relations between producer and consumer as individual actors in the marketplace. In the absence of an actual market in the public domain, the individual consumer is to be protected instead through devices such as charters and customer care initiatives.

Consumerism has however taken on other guises, of a less individualistic nature. Thus the existence of consumer-oriented programmes on radio and television, of consumer journals such as *Which?*, of organisations such as the Consumers' Association and the National Consumer Council and of consumer watchdogs such as Community Health Councils all imply the existence of a certain generality of consumer interest which needs collective expression in addition to any action taken by individual consumers. More specifically those on the left are likely to interpret the relationship between consumer and producer in terms of their relative power and to be less than certain that the individual consumer will always triumph over the producer. This view has considerable relevance for example in relation to 'tenants' choice' and 'parents' choice'. The right has seen these as potential realities under the recent housing and education Acts. The left, more sceptical about the realities of power in these fields, sees the new legislation as more likely to lead to landlords and schools doing the choosing rather than tenants and parents. A purely individualistic consumerism is thus seen as failing to reflect the real world of producer or provider power so that consumerism also needs to take on a collective form.

Rather similar notions were being expressed nearly a century ago by Sidney Webb, who is not perhaps always seen as a champion of the consumer. Nevertheless, he interpreted the gradual emergence of democratic local government as a development in which municipalities hitherto dominated by the producer elements of the guilds, the landowners and the chartered companies were converted into 'associations of consumers', who through representative institutions provided the services that they themselves required (Webb, 1910, p. 734). In addition to the emergence of 'the municipal association of consumers' Webb (1910, pp. 737, 738, 743) also hailed the growth of the retail co-operative movement as 'an essentially similar development of associations of consumers . . . resting on the basis of voluntary membership' and speculated on the 'shifting . . . of the very basis of social organisation from producers to consumers'.

Webb's aspirations for the emergence of collective consumer democracies did perhaps discount too easily the subsequent problems of public sector bureaucracy and commercially minded retail management. They do however have their contemporary heirs in the rise of a variety of self-help, co-operative and mutual aid initiatives in which local groups both produce and consume their own provision to meet needs in fields as diverse as housing, education, handicap, care and health (New Society, 1988). The American futurist Alvin Toffler (1981) sees the emergence of such groups — he puts them at over 500,000 in the USA — as heralding the 'de-marketisation' of many goods and services and the replacement of passive consumers who respond to entrepreneurial initiatives by more active 'prosumers' who define, provide and consume their own requirements outside the marketplace. In both the historic and contemporary versions of such collective consumerism we may find a form of consumerism rather different from that which is organised around the consumer as individual.

If we can thus identify both individualist and collectivist modes of consumerism perhaps the same can also be said about citizenship. The fundamental distinction between the two such approaches is well captured by Luntley (1989) who recognises two models of citizenship, the individual and the social.

> *In the former the source of the bonds that tie people together arises from the individual. The only condition is that individuals have the imaginative resources to reach out to embrace others with their charity . . .On the individual model individuals empower themselves into citizenship . . . On the individual model society does not really exist . . . The onus is squarely on the individual to come up with the moral stamina to reach out to others.*
>
> (p. 133)

In the social model of citizenship however, the bonds that tie people together

> *arise from the community which collectively acts to ensure that certain conditions for citizenship are properly met . . . that society be organised in the appropriate way . . . The social model recognises . . . that individuals need to be empowered by the sort of economic and social arrangements in which they find themselves . . . Meeting the conditions of citizenship . . . is not done to enable success for individuals but to enable success for citizens, people with a moral and social role within a larger framework, a civil polity.*
>
> (pp. 133, 154)

Luntley's references to charity in the case of the individual model and to the polity in the case of the social model suggest that we may also understand the two models as commending respectively philanthropic and political involvements as the true mark of the active citizen.

The philanthropically active citizen is the one whom Douglas Hurd was particularly anxious to prompt: 'We've got to say to those people doing quite well, look, there's a community in which you belong — be an active citizen within it' (quoted in *Sunday Times*, 16 October 1988). In similar vein John Patten (1988) encouraged 'the enterprising individual . . . someone who cares . . . to work for the benefit of others': however he warned against 'those whose only aim is to cause a stir'.

The response from the left to right-wing advocacy of the philanthropically active citizen has been to argue instead for the virtue of political activity. It has been suggested that philanthropy is necessarily inadequate since 'Altruism . . . is inherently discretionary. We choose the people towards whom we wish to be charitable, and a necessary consequence of that is that some are not chosen' (Plant, 1989). Opposing not only the discretionary and therefore discriminatory implications of philanthropic citizenship but also Hurd's 'privatised conception of citizenship that intends to whisk away the notion of political community' the left have placed their emphasis on a citizenship which 'embodies a concept of the common good' (Plant, 1988, p. 3) and which embraces ideas of 'civic activity, public spiritedness and political participation in a community of equals' (Mouffe, 1988, pp. 29 and 30). Such a belief in 'equalized opportunities for effective participation in matters to be decided collectively' reflects a particular strand of concern with citizenship which can be found in that brand of ethical socialism associated with Hobhouse, Marshall and Tawney (Dennis and Halsey, 1988, p. 208). However it also represents one element of that broader enthusiasm on the left for political, rather than philanthropic or market-based, decision-making to which reference has already been made.

The notion of individualist and collectivist approaches to consumerism and citizenship within the public domain can be expressed in tabular form as in Table 4.1.

We have already discussed the various forms taken by consumerism and citizenship — charters and customer care; co-operation and mutual aid; philanthropic citizenship; and social citizenship. The table also identifies the key arenas within which consumerist and citizenship strategies may be formulated and implemented within the public domain and the modes of decision-making which they entail. Public agencies can be the arena for the promotion of either individualist consumerist or collectivist citizenship strategies in that they both revolve around public sector service provision. Public agencies may also offer aid in cash or in kind to charitable or co-operative endeavours. Nonetheless, the philanthropic citizenship of the individualist variety is ultimately the prerogative of the individual deciding on whether and/or where to bestow his or her charitable interest and involvement. Similarly the working out of collectivist consumerist strategies of co-operation and mutual aid depends very much on the ability of groups of consumers to carry through their own exercises in collective self-help.

		Consumerism	Citizenship
Individualist	Form	A Charters and customer care	B Philanthropic citizenship
	Key arena	Public agencies Calculation	Individual Calculation
	Decision mode		
Collectivist	Form	C Co-operation and mutual aid	D Social citizenship
	Key arena	Groups	Public agencies
	Decision mode	Deliberation	Deliberation

Table 4.1   Consumerism and citizenship strategies in the public domain

As for the modes of decision-making involved there is a distinction between the calculative mode of the individualist and the deliberative mode of the collectivist strategies. The individualist strategies focus on individual estimates of value and worth, on whether the consumer is getting value for money or the proper entitlement and on whether a prospective beneficiary is worthy of charitable treatment by the philanthropic citizen (for example the discretionary discrimination referred to by Plant above). Collectivist strategies, however, rely on processes of a deliberative nature in their decision-making — the traditional democratic processes of discussion and debate and of majority or consensus building, within co-operative groups or public bodies.

The above four-fold classification is no doubt something of an over-simplification and is offered largely as a heuristic device. It enables us in particular to recognise that within the recent literature on consumerism and citizenship in the public domain the key debate has often been over the relative merits of strategies A and D — individualist consumerism and collectivist (or social) citizenship. This literature is rich and growing and no doubt open to varying interpretations: what follows reflect merely the present writer's own perspective on the debate.

Running throughout some of the literature we can discern the notion that individualist consumerist strategies are not so much wrong — they may in many ways be benign — but that they are in certain respects inadequate. The limited character of the individual as consumer is, for example, identified in the following remarks:

> *The consumer is a bundle of preferences waiting to be satisfied.*
> (Pollitt, 1993, p. 125)

> *The [Citizen's] Charter has more to do with consumerism than citizenship, for the rights it seeks to realise are those arising out of contractual relations rather than out of the citizen's membership of a political community.*
> (Kearns, 1992, p. 22)

> *Most advocates of consumerism have so far left the idea of empowerment at an entirely rhetorical level.*
> *(Berry, 1988, p. 270)*

> *. . . all consumers [do not] have equal power: the rich and the poor . . . rural and urban; dominant ethnic groups and ethnic minorities; men and women; mobile and immobile.*
> (McConnell and Taylor, 1988, p. 223)

> *As a citizen I may have an interest in the NHS even though I am not a consumer . . . the difference between citizens and consumers is all important . . . participation by citizens and participation by consumers do not necessarily point in the same direction.*
> (Klein, 1984, p. 20)

Those who object to the 'conflation of citizenship with consumerism' (Fyfe, 1993, p. 226) thus argue not that consumerism is of necessity always and wholly inappropriate but rather that it is not enough. It is not enough for a number of reasons enumerated below:

1. The question of *what* is to be consumed, or on what scale, or with what priority is not a question for consumers alone but involves a wider public interest. Thus Klein (1984, p. 20) argues that the citizen 'may well wish to minimise the investment in a particular form of health care' whilst the consumer 'may want to maximise it'.
2. The question of *who* should have access to whatever is available for consumption, and on what terms, is also a matter of public interest. Recent debates about whether young single

mothers should be allowed to 'consume' council housing provide a specific example. More generally it is argued that 'Deciding *who* shall have access to *what* is a political responsibility' (Potter, 1988, p. 151, emphasis in original).

3. Questions of what is to be consumed by whom are properly part of a broader public agenda involving that 'weighing of interests and opinions and not just the narrow pursuit of particular ones, which is a constituent of citizenship' (Wright, 1993, p. 108). 'Consumerism is by itself no guarantee of the public interest' (Stewart and Ranson, 1988, p. 15).

4. An individualist consumerism on its own confines the consumer to a role 'as an individual rather than as a member of a wider community' (Elcock, 1993, p. 167) and tends to define 'almost every relationship . . . as if it involved a cash transaction' rather than by any 'sense of democratic rights and duties' (Straw, 1993).

5. In contrast to the limitations of an individualist consumerism, social citizenship is seen as emphasising the links 'between an individual and a polity' (Heater, 1991, p. 155), as involving 'participation with at least some regard for the whole' (McWilliams and Laudy, quoted in Oldfield, 1990, p. 160) and as entailing 'the promotion of a sense of community, social cohesion and "civic virtue"' (Oliver, 1991, p. 164).

The five points above essentially represent a broadening range of arguments in favour of supplementing, if not necessarily replacing, consumerist strategies by those aiming at the development of social citizenship. In the form suggested by Oliver's reference to the promotion of a sense of community and of civic virtue they begin to approach that civic republican tradition described by Oldfield (1990, p. 159):

A sharp distinction is made in civic republicanism between the public life of the citizen, in which individuals live fuller and more satisfying lives, and the private life of the individual, which is restricted to the immediate concerns of family and friends . . . the clear thought running through civic republicanism is that the public life of the citizen is both a more complete life — it demonstrates more completely than private living what human beings are capable of when they rouse themselves — and a more honourable life.

The link between the civic republican vision of citizenship and such notions as a 'more complete' and 'more honourable' life does perhaps suggest that it is 'a hard school of thought' (Oldfield, 1990, p. 5) from which many ordinary mortals might shrink. In the words of Oscar Wilde's aphorism such a form of citizenship could very well take up too many Thursday evenings. Ultimately of course such a vision of citizenship offers a fundamental challenge not merely to individuals but also to society as a whole. It raises questions about political culture and about the vitality or otherwise of public life as opposed to the privatised life of an individualist consumerism. For the latter, the temptation lies in the gradual shift from the defence of the consumer to the celebration of consumption in all its forms. Its ultimate form of expression — the antipode of civic republicanism as it were — is perhaps to be found in the 'recreational shopping phenomenon' that can be found in the 'pavilioned splendour of the shopping mall' (Thorne, 1993, p. 46; Wright, 1993, p. 122).

Social citizenship and individual consumerism can thus be seen to stand in clear contrast to one another, albeit not always so starkly as when perceived in terms of the polar dichotomy of civic republicanism and recreational shopping. Are they then so far apart as concepts that no bridge can be built between them at the operational level in the world of local public services? Is there no way for example of blending together the calculative mode of individual consumerism and the deliberative mode of social citizenship?

One possible response is suggested by a recent experiment in the Dutch city of Delft, revolving around the setting up of a Citypanel Delft. The panel is described by the city's mayor as

> *a group of households or persons who are regularly (say once a month or once a year) asked to voice their opinion about certain issues. Because it is the same group of people, the changes which take place over a period of time can be detected and explained. . . . [and] developments over a period of time can be analyzed.*
>
> (van Walsum, 1993, p. 5)

The relationship of such a panel to the actual workings of local public services is illustrated by the following example:

> *In Delft every year the major service departments conclude a contract with the court of mayor and aldermen, stating the products to be delivered and the necessary means (financial, personnel etc). In these contracts, targets are specified, as well as the desired quality level of services. To evaluate these targets, we use indicators. Data to measure*

the production of the service departments and to test the quality of the products delivered. We have two sorts of indicators: economic and social. Economic indicators give exact counts (e.g. financial budgets, numbers of workmen, number of inhabitants per metre square etc.). These indicators are supplied by the service departments. The so called social indicators are generated by market research, the Citypanel in particular. They are the opinion of the citizens on certain issues. We feel that the citizens, (not the local authorities) should define the desired quality level of services. In other words, quality equals customer satisfaction. It is clear that the results of this sort of research are estimates and not exact counts.

For example: people of Delft were not happy with the opening hours of the civil service. So was [sic] decided for longer opening hours. The next edition of Citypanel showed clear improvement in this respect: people's opinion of the civil service had become more positive.

(van Walsum, 1993, p. 6)

Such a panel device is of course not unknown in market research and opinion polling, not least for the purpose of tracking shifts in voting intentions during general election campaigns. It is however a device which might be expanded beyond the largely calculative mode of individual panel responses. A randomly chosen city panel might also be asked to operate as, or be paralleled by, one or more city juries, employing the more deliberative style of the jury room, exchanging experiences, uncovering hidden assumptions and exploring possible judgements in a collective form, as social citizens as well as individual consumers.

Clearly, serving on a city jury would be likely to be a more demanding activity than being a respondent to regular surveys as part of a city panel. Like the latter such a jury would need to be drawn randomly from the whole population and would therefore contain people largely or wholly unacquainted either with the workings of local government or with the mechanics of deliberative procedures. In such circumstances the case for some form of 'infrastructure for citizenship', such as that which we encountered in the case of Glasgow's Community Council Resource Centre, might well be demonstrable in order to allow the jurors to do an effective job. There remains however the question of how readily those who might be invited to act as jurors would actually accept the invitation.

Here we enter the realms of speculation: there is however one intriguing possible straw in the wind. Thorne (1993, p. 46) has observed how the consumption of material goods and services has increasingly become supplemented in recent times by 'the consumption of experience, (for example, travel, fitness programmes, New Age therapies and virtual reality)'. Is it possible that at some point the experience of forms of social citizenship such as that afforded by membership of a city jury might become a desired consumption experience as consumers become sated with goods and services?

Oldfield (1990, p. 187) has argued that even if such citizenship activity is not something in which people would 'spontaneously engage . . . it is not thereby inconsistent with what their nature can become'. This suggests that we need to be clearer about the obstacles which have hitherto precluded such spontaneous engagement in citizenship; and having identified those obstacles we would then need to establish what forms of encouragement or assistance might best promote engagement in the future. The design of any infrastructure for citizenship thus needs to be informed by research into the requirements of the prospective citizens.

Could it be that here we will discover another role for marketing in the public sector, a role designed to encourage and maximise the readiness of the public to engage, even if only intermittently, in deliberative and other-regarding approaches to service provision as well as the calculative and self-regarding approaches so assiduously promoted in recent years?

■ REFERENCES

BEISHON, J. (1989) 'Empowering Consumers', *New Socialist*, June/July 1989, pp. 16–17.

BERRY, L. (1988) 'The Rhetoric of Consumerism and the Exclusion of Community', *Community Development Journal*, vol 23, 4, pp. 266–72.

BLUNKETT, D. and JACKSON, K. (1987) *Democracy in Crisis: The Town Halls Respond*, London, The Hogarth Press.

DENNIS, N. and HALSEY, A. H. (1988) *English Ethical Socialism*, Oxford, Oxford University Press.

DUNCAN, T. (1990) 'Community Councils in Glasgow — The Development of an Urban Grassroots Democracy', *Local Government Studies*, vol 16 no 2, pp. 8–16.

ELCOCK, H. (1993) 'Local Government', in Farnham, D. and Horton, S. (eds) *Managing the New Public Services*, Basingstoke, Macmillan, pp. 150–71.

FENWICK, J. (1989) 'Consumerism and Local Government', *Local Government Studies*, vol 16 no 1, pp. 45–52.

FYFE, N. R. (1993) 'Making Space for the Citizen?: The (In)Significance of the UK Citizen's Charter', *Urban Geography*, vol 14, no 3, pp. 224–7.

HAGUE, B. (1989) *Local Authorities and a Public Service Orientation: Ideas into Action*, Local Authority Management Unit Discussion Paper 89/3, Newcastle-upon-Tyne Polytechnic.

HARRIS, R. and SELDON, A. (1979) *Over-ruled on Welfare*, London, Institute of Economic Affairs.

HEATER, D. (1991) 'Citizenship: A remarkable case of sudden interest'. *Parliamentary Affairs*, vol 44, pp. 144–56.

KEARNS, A. (1992) 'Active citizenship and urban governance', *Transactions of the Institute of British Geographers*, NS, vol 17, pp. 20–34.

KLEIN, R. (1984) 'The politics of participation', in Maxwell, R. and Weaver, N. (eds), *Public Participation in Health: Towards a clearer View*, King Edward's Hospital Fund for London, pp. 17–32.

LISTER, J. (1990) *The Exclusive Society: Citizenship and the Poor*, London, Child Poverty Action Group.

LUNTLEY, M. (1989) *The Meaning of Socialism*, London, Duckworth.

McCONNELL, C. and TAYLOR, M. (1988) 'Consumer Action and Community Development', *Community Development Journal*, vol 23, no 4, pp. 222–8.

MOUFFE, C. (1988) 'The civics lesson', *New Statesman*, 7 October 1988, pp. 28–31.

NEW SOCIETY (1988) *Grassroots Initiatives*, London, Bedford Square Press.

OLDFIELD, A. (1990) *Citizenship and Community: Civic Republicanism and the Modern World*, London, Routledge.

OLIVER, D. (1991) 'Active citizenship in the 1990s', *Parliamentary Affairs*, vol 44, No. 2, pp. 157–71.

PATTEN, J. (1988) 'Active citizens who make a stand against life's grim realities', *Sunday Times*, 11 December 1988.

PLANT, R. (1988) *Citizenship, rights and socialism*, Fabian Tract 531, Fabian Society.

PLANT, R. (1989) 'Trinity of Concern', *The Times*, 13 February, 1989.

POLLITT, C. (1993) *Managerialism and the Public Services*, Oxford, Blackwell.

POTTER, J. (1988) 'Consumerism and the public sector: how well does the coat fit?' *Public Administration*, vol 66, no 2, pp. 149–64.

RUSTIN, M. (1985) *For A Pluralist Socialism*, London, Verso.

SMITH, M. (1986) *The Consumer Case for Socialism*, Fabian Tract 51, Fabian Society.

STEWART, J. and RANSON, S. (1988) 'Management in the Public Domain', *Public Money and Management*, vol 8 nos 1/2, pp. 13–19.

STEWART, J. and WALSH, K. (1992) 'Change in the Management of Public Services', *Public Administration*, vol 70 no 4, pp. 419–518.

STRAW, J. (1993) 'Ask no questions, hear no lies', *Independent on Sunday*, 24 October 1993.

THORNE, T. (1993) *Fads, Fashions and Cults*, London, Bloomsbury.

TOFFLER, A. (1981) *The Third Wave*, London Bantam Books.

VAN WALSUM, H. (1993) 'Services for the Citizen: Marketing of Public Services', paper presented at Bertelsmann Foundation symposium on *Democracy and Efficiency in Local Government*, Gutersloh, September 1993.

WALSH, K. (1990) 'Duality of Service in Housing Management' in Harrop, K. and Fenwick, J. (eds) *Consumerism and the Public Services*, Local Authority Management Unit Discussion Paper 90/1, Newcastle-upon-Tyne Polytechnic, pp. 22–31.

WEBB, S. (1910) 'Social Movements' in Ward A. W., Prothero, G. W. and Leathes, S. (eds) *The Cambridge Modern History*, XII, Cambridge, Cambridge University Press, pp. 730–65.

WRIGHT, T. (1993) *Citizens and Subjects: An Essay on British Politics*, London, Routledge.

Chapter 5

EDUCATION AND MARKETING

by Mike Clayden

■ SURVIVAL OF THE FITTEST AND HOW TO BECOME FIT

The education sector has undergone a revolution — from a cosy, supposedly apolitical backwater to centre-stage of policy and socio-economic change; from stable, paternalistic self-satisfaction to jostling atomisation. Schools and LEAs are now picking their way through demand regulation, a crowd of critics and quacks offering advice and instant fixes, and an increasingly discerning and impatient public choosing its supplier with greater care. Theories of democratic centralism, with their related mechanisms of control, consensus and planning, have been dislodged by the marketplace and theories of competition and choice.

Yet a desire for a common framework persists. Despite the exercise of new-found autonomies, despite the new direct pressures on headteachers and governing bodies from the national curriculum, legal regulation, public accountability and inspection, schools have not adopted purely parochial perspectives of self-interest. Equally, despite the considerable fettering of their powers, Local Education Authorities have not forsaken their desire to create coherence and maintain an interactive dialogue with educational providers as a key part of local social provision. Motivation continues to come from beyond market pressures. It is founded, for many individuals and groups at all levels of the local education services, on visions of education being a force not only for individual betterment but for the betterment of communities. It is perceived as a vital impetus for communities and their aspirations which needs to be embedded in community life. These underlying values, shared by many managing and overseeing the various components of the education services, create a climate which still drives the parts together to seek continued collaboration, support and common purpose. The initial flurry of schools' opt-out applications has diminished to a trickle.

This is the world in which the education support services, previously an important part in the holding together of collective endeavour, have to adapt and seek their continuance within a new and rapidly sharpening competitive marketplace.

This chapter is about public sector provision of these services, written from the perspective of local authority services. It examines the forces that create the marketplace, its character, constraints and opportunities and describes one Local Education Authority's approach to reorganising often paternalistic provider organisations into entrepreneurial service sales organisations.

■ THE NATURE OF THE EDUCATION SECTOR

The customer then, in the newly created marketplace, is the school. In a dramatic role reversal, the school has the power to decide, by the single act of a signature on contracts or lack of it, the survival or decimation of those LEA services which must sell or collapse in the attempt. What is the character of this all-powerful animal? Overseeing it is the governing body — a diverse group of mainly lay people who bring with them different perspectives. They are the official voice, the decision- and policy-makers. Increasingly, and logically, the governing body comprises representatives of the school community — parents, political appointees and people from local organisations including the business, commercial and finance sectors. Schools are sometimes keen to attract the latter whom they regard as invaluable in terms of fund-raising, work experience placements, and free budget and management advice. The other key decider is the headteacher who provides the professional leadership but is also chief executive for the school. While, in theory, in relation to LEA services, the headteacher is the dominant decider, in practice, deputy heads, heads of department, school secretaries, caretakers, and other staff members play key roles in making decisions on the use and value of particular services.

LEAs have traditionally performed a paternalistic function. They have provided various key support services to schools within and beyond their boundaries. They have structured and organised the way in which problems were to be perceived and solutions were to be found. Solutions sprang mainly from service-wide policies, local bureaucracies and house styles of working. Even in situations where schools, as in inner London, were given some financial discretion in advance of the introduction of local management legislation, many policy norms persisted which fettered their range of choice.

Now, however, with the delegation of money and, more importantly, the delegation of power, schools are, for the first time, in the driving seat. They decide what to do, when to do it and how to do it. They are no longer the mere recipients of policies determined outside their four walls and imposed upon them. They are the policy creators. It is this freedom which has fired the enthusiasm of the more entrepreneurial schools. They see it as an opportunity to test ideas on policy and approaches to their needs. Only gradually, as pitfalls occur, will it emerge from a diversity of local initiatives that there has been wisdom in the long-term development of some service-wide policies. Many shibboleths have fallen under the critical examination of those at the chalk face. Nevertheless, people are learning that the wheel does not always need to be reinvented.

■ THE LEGAL CONTEXT

The Education Reform Act 1988 introduced Local Management of Schools and with it, the new and challenging environment in which education was to be provided. It laid down that each LEA must come up with a formal scheme which delegated funds through a formula by which its primary, secondary and special, but not nursery, schools were to be allocated money. Even more importantly perhaps, in terms of power, it decreed that schools with more than 200 pupils should take over most of the determining powers of the employer and be responsible for deciding how their budgets were spent. This funding power now includes those with under 200 pupils, and special schools. The thinking behind LMS was that those closest to the service users should know best how to spend the cash. Inevitably, choosing how to spend the money involves management decisions on all aspects of running the school. The governing body is responsible for this. It must also decide the school's educational needs and priorities. It must establish the aims within which the detailed curriculum is set. It must develop a management plan for achieving the school's aims and objectives. Thus it is LMS, together with schools' responsibility for implementing, monitoring and supporting the provisions of the National Curriculum, that has caused the role of the LEA to undergo a sea change.

Although schools can choose to buy in either local authority services or those from the private sector, LEAs, on the other hand, can only sell their services to other public bodies. They are further constrained because they are not allowed to employ extra staff to do this or incur any additional costs. This legislation was laid down in the Local Authority's Goods and Services Act 1970. Obviously, this puts LEAs at a disadvantage with private sector suppliers since they cannot adjust their organisations effectively to maximise economies of scale or to offer specialised services in areas where they could have particular expertise and where they could provide for a wider market.

Compulsory competitive tendering, introduced to local authorities in the early 1980s requires them to seek competitive bids in the marketplace from public and private organisations for the provision of designated services. Local council workforces are able to bid for the contract but have to be set up in accordance with regulations as proper contracted companies and must keep accounts showing their income and notional profits. Initially, the designated areas were largely blue collar services such as cleaning, catering and grounds maintenance. Now, white collar services are to be included in a phased programme over the next few years. This will affect the delivery of education and other council services.

■ THE TASK

As in any system undergoing substantial change, there is a natural tendency for schools to hang on to stability and reduce uncertainty. However, as they become more confident in their own decision-making powers, they are more likely to adopt a serious needs-based review in relation to their own priorities, and to seek alternative solutions. The general attitude prevalent amongst schools is to regard support services specifically in terms of their own children's needs. There is also, amongst many governors and heads, a commitment to ensuring the survival of the comprehensive provision of education and, as a result, some voluntary responsibility for subscribing to services which are perceived as being structured for the common good.

An element in this which needs to be recognised is the loneliness which schools and their governing bodies experience when facing up to considerable change and the continual demands of the education system. It is this sense of isolation which prompts schools to bear in mind, when choosing their services, whether they bring with them a context of general support in terms of both connectivity and collectiveness with other schools, and strategic management support which a LEA can provide.

The change of power and control has been especially traumatic for LEAs and comes on top of parallel changes through CCT legislation which cause a fundamental review of local authority's role as a policy and service provider. Traditionally, councils have been accustomed to express their policy and priorities through shaping and directing service delivery itself. Often, the monitoring of these services has been against high-level corporate policy aspirations rather than practical effectiveness for end-users. The shift of power no longer makes this possible and councils may find that being the provider of a service, where the definition of what is required lies elsewhere, may be a less politically attractive role. However, councils must wrestle with their responsibility, deriving from a democratic mandate, to shape local services to electors' expectations, which is reflected in their desire to remain influential with the schools. This is often coupled with their particular concern, also reflected in residual statutory responsibilities, to ensure comprehensiveness of provision to meet needs. These requirements have led most local authorities to look very carefully at how they can collaborate with institutions to form partnerships to meet common goals.

This aim can be expressed in the concept of joint stewardship where the local authority becomes a facilitator for collaboration between local institutions and leads local initiatives for shared benefit. LEAs that follow this path rapidly discover that effective service provision re-emerges as a key issue in so far as, if the LEA is able to provide for a wide range of managerial and curriculum support needs which go beyond the school, it gains a relationship and rapport with its institutions investing it with a strategic importance as an influential adviser and friend.

■ POLITICAL ASPIRATIONS, ASSUMPTIONS AND CONTRACTS

Schools are not monolithic organisations. Their leadership, through the governing body and senior management, embraces a diversity of people. Many of these are part-time amateurs. All of them have a wide range of backgrounds, motivations and aspirations. Their common ground is concern for the good of the children and the well-being of the institution.

The differences of perspectives contain two important strands of expertise. There are those who are familiar with the education system and the delivery of its support services, and those who have experience of alternative ways of carrying out similar jobs elsewhere. Others, some of them also belonging to the first two groups, bring their parental, local community or political experience. Equally, there is a wide divergence in motivation. This includes the desire to constrain the definition of task and aspiration narrowly either to the immediate cohort of children in the school or to the single institution; to contribute to children's education generally and comprehensively; to embrace a wider concept of the role of education in the community and society. This may manifest itself in terms of commitment to concepts of community schools. It may express itself in terms of collectivity between schools and with other providers in delivering a comprehensive service.

Important components which make up the governing body mixture are:

- local authority appointed governors, often political nominees and sometimes councillors, all of whom may have wider social and political concerns than the immediate institution and often experience of working through Committee structures and community politics to achieve managerial goals.

- Parent governors who, conversely, may be more focused on the particular needs of the institution and the children currently there. They may or may not have other particular expertise.

- An increasingly important group on governing bodies are co-opted governors and those attracted to the new LMS environment where they can use particular expertise gained elsewhere. More and more governors with management skills from the public and private sectors elsewhere have emerged on the governing bodies of schools over the past few years, often giving free advice.

- The staff involvement in the management of schools can display widely differing foci. There are many in the profession who see the provision of education as a universal and indivisible whole and seek to promote their own management concerns so as to contribute to and support such an approach.

Equally, there are others who take the view that substantial progress is best made by focusing solely on their own immediate sphere of responsibility and draw a tight boundary around that without regard to the wider implications of their decisions.

■ BARING THE BONES

For many staff, with long local authority career experiences, the transition to a trading culture is a shock. They are suddenly beached on the shore of self-survival without the comforting raft of authority protection to cling to. Great swathes of the service are faced with having a budget of zero to meet their unavoidable costs. They are obliged to sell their services item by item in order to pay their salaries. The question is how to set about it? This is, after all, fundamentally an alien culture to the thinking of many public sector workers. They tend to regard themselves as professionals or, at the very least, specially experienced in various areas of public work. Not included within that expertise, however, is a fixed priority on counting the cost. Nor, in many cases, has the focus of management been on the viewpoint of the service recipient.

To tackle this, people's ideas clearly need to be shaken up. They need to ask themselves the following questions:

- What do we achieve as far as the people who we hope will buy the service are concerned?

- Which parts of our activity are essential for achieving these outputs and which are optional?

- What supporting frameworks do we need in order to ensure the achievement of these tasks is of a quality which people would want to buy?

- How do we ensure that services are not only valuable to the recipient but also regarded by them as being of value?

To tackle these questions requires a combination of simultaneous approaches. The views of the schools, as potential customers, need to be elucidated, a rigorous operation analysis has to be carried out, descriptions of 'products' have to be developed as a basis not only for contracting but also for describing and marketing the services offered.

Gaining a true picture of schools' views of existing services is not an easy task. A culture of polite relations is not helpful if it prevents dislike or dissatisfaction of particular service areas being expressed. Equally, it is difficult to identify those people within schools whose views are truly influential in advance of the trading culture taking hold.

To address these problems, many authorities have utilised independent organisations to conduct consultative research for them hoping that a third-party agency can obtain more of the hard truth. The methodology adopted seeks to circulate questionnaires and hold discussion groups with a diverse cross-section of governors and management staff trying to elucidate their views and relationships, as stakeholders, to future decision-making.

In Islington, the exercise was successful in providing useful truths, under a cloak of anonymity, about the perception of services. Less successful was the achievement of a cross-section of stakeholders' views. Headteachers and leading governors, hesitant about their own yet-to-be-tried powers, often sought to reduce the involvement of more junior staff, leaving LEAs to guess at their views and future influence.

Nonetheless, the results were vital, showing that some essential core services were poorly regarded whilst other services, seemingly more optional, were held in higher regard. This critical information could be used to shape and focus the parallel task analysis being undertaken, and to focus management effort on the most serious problem areas.

■ BUILDING ENTREPRENEURIAL RIGOUR

A decision was taken at the beginning of the service transformation task that the focus of day-to-day management of the trading operations should be as close to the providing process as possible. It followed, therefore, that each provided service was to be considered as a semi-autonomous, separate organisation. There are some twenty-six individual areas in Islington, ranging from curriculum advice and inspection to payroll, from environmental design to surveying, from employee relations to printing.

Initiation of the task analysis, led and guided by a small dedicated team of senior staff, was entrusted to the lead managers in each of the individual activity areas. An iterative process was undertaken of description, costing and review trying to discern the core and separable tasks which were of value to customer schools. Equally, it tried to ensure a consistent costing basis which took account of associated overheads, in terms of both time taken to do unavoidable supporting tasks, and general overheads such as sickness, holidays, equipment etc. The results of the research into schools' views were used to shape the offer in terms of both form and content. Throughout the process, a painful but productive truth emerged from the structuring of the approach. Those directly involved in the formulation of the proposals were struggling to find a basis for their own jobs. No prevarication could avoid the simple fact that if one wanted to survive, one had to succeed. The quality, speed and profundity of many of the service examinations was a testament to the rigour of the mechanism.

This process made use of tools drawn from the orthodoxy of small-business planning in the form of product definition, cost analysis and control, business planning, quality control, market analysis and market testing. Researching and offering these tools was fundamentally the task of the Senior Management Team and was channelled back to service area managers through regular reviews and critique of the progress being made.

The result of the process was a set of radically redesigned draft service offers, representing hundreds of hours of work at all levels of the service and not a few tears. The common feature was a manager in charge of each area with a clear sense of focused saleable services for which s/he was responsible and in control of the costs of delivering them.

■ DESCRIBING THE PRODUCT

In order to communicate to potential customers in schools what the reformed service had to offer, it had to be defined and described. These are not the same task.

Quite clearly, in a market system, if a service is to be sold there must be a definition of the transaction in the form of a contract which sets out its extent and terms. Between a Local Education Authority and its own schools, we termed this a 'Service Level Agreement' since contract law could not apply. Its purpose, however, was similar and, for each service, a common format document was drawn up setting out the nature of the service offered, its extent and frequency, the related undertakings of the service provider, the requirements of the service recipient, the quality monitoring arrangements, procedures for dealing with complaints and service failures and, last but not least, the price.

Although the re-design of each area had been a matter of individual responsibility of the relevant service manager, it was at this point of service description that a corporate framework was introduced. The key decisions were to unify the reliability of delivery by a superimposed common arrangement for quality control by means of precise definition of outputs and expectations, a regular customer feedback and a service-wide means of dealing with shortcomings, complaints or service failures. This provided the Council with a proper role as the guarantor of quality of services provided in its name, without having to seek to centralise day-to-day management.

Contract documents, by their nature, are not marketing tools especially when the purchasing decision-makers are a diverse and ill-defined group of lay and professional interests differing from school to school. To complement the Service Level Agreements, therefore, a marketing document was prepared for each service focusing on purpose, benefits, quality and costs. At the same time, especially for those services likely to need to appeal to a wider cross-section of school interests, such as environmental centres, library and artefacts collections, etc., further publicity, brochures and handbills were produced to raise the marketing profile and attract interest. The stage was set for the final effort of market testing and sales.

■ TESTING THE MARKET

Copies of the marketing documents and draft contracts were sent out to all school heads and governors for consultation. The problem now was to establish proper communications. A two-pronged attack was undertaken. Firstly, a set of formal events and consultations; two exhibitions of services targeted at school staff and governors; a range of formal consultation meetings with heads and governors; offers to attend meetings with individual governing bodies to which others were invited. Secondly, less formal routes were to be used, capitalising on existing networks, contacts and relationships to open up dialogue and stimulate interest and feedback. In the course of deciding this latter approach, the question whether such contacts should be centralised through senior staff, or whether each area should be free to make its own arrangements, gave rise to much anguish. The concern was that, whilst the latter might achieve informed discussion, it might also be counter-productive if headteachers and governors received 20+ individual approaches. In practice, these concerns were groundless and senior and area-specific staff were able to utilise their own contact networks without falling over each other to obtain vital intelligence about how the packages were being perceived.

It was of key importance, however, not to be carried away solely by what one heard through such formal and informal contacts. Just as important was the awareness of who was not in contact with the service and why. It soon emerged that a tiny minority of schools was determined not to participate in the LEA's service level discussions on provision in some areas and to seek other providers.

This led to rapid focus in these areas on the key aspect of market analysis, namely considering the products of the opposition. Despite preliminary market analysis during the initial design stage, it quickly became apparent that we still fell short of market competitors' offers in a few key service areas. Fundamental re-design of these areas was undertaken and, for example, in one area, costs were reduced by a factor of 4 to undercut the market, and to provide a more robust but radically different high technology solution — a task completed from review to re-design and re-offer in ten weeks.

Other services needed less modification but formal and informal contacts indicated where flexibility of offers should be increased or wider or narrower options should be provided.

The service offer was finalised and despatched as schools received their budgets for the following financial year. Service area managers recharged their batteries to obtain the key signatures to confirm the necessary sales which they needed for viability. Once again a multi-faceted approach was adopted. Formal processes for channelling and monitoring the despatch and receipt of Service Level Agreement documents, clarifying details and responding to formal requests for advice, ran alongside service area and senior managers networking their contacts to support the sales process.

One year on, and the process can be counted a success. Of twenty-six initial areas, only one failed to achieve reformulation on an entrepreneurial basis (but the work was salvaged under the banner of management of another area). After twelve months of trading, only one area has failed to establish a viable trading base, whilst many have exceeded their planned volume, bringing vital flexibility to future resources for development and improvement.

■ MANAGEMENT AND CONTROL

In the above account only a little has been said about central management and control. The emphasis on empowering entrepreneurial effort within each work area does not mean that there is no overall embracing philosophy or that there is a loss of strategic purpose.

Although a council has an interest in its schools having access to efficient services, often equally important are the motives that help underpin a partnership between the LEA and its schools. Through this partnership, LEAs can nurture a continuing collective view of the education service and community needs. Some services, such as personnel management, financial management, and inspection and advice are central areas where interest in generating shared intiatives and policy may be mutually beneficial. Joint projects may be developed, derived from the sharing of ideas and aspirations.

There are essential risks in delivering services as far as a council is concerned, by owning the services in-house. Its own reputation depends on delivering quality. As always, there is a financial risk in any trading operation. In seeking to control these risks there is a counterbalancing problem that the costs of a heavy management structure over the service areas might drive prices up and make the services unmarketable. All these factors come together to shape a management control system for the Service Level Agreement areas which seeks to focus on financial control, quality monitoring and the structure of minimum supervision. The conceptual framework is that of a parent company and its subsidiaries. Systematic quality monitoring and customer feedback are the basis of quality mechanisms. A formal and periodic review of the balance sheets and forward commitments is the basis of the financial control. The head of the individual service area remains responsible for financial integrity and market viability, sales and costs. The senior management (the parent company) seeks to provide formal assurance of viability and quality control through a minimum system of formal periodic review, perhaps three or four times a year. At these formal meetings, they also seek to offer some resources to facilitate strategic forward planning and development. This latter role is particularly important for the Local Education Authority for it can encourage and develop new services to meet needs and objectives identified through collective collaboration with schools. This can, in turn, nurture continued partnership.

At present, these arrangements are held solely within the officer management hierarchy. It remains to be seen whether the parent company concept may, in time, develop as a member-level board.

■ THE FUTURE

So far, the Service Level Arrangement for most services has been developed solely in relation to the local management of schools' initiatives. However, white collar work, like much existing blue collar work, is planned to be subject to compulsory competitive tendering. The current CCT regulations would add further anti-competitive restrictions to the viability of local education authorities as trading organisations. LEAs will have to see whether it is practicable to compete effectively with private-sector organisations. If this system becomes less viable, consideration will have to be given to whether there may be other ways of sustaining clusters of services related to local communities, their elected councils, the schools, and other services which can still support the notion of collectivity for local social benefit. Some councils are already exploring 'off-shore' organisations, related in a variety of ways to councils, and management buy-outs by staff committed to council objectives. These may, if necessary, provide ways in which the benefits of continuing partnerships between schools and local authorities can be maintained but may raise new risks and problems.

Chapter 6

THE CUSTOMER'S OPINIONS

by Brian Gosschalk and Warren Hatter

■ MARKET RESEARCH AS A MANAGEMENT TOOL

The extent to which market research is used in the public sector has grown enormously over the past decade. This, in itself, is evidence of a massive sea change. The customer, if not yet king, is now deemed to be worth consulting, and recognised as a key stakeholder by public service managers.

Prior to this, the prevailing attitude — with honourable exceptions — tended to be 'we know best', or 'we know what people want'. Examples of this are local authority members insisting that they knew what local people thought, because they were in touch with hundreds of residents each year, therefore why waste money on consulting residents? This attitude, of course, is still alive in some quarters, but is now less likely to remain unchallenged by those who, these days, appreciate the importance of having a representative view, rather than the views of the minority who contact a member or officer.

Another example would be the hospital manager who knows that the quality of medical care offered is good, and sees patients grateful to have access to this expertise. Making people well is the core function of the hospital, therefore customer care — making the service user-friendly — simply diverts resources from beds and operations. This sort of approach was often backed by hospital staff, dedicated to serving the public, yet failing to see that the personal service offered was poor; if you make people well, then why treat them like valued customers, when their gratitude is clearly visible? Everyone reading this will have their own examples of public sector managers 'knowing best'.

It is important to recognise that the views of people who make the effort to tell managers or staff (or members) their views are unlikely to be representative. Rather, they tend to be people who have the time and motivation to get in touch. Our research has shown that, on average, just seven per cent of adults will be in contact with a local Councillor during the course of the year. They are more likely to be middle-aged and middle-class.

One response to this is that those who make the effort to get in touch are the ones who have opinions, and should therefore be taken notice of. The best example of why this does not work, in marketing terms, is complaints. Those who are dissatisfied with a service tell more than twice as many people about it than those who are satisfied. If you only get to know the views of those who complain about a service — that is, those who feel strongly enough *and* who know how to complain — then you are already having problems in marketing your message and your service. If the public sector is to play a valuable role, it needs to recognise its responsibilities to *all* its customers.

It is beyond doubt that these attitudes are becoming a thing of the past. Having overcome this central dilemma — genuine interest in serving the public but resistance to seeking out customers' views — we now have a public service ethos which views the public as (potential) customers. It is a short step to measuring customers' views systematically.

The bottom line for anyone involved in marketing in the public sector is that you can only deliver services effectively when you know how customers and potential customers feel about a service, product or message, and when you know what they want. Research should always be seen as an investment in the future; if this argument cannot be justified, then research should not be commissioned.

Additionally, to be effective as a management tool, research and the changes which result from it need to carry the approval of staff. Communication is, therefore, important in ensuring that the positive effect of research is maximised. The key to eliminating cynicism and negativity is 'ownership'. The more people feel they own the data, the more can be achieved. If staff feel that they have been consulted, that they have an input into how research data is acted upon, then they will be closer to the customer and more motivated to improve the service.

Our experience is that once staff see the benefits of research, it can be a powerful motivating tool. They are keen to improve performance ratings in subsequent evaluation, and come up with ways of solving problems identified by the research.

When an organisation's culture changes to the extent that there is widespread understanding of the benefits of research, the type of research programmes initiated can be very cost-effective, as in-house resources are used, and proportionately less time is spent communicating findings and ensuring ownership of the data. Additionally, in-house research can avoid the necessity of a tendering process. Later in this chapter, we shall look at the use of an external agency as research consultants as one of the recent developments in the public sector.

We should not, of course, lose sight of the fact that money invested in research by a public sector organisation is tax-payers' money, and the public, too, may need convincing that a decision to spend £X thousand on a survey is the right one. Some of the public may also feel that surveys divert resources from core activities, and are therefore a waste of money. The best approach in our experience, is to put the cost in perspective as a proportion of the annual spend, and to assert that 'the proof of the pudding is in the eating'; enhanced efficiency and effectiveness can arise out of the findings. Going public with 'warts and all' survey findings that include critical aspects, along with a list of areas that will be targeted for improvement, is an approach that attracts less criticism than attempting to 'massage' the findings to make them appear favourable.

Our experience of public attitudes to research is favourable. Generally speaking, the concept of the public sector listening to what its customers think about the way it spends their money is fairly new to most. On the whole, respondents are pleased to be able to help, in some cases flattered to be asked to help improve services.

This raises the issue of a supplementary benefit of research. It can be an outreach exercise, since it communicates that the organisation cares about its customers' views. This is a public relations benefit that can aid the marketing of the organisation's message.

■ RESEARCH METHODS — QUALITATIVE AND QUANTITATIVE

The research techniques used to provide management information for public sector bodies come under two categories: qualitative and quantitative. Before looking at the ways in which public sector bodies make use of research, it is useful to outline the methods briefly.

Qualitative research is often a good starting point for an organisation new to research, or beginning to research an area about which little is known of customers' views. The approach most frequently used is to recruit respondents to attend a series of group discussions.

Qualitative research does not give a statistically representative view; instead it offers insight and understanding, in a detailed way. It can be particularly useful as an initial attempt to understand what influences views of the service or organisation in question.

This starting point emphasises the principle of not claiming to 'know best'. It ensures that, if and when a statistically representative view is taken, the issues explored are those of importance to customers, not necessarily those that managers think matter. For instance, group discussions among housing association tenants may raise the issue of quality of repairs, enabling this issue to be explored further in subsequent quantitative research.

Qualitative research has other functions, too. One technique which tends to be under-used is following up noteworthy findings to seek to understand the perceptions that lie behind them. Sometimes, findings from a quantitative survey stand out as requiring further explanation. If the joint expertise of management and agency does not properly understand a finding, then clearly managers will not be able to act on it. If, for example, a certain aspect of a particular service has an unusually high dissatisfaction rating, then the managers of that service need to know why.

Qualitative research does not always consist of group discussions; in some case, the most effective approach is a series of depth interviews. For example, a survey exploring the views of carers for a Social Services department would encounter logistic problems if relying on group discussions, as finding a time and place where a fair number could attend is not realistic. Visiting carers in turn, however, can achieve almost as much. On the plus side, the researcher has the opportunity to explore respondents' views fully, which may be difficult in a group discussion. On the other hand, respondents in depth interviews do not have the opportunity to share experiences and find common threads.

When a representative picture is needed, quantitative research should come into play. If it follows qualitative research, then it is an opportunity to measure the extent of certain perceptions on the issues that have been raised.

In the public sector, a general public survey is often relevant. Interviews with a representative sample of residents of a health authority area or local authority area will give a representative picture of the views of all users and potential users of the services provided. Sometimes, of course, a quantitative survey may be conducted among, say, users of a service, non-users of a service, people who have complained in the past year, or visitors to a particular office or attraction.

There is enormous variation in the way that surveys can be, and are, carried out. It is rare indeed that a cost-effective research solution cannot be found to a challenge faced by a manager. The input that research provides, by telling managers what customers think, and why they think it, has helped many managers optimise the service they provide and the message they send.

■ WAYS IN WHICH THE PUBLIC SECTOR HAS USED MARKET RESEARCH AS PART OF A MARKETING STRATEGY

Over the following pages, we will examine a number of examples of market research being used to provide an input into various facets of marketing strategy. Among the aspects covered are: service delivery, customer care, communications/press and public relations, investment/spending plans and human resources. The case studies are taken from a variety of sectors, including policing, health care, utilities and local government services, including housing.

Space constrains our ability to examine findings and action taken in great detail; rather, we trust that these examples give a flavour of what research can help achieve — and how this can be done. In each case, a particular challenge or set of challenges needed to be addressed, and research was identified as a tool to help achieve this.

Staff surveys — Dorset County Council

Perhaps the most fundamental change required for any organisation to become successfully customer-oriented is a change in its employment culture. Often, staff are driven by a concept of serving the public, and yet find it difficult to see that the service they provide can be unresponsive and far from customer-friendly. There is often resistance to change, which can reduce morale. A workforce that is not motivated will not provide a high quality service, and its front-line staff will project an image some distance from the customer-friendly message that management are seeking to get across.

Additionally, comparison of different survey data has shown that customer-friendly staff have a substantial positive effect on the way that organisations are viewed overall. In the field of local government, for example, the data from two specific residents' surveys demonstrated that authority A's services consistently elicited more satisfaction than those of Authority B. The latter authority was, however, more favourably viewed overall. The reason seems to be the positive image of Authority B's staff who were widely perceived as helpful, efficient and accessible by those who contact the Council. The grapevine worked in Council B's favour.

How, then, can research be used to address the issues that concern staff and to improve motivation? Dorset County Council's use of MORI's employee attitude research is a good example.

The findings of a postal survey of over 8,000 staff showed that almost as many rated the Council below average (14 per cent) in terms of customer care provided to those who visit the Council as rated the County Council above average (16 per cent). Generally, of course, service providers tend to rate the service they provide more favourably than do users of the service, so there was clearly an encouraging awareness of the limitations of the service provided.

Training is a key element in ensuring that standards of customer-care provided improve an organisation's image. At Dorset County Council, one in three staff felt they needed a lot or a little more training to deal with members of the public. As many disagreed as agreed with the statement 'I receive sufficient training for my job'. Clearly, staff perceived a training need to be met.

The survey also explored problems preventing staff from giving a higher standard of service. Lack of money and resources headed the list, followed by lack of staff, ineffective decision-making higher up and too many unnecessary procedures. There were also concerns about the perceived lack of encouragement for taking initiative and the lack of information available to staff. What are the implications of these findings, in terms of improving personal service? It is clear that staff can feel emasculated by the decision-making process and resources. Increasing resources may be difficult, but much can be done to empower employees, to make them recognise that they have a crucial role to plan in improving the customer's lot. Internal communications also have a role to play — if staff feel informed, then they do not feel cut off from the decision-making process, and are hence more motivated.

Corporate research for a local authority — Colchester

The research used by local authorities falls into two main categories; corporate research, which provides an input for a number of departments — perhaps all departments — and service-specific research, which usually has a narrower focus and objectives.

Key questions asked by local authority clients include the following: what are the particular problem areas for residents? (What, for example, do local residents like most and least about the area in which they live; what problems would they most like to see addressed?). Second, in specific areas of service provision, does service delivery match up to expectations? And if not, what are the main causes of dissatisfaction? Third, how would local residents like to see their locality developed in terms of amenities, traffic control, shopping facilities, tourist attractions and so on?

Corporate research often comes about as a result of an attitudinal shift among officers and members; results often have a considerable impact on the authority, as they represent the first time that an authority has had a representative view of what its residents — or customers — want. This is no small thing when, for years, councillors have been convinced that they know what residents want and what they think of the council and its services, through their limited contact with a small minority of 'active' residents. Since 1980, many councils have come to appreciate the benefits of feeding in the views of local residents into their decision-making processes. One major advantage of a professionally conducted survey is that you can cover the needs of several council departments within the context of one questionnaire. Many councils now undertake surveys on a regular basis, for example every two to three years, to see how far the actions taken as a result of one survey are reflected in the views of local residents in the next survey.

Research commissioned by Colchester Borough Council is fairly typical, but also particularly interesting because the actions taken as a result of its first MORI survey in 1988 have been well documented, and the effects of these actions are reflected in the results of a follow-up survey conducted in 1992.

In 1988, we found that 86 per cent of residents were satisfied with the neighbourhood in which they lived, while one in ten was dissatisfied. The questionnaire asked those one in ten to explain why they were dissatisfied. A quarter of these talked about the area being dirty or littered; one in six thought there was too much traffic, and a similar proportion talked of vandalism and hooliganism. Following on from the survey the council introduced an Environmental Initiative which had been a main plank of the administration's policy, supported by the research findings. The Initiative included introducing a Charter for the Environment, appointing an Environmental Co-ordinator and undertaking a policy of enhancing the cleansing standards in the town centre including the acquisition of a specialist street washer. On the traffic side it introduced a 'Keep Colchester Moving' campaign. A series of additional traffic management measurements such as lower speed limits and road humps were also planned.

Four years later the repeat survey showed a significant improvement in satisfaction, with 90 per cent of residents now expressing satisfaction with the neighbourhood in which they lived and only 6 per cent dissatisfaction. Although the top three reasons for dissatisfaction remained litter, traffic and vandalism or hooliganism, the proportion mentioning litter had declined from 24 per cent of those dissatisfied to 15 per cent of those dissatisfied. The proportion mentioning traffic and vandalism remained about the same, although this was, of course, on a lower base of dissatisfied respondents.

A rather more marked change came in residents' ratings of satisfaction with the way the Council was running the Borough. In 1988 just 57 per cent of residents expressed satisfaction and 21 per cent dissatisfaction. By 1992 those satisfied had increased to 73 per cent and those dissatisfied had declined to only 8 per cent.

Part of the Council's strategy had been to tackle the three most important issues identified by residents with a series of measures. The top three issues in 1988 were:

- traffic control
- maintenance of roads and pavements
- housing

On the first of these, the Council had taken further initiatives with respect to their 'park and ride' scheme, reviewed their parking charge strategy, which had come in for some criticism in the research, and looked for continued ways of easing traffic congestion. Although roads and pavements were, strictly speaking, County Council functions they also considered injecting Borough funds into this problem and a County/District review was implemented.

On the housing front the Council worked with housing associations and instigated a £1.5 million capital programme. They also introduced schemes to free up under-occupied council houses and acquired property for letting.

The results of the 1992 survey suggested that these efforts bore fruit. Satisfaction with roads and footpath maintenance increased from 27 per cent to 38 per cent; satisfaction with car parking or parking in the town centre increased from 26 per cent to 33 per cent, and there were marked increases in a number of other areas in which the Council had focused its efforts. In 1988, for example, the Council already had a very good reputation in terms of its refuse collection service — 88 per cent were satisfied and only 7 per cent dissatisfied — by 1992 this had improved still further to 91 per cent satisfied and just 5 per cent dissatisfied, and street cleaning also showed an improvement from 60 per cent to 68 per cent satisfied.

The 1988 survey had also shown how leisure facilities were high on the public's list of requirements. The opening of a large water-based complex, Leisure World, between the two surveys resulted in marked improvements in the Council's ratings on the provision of leisure facilities generally and satisfaction with swimming pools and sports facilities increased from 53 per cent of users to 66 per cent while satisfaction with parks, playgrounds and open spaces also improved from 55 per cent to 60 per cent.

The research illustrates how research can provide an objective and independent measure of residents' perceptions and priorities. If a Council honestly believes in a mission to improve the quality of life for local residents, action on the basis of this input can achieve real, measurable improvement overall and in different service areas.

Utilities — water companies

The ways in which utilities have changed over the past ten years justify their inclusion here. Although no longer in the public sector, their service provision and pricing remain regulated, and the key changes they have undergone in moving from public sector to private sector mirror those of other organisations which have remained publicly owned. This latter group have, similarly, introduced market disciplines and elements previously confined to the private sector (customer care, etc.), while retaining largely the same workforce.

Listening to the customer — via research — has enabled some newly formed water companies to identify customers' problems and priorities. By distinguishing these from the problems and priorities of engineers, technicians and scientists, they have been able to prioritise investment to meet customers' needs in a way that customers are prepared to pay for.

The context of this research is a requirement to show that customers are willing to pay for improvements that lead to prices rising above a statutory maximum. The onus is on engineers to spell out their proposals in terms of customer benefits, expressed in a way that the customer can understand. Customers are, of course, in no position to say whether or not there should be investment in a new treatment works, or speeding up the pipe replacement programme or introducing multi-stage filtration. They can, though, say whether or not they would be prepared to pay more for improving the appearance of water or to eliminate the smell of chlorine or to prevent the possibility of raw sewage discharges into local rivers. Getting what they want at a price they are willing to pay is the concern of the customer. How this is achieved in terms of the appropriate engineering solution and capital investment is the concern of the specialist and the manager.

The water industry is a case where the world of the engineer and that of the market researcher have come together. This has inevitably meant compromises in thinking on both sides. Market researchers have had to rewrite some of the rules of questionnaire design, while engineers have also had to revise their way of thinking. Human behaviour and attitudes do not conform to laws in the same way as the physical world does. Understanding customer preferences is not just a question of asking whether they want this built or that built. It usually involves a series of questions designed to identify needs and underlying rationales. Often it involves in-depth qualitative research with small groups of customers as well as larger-scale quantitative surveys of representative cross-sections of local communities.

Policing — Merseyside Police Authority

In recent years, pressure has been building on police forces to be more responsive to the public's needs, perceptions and priorities. All forces have now moved in this direction, some quicker than others: for example, in some areas, substantial parts of the policing budget have been devolved to a relatively local level.

The main issue for public input into policing, given that demands far outstrip resources, is in terms of policing priorities. One of the three principal areas of change recommended by the Audit Commission in *Helping with Enquiries: Tackling Crime Effectively* (published in November 1993) is making police priorities more explicit. The need for research is clear when one considers the potential divergence of nationally identified priorities and the issues which most concern the public in a particular constabulary's area. Additionally, the introduction of Performance Indicators has put perceptions of the police into sharp relief; the need to balance PIs with 'non-statutory' measures of performance, such as public satisfaction and perceptions is becoming increasingly clear. These are issues which MORI has sought to address in a number of areas. One illustrative case study is from Merseyside, where priorities were an issue, as were the image of the police in this sensitive area, and communications.

The project began in 1992 with a series of group discussions with residents and among representatives of the voluntary sector. These explored the background factors which influence people's views of the police. Subsequently, a wide-ranging questionnaire was developed and used on a representative sample across the five Districts on Merseyside. In addition, there was a 'booster' sample of black residents of Granby, Liverpool.

One subject area covered by the questionnaire was police/community relations, as this impacts both on communications and on priorities. Around one in seven feel that relations between local people and the police are poor (14 per cent), while the majority rate relations as good (58 per cent).

The follow-up question is an example of the way in which priorities can be established in a quite straightforward way. Asked to suggest ways of improving relations, responses focused on the interaction between the police and local people. Most popular were more police on the beat, the police making more effort to get to know local people, retaining individual officers in the same area for longer, more activities with the young and more feedback to the public on the outcome of investigations.

In Knowsley and Liverpool, residents were notably more negative about relations than those elsewhere. The most striking disparity in views, however, was found among the black population of Granby, where three in four rated relations with the police as poor. The top priority in this area — bearing in mind that Merseyside's black population is narrowly focused geographically — is an improvement in the attitude of the police towards the public. Here, there is much less enthusiasm for more police on the streets.

The information provided has enabled the Police Authority to identify, area by area, the priorities for improving community relations. The Authority and Merseyside Police are now addressing the issues raised by the survey. The survey will also prove useful in measuring changes in public opinion resulting from force reorganisation, which is currently being phased in, and which will devolve policing management to local level.

Housing — Warwick

Housing is another area of public sector service provision that has been subject to major legislative change, leading to considerable changes in organising the delivery of services. Nevertheless, the vast majority of social housing in Britain is still provided by local authority housing departments. One such department, Warwick District Council's Housing Department, employed MORI in 1988 to carry out its first survey of tenants. Until then, managers and staff had assumed that they offered a high quality housing service. Indeed, the survey was fuelled by the arrival of a new Chief Housing Officer who wished to challenge existing views.

The research revealed high levels of satisfaction with most aspects of the service offered. In a number of areas, however, the research showed that Warwick was below par, and the Housing Department set out to identify areas where policy initiatives were required.

Communications and marketing featured strongly in the identified areas, since there were relatively poor ratings on communicating with tenants, consultation on proposed improvements and low awareness of Tenants' Choice legislation.

Among the communications measures introduced as a result of the survey were:

- The introduction of consultation on improvement, providing tenants with a choice

- The creation of a budget for marketing

- Publishing a Tenants' Handbook, providing information on Council services, contact points and procedures

- The publication of a Newsletter for tenants, on topical issues relating to tenants, tenants' associations and housing in general locally

- A series of meetings on Tenants' Choice was set up

Two years later, the survey was repeated to measure the success of the initiatives. Over two in five had read all or nearly all of both the newsletter and handbook. Questions were asked about the usefulness and clarity of both publications; residents were, on balance, positive. The overall effect of increasing efforts to communicate was clear to see: the proportion who felt well-informed had doubled from 30 per cent to 61 per cent.

Health — NHS in Scotland

Most of our examples of use of research are locally based. MORI's research for the Scottish Office on the NHS in Scotland, however, is an example of how larger-scale survey work can feed into policy and communications.

Following a large-scale staff survey and a preliminary qualitative study, MORI was commissioned in 1992 to carry out a quantitative survey. A wide-ranging questionnaire covered the key issues that local researchers had identified during qualitative work. Among the service areas investigated were: accident and emergency, maternity, GPs, community services, out-patients and in-patients. The service delivery issues included: access to services, waiting times, linkages, communications, treatment and feedback to patients.

In addition to 2,500 members of the general public, MORI interviewed 'booster' samples of 130 carers and 650 parents, to ensure that adequate coverage of their views and specific needs was obtained. The research contained a great deal of probing, in order to overcome what is often called the 'halo effect': a reluctance to criticise due to gratitude for the health care received.

The output of the survey was *The Patient's Charter — What Users Think*, a user-friendly report jointly produced by MORI and the Scottish Office. This was sent to all GPs and NHS managers in Scotland, to give them an insight into their customers' views. Additionally, steering committees have been set up to examine how to improve services in the key problem areas identified.

■ RECENT DEVELOPMENTS

Government Initiatives — Performance Indicators and the Citizen's Charter

The key developments in the past two to three years affecting the public sector define the context in which most public sector research takes place. The changing culture of public sector service provision is, most recently, embodied by the introduction of a series of around thirty Charters and, following on from the Citizen's Charter, Performance Indicators.

To some extent, then, change has been forced on public sector organisations. This, in itself, can cause difficulties. For instance, it is all the harder to motivate staff to be involved in customer-friendly initiatives if the new culture is seen as being Government-driven, rather than customer-led. The wider the 'ownership' of research, the more organisational and cultural changes will be identified with the organisation concerned, rather than with government.

Successful public sector organisations — if success is defined as efficiently providing high quality services — tend to approach Charters and Performance Indicators as pegs on which to hang improvements, rather than taking a reactive approach and doing the absolute minimum required. This is not to say that the Citizen's Charter is flawless; nevertheless its contents should not be rejected out of hand.

This concept of building on PIs and on concepts of citizenship is vital, because national guidelines take little account of local factors. If quality measurement relies solely on measuring hard data for national comparisons, then it will be too production-oriented. If it looks at 'soft' data from customer research in tandem, then supply-side and demand-side considerations can be married.

Complaints

One increasingly important issue for public sector managers is responding to complaints. The number of complaints is rising as expectations rise, fuelled in part by Charters, in part by the public sector's increasing openness, but mostly by a general increase in the extent to which people see themselves as consumers. Increasingly, people are less prepared to accept what they see as poor-quality services or goods.

The first stage of deciding how to deal with complaints is defining what constitutes a complaint. For example, when a resident rings a transport department to say that a street light bulb has blown, is he or she making a complaint? In our experience, the answer is 'no' (although it can soon become 'yes' if the caller is passed from pillar to post and then asked to ring back when they have noted the serial number shown on the base of the lamp!).

We have already noted the importance of the grapevine in defining the image of a public sector organisation. Clearly, dealing effectively with complaints will become increasingly important for the public sector. In the most progressive quarters, this issue is being addressed, and researchers are helping to ascertain customers' priorities. It has even been suggested that the quickest way of raising satisfaction is to encourage complaints and then deal with these efficiently and effectively.

How acceptable is it to be in contact with a number of different staff members while a complaint is being dealt with? How helpful would it be to be given a leaflet outlining the complaints procedure? What speed of response is expected? These are among the questions that need to be asked if responsiveness to complaints is going to be taken seriously.

A London Borough, aware that it appeared to receive a low level of complaints, wanted to know why. Was it because services were satisfactory, or were residents not complaining when they might have? MORI was commissioned to find out. A qualitative and quantitative survey found that, among other things, many do not complain because they feel that nothing would be done as a result. Importantly, many of those who had not complained wanted contact information on whom they should call with complaints. One aspect that featured strongly in the views of those who had already complained was that there should be identical procedures throughout the different Council departments for dealing with complaints. As a result of the findings, the Council in question is reviewing its complaints procedures.

Developments in the use of research

There are a number of trends evident in the way research is commissioned and used.

Firstly, there is a growing tendency for general public research in an area to be a shared resource for different public agencies. This is a product of pressure on financial resources and of the way in which inter-agency co-operation is increasing. Examples of this in MORI's experience are surveys carrying questions for combinations of: different tiers of local authority, the police force, the Regional Health Authority, the local TEC and an NHS Trust. Economies of scale offer real savings as setting-up costs are shared between all participating parties. It can also lead to closer working relationships.

Secondly, as research is recognised as an important management tool in an organisation, surveys are increasingly run internally, with little or no outside involvement. This enables small-scale surveys to be done relatively cost-effectively. Additionally, research agencies are being used in an increasingly consultative role, to provide guidance on sampling and questionnaire design.

An example of this approach is MORI's work with Kent County Council. This began with corporate research, and developed into research for individual departments. Many of these departments now conduct their own research, using MORI in a consultative capacity, to assist in identifying research to meet departments' information needs.

Such an approach is not without its possible pitfalls. For example, it may be possible to 'lose' some of the costs (such as staff time, printing, postage) in other budgets. Thus, internally managed research may not be as cost-effective as it appears to be. Additionally, the issue of the opportunity cost of internal staff managing surveys needs to be considered. There are also methodological considerations; for example, a postal survey whose return address that can be identified with the organisation conducting the survey is likely to achieve a biased response and, possibly, a lower response rate than would be achieved by an independent research company. Despite these 'health warnings', there are occasions when research is appropriately handled internally, and others when it would be more effective to do this externally.

These developments mean that the relationship between public sector and research agency is changing. The researcher's function, however, remains the same: to identify ways to fill information gaps in a way that enables managers to make decisions to fulfil their objectives better.

■ ASPECTS TO CONSIDER IF COMMISSIONING RESEARCH

We could give dozens of examples of poor 'research' we have encountered. With this in mind, it seems useful to set out some of the key questions which managers considering undertaking research should ask themselves. The aim of asking these questions is to maximise the benefit an organisation might get from research and to rule out the possibility of commissioning — or setting up — bad research.

At a strategic level, survey research must be able to help solve the problem being dealt with. The objectives must be clear and there must be willingness to act on the findings, along with an understanding that research will solve nothing if not acted upon. One important issue is whether the cost of the research bears a reasonable relationship to the importance of the policies or measures that might be introduced as a result.

A number of questions centre around deciding whether to use internal or external researchers. For example, if internal staff do not have the expertise or time, an internally managed survey is a non-starter. If internal staff are used, they must have access to suitable facilities for data collection (such as interviewing) and data processing, and be able to deliver results and appropriate conclusions within the necessary timescale. When considering an outside agency, can they provide comparative data from other surveys to put the proposed survey into context? And do they have relevant experience and expertise? Cost is, of course a vital factor if a choice has to be made — what are the *real* comparative costs (including opportunity costs) of the different options?

On the practical side, survey design is crucial. We do not propose to present a full list of the questions which those considering commissioning should ask, rather a selection of the most important. Among the aspects which need to be decided upon are: sampling (which is the 'universe' to be sampled and what is the best way to sample it?); sample size (how many interviews are needed, and how much analysis is needed of different parts of the sample?); the questionnaire (how long? are there existing questions that can be used to provide comparison? are there enough questions which explore respondents' thinking?); fieldwork (how is the data going to be collected?); data processing and analysis (what are the quality control procedures? will the final output meet the organisation's needs?).

The survey output also needs to be considered at the planning stage. For instance, how to ensure that the survey data are presented in a way that will enable those who will have responsibility for taking action to use them easily? It may be that more than one reporting format would help maximise the effect of the research; for instance, a written report for those closest to the research, plus a presentation of key findings to the most senior executives.

In brief, the key to successful use of research is planning; in this way, expectations will not be dashed. On the one hand, the research option, when considered, can very often offer a cost-effective solution to a management challenge. On the other, research for its own sake, or to use up an allocated research budget, is of little use to anyone.

■ CONCLUSION

Research can help public sector managers meet the increasing challenges they face. It should be viewed as a potentially useful tool for management, not as a solution in its own right. It must be accompanied by the will to act, as it does not make decisions for managers; it helps managers make more effective, because better informed, decisions.

Whether it be in deciding on priorities between services, helping evaluate   policy   initiatives,   monitoring   and   targeting communications messages, or helping improve customer care and service delivery, survey research can play a valuable role for public sector managers.

PART C
Competition

Chapter 7

HEALTH IN THE MARKETPLACE

By David Fillingham

■ INTRODUCTION

The job of the Health Service Manager is to improve health and improve healthcare services. This is no easy task, as the 'end product' consists of thousands and thousands of intense personal experiences, each of which is a domestic drama in its own right. This chapter explores how the creation of a purchasing role for health authorities can help the health service rise to this challenge more effectively. The 'internal market' for health services in the NHS is intended to combine higher quality and greater cost-effectiveness with a continuing social concern. This can only be done if 'purchasers' adopt a way of working that is very different from the way management has traditionally operated in the NHS. What is needed are not efficient corporate bureaucrats, or even astute contract negotiators — to be successful, purchasers must act as 'social entrepreneurs'.

The chapter begins with an explanation of the NHS reforms as a response to the difficulties which the NHS faced during the late 1980s, in particular the perverse incentives that were built into its funding system. The internal market and the development of a purchasing role for health authorities are then depicted in the wider context of a restructuring of public sector services in the UK. The introduction of 'market forces' into health, education and the Civil Service is an attempt to make services more responsive to the consumer whilst at the same time containing their expenditure within the constraints on public spending.

The tendency for health service managers to form a naive interpretation of the new market arrangements is potentially highly damaging. This is not least true because of the high potential for market failure within the internal market arrangements in the NHS.

The actual agents of change — the GPs via their referral behaviour — are neither the official 'purchasers' nor the ultimate end-users of the services provided. Consequently, an alternative conception of the 'market' is needed.

Developments within the private sector provide just one such alternative in the emergence of dynamic networks or value-adding partnerships. The behaviours and skills needed within such arrangements are very different to those which are required within classical competitive markets. Moreover, the purchasing of health services is only part of the role of health authorities. Improving health which forms the rest of the remit, can only be done through advocacy, influence and persuasion. Health authority purchasers need to act as brokers both within the NHS internal network for services and in the wider network of community interests in regard to health.

On the basis of this analysis, the second part of the chapter outlines a number of challenges facing health authority purchasers:

- How to organise themselves and what skills and behaviours to adopt in order to operate effectively: the method of operation needs to be very different both from the traditional bureaucratic style of public sector monopolies and from the naive 'cut and thrust' approach to management suggested by some competitive market models.

- How to make the NHS internal market work effectively: this will involve understanding and influencing the clinical dynamics of the system which are what really determines what resources are used. This will require a chain to be established from patients, through general practitioners, to hospitals and consultants in order to develop more rational cost-effective behaviours which will be in the best interests both of patients and of the wider community,

- How to discharge their responsibilities for improving health: this will involve the creation of healthy partnerships with a diverse range of organisations and individuals. These partnerships must be mobilised in order to make change happen in situations where health authorities have no direct control. To do this they will need a greater breadth of outlook and more creative relations with the media, with local politicians and with influential power brokers.

- How to create a new relationship with residents: health authorities are purchasing on behalf of residents and must develop imaginative and systematic methods of finding out their needs and wants; they must be able to stimulate community action and lend support and help without disempowering those whose health they are trying to improve.

- How to 'connect': health authorities need to recognise that all of these activities are inter-related. Health is not a straightforward product which can be delivered off a production line in standardised packages. Health and health services involve highly complex interactions between individuals and their environments. Improving health and health services is about developing communities. An holistic approach is needed to integrate the fragmented elements of modern living, and fuse them into something of greater value.

This is an exciting if somewhat daunting task. Those working in health authorities who will carry this work forward successfully, are likely to be a long way removed from the traditional image of the bureaucratic health service administrator. The 'internal market' is a curious hybrid of a competitive market, managed public service, and a sophisticated dynamic network. Success in such an environment requires more than just marketing skills. It entails a fusion of entrepreneurial spirit with the ethics of public service.

■ THE NHS REFORMS: THE INTRODUCTION OF AN INTERNAL MARKET

Although the UK invests less in its health services than most other developed countries, the NHS is generally regarded as giving good value for money. The USA invests 11 per cent of GNP in health care compared to only 6 per cent in the UK, but in the United States, using an insurance-based system, 30 per cent of the population are not even covered by the States' safety net and effectively have no rights to any health care all (Ham, 1991a, p. 5).

The National Health Service, established in 1948, is a publicly funded system which gives equal access to health care to all citizens free at the point of delivery. However, during the 1980s it became clear that there were a number of problems with the operation of the NHS. More sensationalist accounts concentrated on alleged underfunding, and reports of the NHS 'in crisis' received high publicity (Cooke, 1987, p. 7).

More considered commentaries recorded a number of underlying structural problems quite apart from the issues of adequacy of funding (Ham, 1991a, p. 5; Enthoven, 1985, p. 9; Harrison *et al.*, 1989, p. 10). These included the following:

- Problems caused by increasing pressure on costs arising from the demands of an ageing population and the possibilities created by new medical technology and drug developments within the context of a publicly funded cash limited system.

- A very powerful lobby of hospital consultants with long-term employment contracts and enshrined rights to clinical freedom. This allowed consultants to specialise in their area of particular interest rather than concentrating on what consumers actually wanted or needed.

- Perverse incentives in funding arrangements, with those hospitals which were the most efficient and attracted the most patients being under the greatest pressure on resources as a consequence.

- A complete absence of incentives for innovation — managers were unlikely to 'rock the boat' by attempting to engineer any change, particularly in such a highly politicised environment as the NHS.

- Virtually no choice for patients — the pre-reform NHS was a service apparently run more in the interests of providers than for the benefit of the consumers.

The 1990 NHS and Community Care Act — *Working for Patients* — sought to redress these deficiencies in the service. Its declared aims were two-fold — to give patients better healthcare and greater choice of the services available and to produce greater satisfaction and rewards for NHS staff who successfully responded to local needs and preferences (Department of Health, 1989).

This was to be done through new funding arrangements which were an attempt to introduce an intermediate model part-way between a free market in healthcare and a centrally managed hierarchical system. This form of internal or social market had been mooted by Enthoven in 1985 in a pamphlet which was to become the cornerstone of the NHS Reforms (Enthoven, 1985). The system was to remain publicly funded but health authorities were to be given resources in respect of their resident populations and to procure healthcare from hospital and community unit providers.

Whilst these new arrangements would not necessarily create positive incentives for change, they did at least remove some of the disincentives embodied in the former bureaucratic system. However, *Working for Patients*, although it outlined the principles of the new funding arrangements, was very short indeed on the details of how they would work. Indeed, early guidance accompanying the NHS reforms focused much more strongly on the formation of NHS Trusts than on the creation of effective purchasing authorities. The Department of Health's official guidance (Department of Health, 1990) was heavily weighted toward the detailed establishment of contracts rather than a broader purchasing perspective.

Across the country, a wide variety of models has developed as health authorities have striven to implement the reforms, and to 'make the market work'. Understandably there has been confusion. Many sections of the media, and consequently a large part of the public, equate an 'internal market' with the commercialisation or even privatisation of healthcare. Some NHS managers have taken a somewhat naive view of the new arrangements and have indiscriminately applied what they believe to be private sector marketing techniques and behaviour. An essential prerequisite to determining the 'marketing' approach appropriate to an internal or social market is a more sophisticated understanding of how that market functions.

■ A MARKET OR NOT A MARKET? — MARKETS, HIERARCHIES AND NETWORKS

Those health service managers, on both sides of the purchaser/provider divide, who have adopted a 'naive' interpretation of the new market arrangements (Culyer et al., 1990, p. 3) appear to have been inspired by some models of business strategy which have been developed in the private sector. They have tended to see the marketplace as a battleground and the contracting process as analogous to warfare (Ries and Trout, 1986, p. vi). This has led hospitals and community units to develop strategies for attack and defence with an emphasis on success at all costs and a view of patients as the ground to be fought over and won.

In some places this approach to the market has gone spectacularly wrong. Purchasers have set out in aggressive, business-like mode, intending to 'market-test' services and move large numbers of treatments from one hospital to another. But then well-orchestrated pressure from providers, local people, general practitioners and, often, MPs, has forced the purchaser to back down and take a different approach. It is revealing that the large-scale rationalisation of hospital services in London has not been driven entirely by a 'free market' approach. A much more managed process has been applied which recognises the political and clinical complexities and seeks to build alliances supportive of change (Donaldson, 1992).

As a result, a number of commentators have begun to question whether market forces will actually be allowed to operate freely in practice despite the sometimes aggressive rhetoric (Ham, 1991a). It has been argued that a balance between management and competition is what is really needed. This is a different conception of the market — one which is less 'red in tooth and claw' and which operates along more collaborative lines as is the case in some segments of the private sector (Maynard, 1991). Contestability and competition are still important as a spur to greater efficiency and quality, but they are contained within a supportive set of long-term relationships.

Limitations of the market model

Advocates of free markets argue that they are the most effective way of co-ordinating a large number of complex interactions, However, critics of this classic approach point to the capacity for market failures. When a market fails the equilibrium between supply and demand which is achieved under perfect competition is not realised and the total resources of the marketplace are no longer being used to best effect.

There is significant potential for market failure within the NHS internal market. Competition is, in reality, very limited. Hospitals represent huge capital investments and neither entry into the market nor exit from it can take place easily. Whilst health authority purchasers will seek to use competition at the margins to improve quality and efficiency, it is not feasible to switch large volumes of business from one hospital to another in response to market forces. This means that power tends to become concentrated in the hands of a small number of important hospital or community services providers within any particular geographic locality.

In terms of 'externalities' — that is 'side-effects' of the market that are not reflected in a financial bottomline, the internal market is even further from the perfect competition model. The raison d'être of the NHS is social and not economic. The bottom line of the organisation

— improved health and better-quality health services — is intangible and cannot be simply captured in a pricing mechanism. Despite a large investment in information technology, the NHS internal market is a long way from having perfect information sharing between buyers and sellers. The market has been established on the basis that price should be equivalent to cost, but inadequate and inconsistent accounting systems means that price signals are inevitably strained and distorted (Culyer et al., 1990).

To add a further complication, the health authorities who make purchasing decisions are not the end-users of the services they are buying. Furthermore, they cannot actually control the way the system works in practice. Whilst contracts within the internal market might regulate the flow of resources, it is the general practitioners' act of referral which regulates the flow of patients around the system. Consequently, neither the proxy purchaser — the health authority — nor the actual end-user — the patient — has effective power to determine the way the market works.

The difficulties faced by those operating the internal market are not restricted to getting it to deliver high-quality health services — the market must also fulfil the other part of the remit of the NHS — improving the health of the individual and the community. It is questionable whether a market model is helpful in achieving this. Indeed, there are some who feel that the medical model of the compliant patient has simply been replaced by a managerial model of individuals as consumers making choices within a healthcare market. Neither view gets to the heart of what is needed to improve the health of individuals and communities. The 'new Public Health' Movement, believes this can only be achieved by creating a healthy environment, reducing poverty and improving housing and other conditions by working with local communities (Ashton and Seymour, 1988). Historically, however, the NHS has been peripheral to these initiatives and the resources needed to achieve success are not under its direct control (Hogg, 1991, p. 6).

In order to achieve the aim of bringing about improved health, therefore, health authority purchasers must learn the skills of inter-sectoral collaboration. Improving health means tackling issues concerning jobs, housing, education and leisure opportunities. None of these are financed by NHS resources, or come under health authority control. To achieve action, health authorities must learn to advocate, influence and persuade.

Less striking, but perhaps more concrete instances of the need for health authorities to work in a collaborative way are evidenced by the new community care arrangements. Under these arrangements, local authority social services departments hold a budget which can be used to support individuals who wish to live independently in the community, but who need some form of clinical or social support to do so. If the new arrangements are not to become 'lack of care in the community', then it is essential that the various agencies involved learn to put collaboration before competition (Wolstenholme and Davidson, 1993).

For those working in health services, recent policy developments thus appear to contain an apparent paradox between, on the one hand, the pressure of market driven reforms emphasising choice and competition, and on the other exhortations to greater collaboration and working together (Smith et al., 1993). What is needed is a model which can be successfully adopted to help resolve these contradictions. The challenge to health authority purchasers is how to organise themselves and what skills and behaviours to deploy to be successful in this new environment. They must demonstrate that they can achieve results as the purchasing component within the health services internal market, whilst at the same time working collaboratively with a vast array of agencies and individuals to bring about better health within the community. Some aspects of classical private sector marketing may be applicable here. But there are great dangers if health service managers adopt these approaches unthinkingly.

It can clearly be seen from this that the way in which the market is perceived is crucial. Managers interpret the world through metaphors and that interpretation shapes and influences their thinking and, ultimately, their behaviour (Morgan, 1986). What is needed is a more productive mental model of the internal market (Senge, 1992), one which will lead health service managers to adopt attitudes and behaviours that will be the most conducive to bringing about improvements in health care delivery and in health.

An alternative approach — The dynamic network

The internal market must enable health service managers to combine a strategic overview with the benefits to be gained from choice and competition. It has to bring about simultaneously 'the orderliness of order and the disorderliness of creative freedom' (Schumacher, 1974, p. 203). This balancing act is not something which the public sector alone is faced with, but is also pertinent to firms operating in the private sector. In many fields, including manufacturing, publishing and the entertainment industry, examples are emerging of a new organisational form which attempts to do this. The form lies part-way between traditional corporate hierarchies and free markets, and is being called variously strategic alliances (Jarillo, 1988), dynamic networks (Miles and Snow, 1986) or value-adding partnerships (Johnston and Lawrence, 1988).

The existence of networks has long been recognised. However, these have normally been thought of as informal associations of professionals, either within or across organisations. These often come together as 'policy communities' to influence corporate or governmental thinking in respect of a particular area of interest. (Thompson et al., 1991 p. 204). But now networks are being consciously managed by entrepreneurs as firms begin to use co-operative behaviour to improve their individual competitive positions. The main features of emerging dynamic networks have been identified as follows (Miles and Snow, 1986):

● Vertical disaggregation: firms specialise in different parts of the value chain from raw material processing through manufacture to distribution.

● The role of the broker: a hub firm develops which takes on a lead role in directing the network and co-ordinating the activities of other firms.

● Market mechanisms: the major functions of the network are held together by market mechanisms rather than by plans and controls; contracts and payment for results are used more frequently than personal supervision.

● Full disclosure information systems: broadly accessed computer systems are often used as a substitute in dynamic networks for lengthy trust-building processes based on experience.

The components of the network are thus complementary rather than competing, as is shown in Figure 7.1.

Perhaps the most striking example of network development is to be found in the movie industry:

full blown movie studios that hold exclusive long term contracts with actors and directors, have a staff of full time composers and script writers, and own and operate fully equipped production studios are a thing of the past. Now the studios act like brokers who negotiate a set of contracts for film production. Old fashioned studios have been unable to compete

(Johnston and Lawrence, 1988, p. 98)

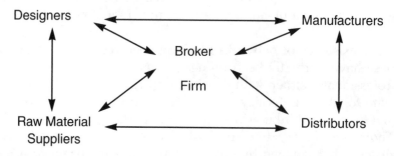

Figure 7.1

This provides an excellent analogy for the internal market within the NHS. NHS purchasers do engage in transactions to secure services. However, they are doing so not for their own benefit, but so that a complex network of providers can work together in a co-ordinated way to offer a product that is of value to the end-user. In movie industry terms this is the punter who attends the cinema to watch the film. In health service terms, it is the patient who is on the receiving end of treatment or care. It is perhaps going too far to suggest that dynamic networks are a post-entrepreneurial model that is becoming the norm. But there is no doubt that making the best use of synergies is the key to success in an increasingly competitive environment. To be successful in this new climate, however, managers need a new set of attributes (Moss-Kanter, 1989, p. 361).

They must:

- learn to operate without the might of the hierarchy behind them and use their individual skills rather than their formal position to achieve results.

- be able to compete in a way that enhances rather than undercuts the competition; to do this managers must become skilful collaborators.

- conduct their business to the highest ethical standards; trust is crucial to successful alliance building.

- develop a process focus — concentrating not only on what is to be achieved but on how.

● have an approach which is multi-faceted and ambidextrous —
be able to work across functions and business units in a way
that spots synergies and opportunities for alliance building

These are skills and attributes that must be developed by NHS
managers if the internal market arrangements are to operate
successfully and to the benefit of patients.

■ HOW SHOULD NHS PURCHASERS ORGANISE
THEMSELVES AND WHAT SKILLS AND ATTITUDES DO
THEY NEED?

The provision of health services is something which the NHS has
been practising for over forty years and of which it has substantial
experience. The creation of self-governing provider units as NHS
Trusts devolved more authority to those running hospitals and
community units. The need to 'compete' within the internal market
may be a totally new dimension but the vast majority of processes
and activities in which health service managers and provider units
are engaged has remained substantially the same as prior to the
reforms.

Purchasing however, is an entirely new discipline, and as Health
Ministers have recently recognised, success in purchasing is the key
to achieving results from the internal market. The danger is that
health service managers adopt too naive an interpretation of this
'market', seeing it is a classical, competitive enrivonment rather
than as a dynamic network. Early guidance from the Department of
Health with its heavy emphasis on the contracting process, did not
help in this regard (Department of Health, 1990). Consequently, the
skills which health authority purchasers saw themselves as most in
need of developing in the early years of the reforms were those of
contract specification and negotiation (Appleby, 1992, p. 7) Whilst
contracting does form part of the purchasing process, it is only a
small part and health authority purchasers require a much broader
range of skills, and indeed, a fundamentally different set of
attitudes.

Most health authority purchasers, however, in developing their
organisations, have maintained the traditional NHS 'boxed set' of a
District General Manager, Finance Director, Planning Director, a
Director of Public Health and a Quality Assurance Director. The
requirement for District Health Authorities to have five executive

directors seems to have constrained thinking in developing organisation structures for purchasing, and most purchasing teams are organised along functional lines (Appleby, 1992). The responsibilities for the various elements of the purchasing cycle are thus divided up functionally with needs assessment being carried out by public health doctors, review of services and strategy development by planners, contracts being negotiated by the finance department, and the nurses becoming Quality Assurance Directors responsible for setting standards and monitoring outcomes. The size of purchasing organisations varies greatly from as many as 200–300 staff down to as few as 30–40. The larger authorities have developed traditional-looking hierarchies built around their functional directorates.

It would seem that the inherent dangers of this approach are beginning to be realised. Unless purchasers are organised in a way that encourages innovation, the powerful lobbies opposing change can institutionalise the purchasing process to such a degree that it becomes simply a sophisticated way of allocating budgets to existing service providers. This is not because purchasers are lacking in power or failing to act aggressively enough. It is because they are not organised in the right manner to generate innovation, and consequently are behaving in such a way as will tend to maintain the status quo. What purchasers need are looser structures; a blurred matrix or cluster approach, which creates multi-disciplinary project teams with a strong customer focus. Experiences in the private sector have shown that this is by far the most reliable way of generating innovation. (Moss-Kanter, 1985; Quinn-Mills, 1991; Schonberger, 1990).

Developing new skills and behaviours

The skills which health service managers have traditionally needed have been those which have helped them to work effectively within hierarchies. The NHS has been dominated by a variety of herarchies from the medical model of the autocratic consultant through the regimented nursing battalions to the corporate hierarchies of general managers. The skills and behaviours required of health services purchasers do not fit neatly with this traditional model. Rather a premium should be placed on the ability to develop partnerships and to work towards effective decisions based on a sound analysis of data and evidence. (Jarrold, 1991). Skills and behaviours which are required of purchasers will include good interpersonal skills, effective informal and formal negotiating ability and a predilection for change. Pamela Charlwood, formerly Regional General Manager of South Western Region, and Director of the Institute of Health Service Management, has summed this up by saying that: 'Purchasing is about lateral thinking, imagination and vision, and about being innovative, taking risks and being courageous. An effective purchaser will need a lot of bottle' (Charlwood, 1992, p. 10).

The need for long-term vision

Purchasing organisations thus need to become more effective by developing customer focused multi-disciplinary ways of working and by identifying and developing the new skills and attributes which purchasing managers will require. There is a danger, however, that this purchasing activity proceeds in a vacuum. What is needed is a coherent long-term vision — a strategy for the development of health and health services over a five- to ten-year period, which can inform and invigorate year-on-year purchasing plans. To return to an earlier analogy, the film production industry is now a diverse network of many different types of company. They are able to collaborate successfully in the enterprise of film production because they have an overall unifying sense of purpose. The mechanism for drawing them all together exists in the film concept and script outline. Within the internal market some providers currently appear to be acting out scenes from *Macbeth* whilst others seem to believe that the production is actually a version of *The Sound of Music*. The equivalent of a clear script is needed to draw the different players in the network together in an effective manner. This long-term strategy should be developed in an iterative way with the full involvement of the relevant stakeholders. It should not be a firm blueprint as to how health services will develop, but should establish some common values and principles and be bold enough to quantify what is to be achieved over the coming years. Quantifiable targets should be set for improvements in health and the quality of services and in achieving better value for taxpayers' money. These have often been seen in the past as intangibles which are difficult to quantify. There is no doubt there are difficulties involved, but the *Health of the Nation* strategy and the Patients' Charter are a step in the right direction. These strategy documents now need extending and localising so that there is a coherent shared vision amongst all the stakeholders in the network as to how health and health services will develop. The development of such a long-term strategy will be an essential part of the process of becoming an effective purchaser. In the shorter term, however, there are more immediate challenges in getting the 'market' to work at all. These arise out of the fact that the purchasers' 'contracts' are not in reality the dynamic which drives the system. The key to making the market work in practice rests in the hands of the general practitioner.

■ HOW CAN THE NHS INTERNAL MARKET BE MADE TO WORK IN PRACTICE?

The market in reality — the role of the general practitioner

The NHS internal market is likely to be prone to market failure due to lack of perfect competition, the absence of good information and the existence of externalities that are not reflected in the price mechanism. This likelihood is strengthened by a more fundamental problem, that those who actually commit resources in the market are not the same as either the ultimate end-users (i.e. patients) nor the official purchaser, the health authorities. The real drivers of the market are the general practitioners who, by their referrals, move patients around the system. In reality, it is the act of referral that is the act of purchase. It is this which commits the use of health service resources. Unless health authorities can find a way of shaping and influencing GP referral patterns, then contracting will simply be a paper exercise.

GP fundholding

The GP fundholding scheme is an attempt to overcome this problem by allocating a budget directly to general practitioners. Only larger practices with over 7,000 patients are eligible although consortia of smaller practices can form themselves into fundholding units. A budget is allocated to the practice on the basis of historic activity in regard to the practice's own prescribing costs, staff employed within the practice, such as nurses, managers and receptionists, and the cost of the GP's referrals for a limited list of diagnostic and treatment procedures. The fundholding practice then sets its own contracts with hospitals and community units for the provision of services. Health authority purchasers in the main are still using simple block contracts which pay an annual amount for a given facility, and which are not particularly sensitive to changes in volume. GP fundholders, however, have been quicker to adopt more sensitive cost and volume or cost per case contracts. It is more likely therefore that in the case of GP fundholding, money will actually follow the patient as GPs switch their referral patterns to achieve shorter waiting times, higher quality treatment or a lower price. Hospital providers have, not surprisingly, been quick to seek to win the favours of GP fundholders. GP fundholding has the potential to initiate significant change as a result. Benefits which have been established by fundholders throughout the country, have included developments such as out-patient clinics held in the practices' own surgery, and improvements in communication between the hospital and the practice. The practice is also allowed to retain any savings made from the fund and reinvest them in additional patient care services. This provides an incentive to scrutinise activity more closely in order to reduce inappropriate referrals or prescribing where possible. There are instances where this has been shown to provide both a more cost-effective service and a higher quality of treatment for the patient. For example, the use of physiotherapy instead of an orthopaedic outpatients' referral, or of referral to an in-surgery counsellor instead of a tranquiliser prescription.

Locality sensitive purchasing

Health authority purchasers have found it feasible to liaise with fundholding practices as these are relatively small in number and often amongst the most articulate and politically aware of general practices. A greater challenge lies in the need to engage non-fundholding GPs as it is their referral behaviour which still provides the engine for the greater part of the internal market.

Purchasers most certainly recognise the importance of working with general practitioners but have not always found this easy. (Kings Fund College Learning Set). As seen by the Secretary of State from the top down, the health service looks relatively neat and tidy, with its well-defined hospitals and community unit trusts, family health service and district health authorities. Seen from the bottom up, however, it looks a lot less structured with a plethora of independent contractors — general practitioners, pharmacists, dentists and opticians — who filter out patients as they move through the system (Jarrold, 1991). Purchasers have tried a range of initiatives to engage general practitioners in a dialogue, including visits to practices, questionnaires, interviews, and general practitioner representatives on purchasing teams (Kings Fund College Learning Set). An emerging notion which has the benefit of reinforcing the connection with GPs in a structural manner, is to group general practitioners into localities in order to engage them in a debate about purchasing priorities. Those elements of the profession itself which are sceptical about benefits of fundholding, see locality purchasing as an effective way forward (Medical Practitioners Union, 1992b; GMSC, 1992). The concept can be understood diagrammatically as shown in Figure 7.2:

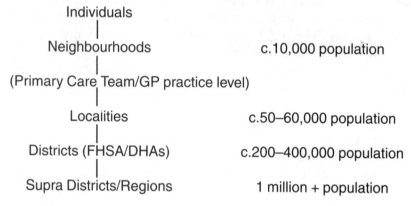

Individuals
|
Neighbourhoods   c.10,000 population
|
(Primary Care Team/GP practice level)
|
Localities   c.50–60,000 population
|
Districts (FHSA/DHAs)   c.200–400,000 population
|
Supra Districts/Regions   1 million + population

Figure 7.2

This form of structure mirrors to some extent what happens in the real world. An individual's first point of contact with the health service is normally his or her general practitioner, operating at a neighbourhood level with a list size of between 3,000 and 10,000 patients. If the individual needs referral for diagnosis or treatment, this normally occurs to a hospital operating at the district level on a population of between 200,000 and 400,000 residents. Exceptionally, if specialist referral is needed, the resident may eventually move on to a tertiary centre operating at a supra-district level. Most planning and management of health services has traditionally been carried out at district level. Prior to the health service reforms, there was very little dialogue between health authorities and general practitioners and little opportunity for either the individual receiving the treatment or staff working at a grass roots level to shape and influence the development of health services.

Health authority purchasers have found it difficult to engage with the large number of independent general practitioners — in a district of 350,000 residents, there would be around 180 GPs. This is not helped by the fact that general practitioners are fiercely jealous of their independent contractor status and many of them are focused narrowly on their own practice populations and may well be idiosyncratic in their referral behaviour. The locality is a link which can help health authorities to engage GPs and seek to influence their clinical behaviour. A number of health authorities around the country are currently developing locality arrangements of one form or other (Ham, 1992b). Stockport Health Authority is perhaps the most often quoted example of a locality-managed system. In Stockport District, managers from the health authority purchaser are each linked to a locality and are responsible for identifying needs and assessing service strengths and weaknesses in regard to that locality, in consultation with general practitioners and other stakeholders. Some authorities have used the locality more explicitly as a focus for community involvement. In Dorset, for example, patch workers have been appointed and in the South East London Commissioning Agency, locality co-ordinators work closely with GPs and others at a neighbourhood level. In some districts such as Bath and North Derbyshire, slightly more formal practice-sensitive purchasing arrangements have been developed. In these areas, notional or indicative budgets are established at practice and locality level, and the health authority purchaser seeks to influence the development of services in line with these notional resources, in an attempt to mirror GP fundholding without the burden of administration falling on the GPs themselves (Ham, 1992b).

Wirral Health Authorities have taken the approach of seeing localities, not only as a means of intelligence gathering for purchasers, but also as a way of developing primary care and community health services and of developing a dialogue with local residents.

Health authority purchasers are thus developing a locality approach in order to create an intelligence network whereby issues and needs can be identified from the bottom up. Emerging purchasing strategies can be tested out through this network, whilst they are still being formulated. These locality arrangements are at their most powerful where GP fundholders and non-fundholders work closely together so that the benefits of fundholding can be extended to a wider section of the population. The involvement of GPs in this way, through locality-sensitive purchasing, gives the health authorities a better chance of achieving their commitment to service changes such as the movement of a particular category of work from one hospital provider to another. It is more likely, if GPs have been involved, that they will feel committed to the proposed changes and will switch referrals as a result. Only if this is achieved will the contracts developed by health authority purchasers actually become meaningful and the market be made to work in practice.

The role of the general practitioner complicates the 'market' for health services. The marketplace for health, however, is even more complex! For purchasers to be successful in it, they must be able to develop partnerships with a wide and highly diverse range of agencies:

■ HOW CAN 'THE MARKET' IMPROVE HEALTH?

As was indicated earlier in this chapter, the causes of ill-health are multi-factorial and have their roots as much in society as in biology (Ashton, 1984). It has been shown that there is a strong correlation between social deprivation and ill-health (Townsend, Davidson and Whitehead, 1988; Smith and Jacobson (eds), 1988). Consequently tackling this problem and seeking to bring about improved health requires intersectoral action — many agencies and individuals working together towards a common aim.

Those partnerships for health which have proved the most successful have focused on recognisable communities. It is at the level of the city, the village or the neighbourhood that action is needed. Because these are communities with which citizens can readily identify, there are good prospects for participation, harnessing neighbourhood or civic pride. As long as the community is large enough to muster the necessary resources and to secure the political mandate and authority to develop and implement multisectoral approaches to health, it stands a better chance if it is small enough to establish strong partnerships based on personal working relationships (Ashton et al., 1986, pp. 319–24).

A significant help to effective joint working in many areas has been the existence of government aid for the inner cities through the City Challenge programme. Although aimed primarily at economic regeneration and the improvement of housing and community facilities, these programmes stand to impact enormously upon health. By requiring community groups, local government and the private sector to work together effectively, they are following the best principles of intersectoral working. Arising out of these practical instances of success, a number of guidelines can be identified for the creation of healthy partnerships:

- Focus on recognisable communities that can empower citizens and harness their energies and enthusiasm.
- Include all partners in strategy formulation through joint vision-building events and constant communication (Hancock in Ashton *et al.*, 1992).
- Adopt a flexible approach which allows opportunistic action based upon the shared vision — 'goal-directed muddling through' (Hancock in Ashton *et al.*, 1992).
- Erode hierarchical structures in favour of looser, more flexible networks.
- Recognise and allow for the differences in culture and in perspective between organisations.
- Develop a shared language and avoid alienating professional jargon.
- Create a new relationship with the media and harness their potential for raising awareness and stimulating action.
- Train all those involved in the skills for intersectoral collaboration.

Those who are facilitating healthy partnerships are likely to be coaches and catalysts rather than prescriptive bosses (Ashton *et al.*, 1986, p. 322). They will need to operate as social entrepreneurs who are able to use good business skills but who will have public service values (Duhl in Ashton *et al.*, 1992, p. 18). Such individuals are likely to be in short supply and will have to be trained rather than discovered. Lessons from the private sector world of dynamic networks and value-adding partnerships may well be helpful in that development. In particular, successful commercial businesses have found ways of fostering a culture which is responsive to the customer. A major criticism of the managed public sector has traditionally been that it is a self-sustaining bureaucracy that fails to understand or respond to the views of service users. A difficulty exists for health authority purchasers, however, in identifying who the 'customer' actually is! Patients are only that minority group in the population that happens to be sick at any particular time. Health service purchasers need to cast their net wider than this — and in doing so they will need to adopt new techniques and behaviours if they are to become truly responsive to their customers.

◾ HOW CAN A NEW RELATIONSHIP BE FORGED WITH RESIDENTS?

Working for Patients, as its title suggests, was mainly about the provision of health services. The assumptions underlying it were those of the medical model of patients as passive recipients of professional intervention. Purchasers tend to be less concerned with patients and more with residents. Residents might be ill or well, healthy or unhealthy, and the challenge for the purchaser is to see them as empowered citizens rather than as compliant patients. A White Paper for purchasing ought perhaps to be entitled *Working for Residents.*

Since the introduction of the NHS reforms, there has been a dramatic increase in attempts to discover what residents actually think about health services. A critical review of literature in 1987 produced a fairly sparse collection of studies of consumer views. The majority of these were inspired or actively supported by community health councils (Jones *et al.,* 1990). By the time the Department of Health's Local Voices document had been published in 1992, health authorities themselves had become the main instigators of consumer research projects. There are now a variety of guides and toolkits being produced to assist them in this process, such as *The Public as Partners* (Healthgain Conference, 1992) and the *Kings Fund Consumer Feedback* series. (Jones, Leneham and MacLean, 1990).

Potential pitfalls of adopting market research techniques

Effective market research is at a premium in any field. It requires careful planning, preparation and execution. This is particularly so in health care, where the nature of the services delivered and of the client groups creates some particular difficulties. These include:

- Tokenism: a 'tick in a box' mentality with the activity being marginal to the health authority's main role.

- Failure to make use of the results.

- Over-mechanistic application: The policy making process is essentially a political one, where wide debate and dialogue are needed in order to reach effective judgements. Good consumer research can play an important part in this, but ought not to drive the process in too mechanistic a way (Hunter, 1993).

- Poor design or implementation of research can undermine its validity and usefulness.

- Over-intrusiveness of research studies. Some studies of residents' views may entail an exploration of very personal ideas, feelings and emotions and a great deal of sensivity and care is needed in their implementation.

- Paralysis by analysis: the NHS as a public sector monopoly, has a tendency to bureaucratise its activities. Developing an effective dialogue with residents ought to be an exciting and energising process for health service managers and for residents alike, but the bureaucratisation of it can have the opposite effect.

Developing an effective dialogue with residents

The development of an effective dialogue with residents must not be seen as a separate initiative taking place on the margin of the organisation. It is central to the health authorities' role and should be built into all purchasing processes. What is required is a gradual change to a culture which naturally and readily considers the views of residents and seeks to make health authority decisions more explicit and understandable. A number of principles have proved to be effective in practice:

- Small scale can be powerful: research into residents' views is most useful when it is initiated by those who are able to make meaningful changes as a result of what is learned. This can often be done very effectively at the level of the general practice, the community clinic or the hospital ward.

- Adopt techniques suited to the purpose: There are a number of different aims both for research into residents' views and for communications from health authorities. Appropriate techniques need to be selected to suit the purpose of the research and the target audience.

- Focus on specific groups: the population and the task at hand need to be effectively segmented.

- Be clear about the aims and intended benefits: it is essential that health service managers are clear at the outset how they are to use the results of any particular research or communications exercise.

- Clarity of language: avoidance of NHS jargon and professional bias is another essential prerequisite whether in giving or receiving information.

- Underpromise and overdeliver: the initiation of a communications or consumer research programme can raise expectations amongst a wide range of groups. This can quickly turn to cynicism if results are not delivered quickly and if action is not seen to follow.

- Have patience: the development of an effective dialogue is a long-term process. It is essential that purchasers have patience and retain a sense of humour as some setbacks will be inevitable.

Tools and techniques

A wide range of tools and techniques exist for establishing a dialogue with residents, and some useful guidance has been developed on how to use these appropriately. These include:

- questionnaires
- focus group discussions
- observation of real service situations
- the use of advocacy for vulnerable or less articulate groups
- rapid appraisal — a means of obtaining quick feedback from 'key informants' within a community.

Health authorities are also discovering that there are many agencies that already have effective networks within the community including community education colleges, leisure centres, residents' and tenants' associations, voluntary groups and the neighbourhood watch system. These existing networks can effectively be used for the dissemination of information about health and health services and to seek views in return. Some health authorities are currently exploring ideas such as a health shop or resource centre, a mobile unit such as a health bus, and even a community radio station which would enable a lively debate on health and health service issues. Whatever means are adopted, it is crucial that health authority purchasers place the development of an effective dialogue with residents at the very centre of their activities. Even though the NHS may not have a 'real' market, it is essential that the voice of the consumer is heard if the quasi-market is to secure the desired benefits.

■ ENDNOTE: HOW TO 'CONNECT'

The field of health and health services is a complex one, involving a morass of moral, legal, political, social and economic issues. Health authority purchasers must be able to command a vast range of technical detail from chiropody to Creutzfeldt-Jakob disease, from bed-baths to bypass grafts. This complexity is compounded by the NHS focus on structures and on processes rather than on outcomes. The Department of Health and the NHS management executive, through regions, still attempt to manage the day-to-day activities of health services rather than setting a strategic framework and clarifying what is to be achieved over the long term This approach results in management by 'executive letter' — missives which emerge from the Department of Health stipulating action to be taken across a wide range of disparate initiatives.

The Department of Health itself is a classic bureaucracy, organised in a highly compartmentalised manner with separate sections dealing with every aspect of health services, from GP fundholding to the Patients' Charter, from Care in the Community to Health of the Nation. Consequently there is a danger that health service managers see their job merely as a series of separate unconnected initiatives. To be effective, purchasing cannot possibly operate in this manner. It must take an holistic, integrative approach; one which sees individual patients as part of wider communities, and health services as an integral part of our social structure.

Purchasers must be able to make connections. They must be able to make connections between many different dimensions:

● Connections between ostensibly separate issues, the Patients' Charter, Health of the Nation, Local Voices, Needs Assessment and the Development of Purchasing Plans.

● Connections between the different stakeholders within the health services network and the wider networks for health, including GPs, hospital and community services professionals, Local Authority managers and councillors, voluntary organisations and residents themselves.

- Connections up and down the system between those at grass roots level and policymakers, and laterally across the system, between the different agencies who need to work together more effectively.

- Connections between health and the wider issues of community development. Between the work of health professionals and that of economic regeneration, housing action, and better education.

- Connections between the present state and their vision of the future. This involves the development of a creative tension to provide sufficient energy to make change happen.

To do all this, health service purchasers must work very differently from the way in which they have operated in the past. They must be able to integrate rationality and intellect with intuition and values. In this sense, purchasing is a creative process. The concept of the purchaser as a social entrepreneur is a useful one. Purchasers must hold dear a clear, passionate picture of better health and better services, but at the same time must be quick on their feet and able to act opportunistically to achieve their goals. They must be able to make effective connections within a delicately balanced network, full of competitive pressures arising from individual and organisational hopes, ambitions, paranoias and rivalries. Above all, they must be able to make the connection between an all-absorbing, often frustrating but ultimately highly satisfying job of work for themselves and the wider social good of better services and better health for the residents they serve.

■ REFERENCES

APPLEBY (1984) *et al.* (1992) *Second Survey of DGMs*, NAHAT Project Paper No 7.

ASHTON, J. *Health in Mersey — A Review*, Liverpool; University of Liverpool.

ASHTON, J., GREY, P. and BARNARD, K. (1986) 'Healthy Cities —

WHO's New Public Health Initiative', *Health Promotion*, vol No 3, pp. 319–24.

ASHTON, J. and SEYMOUR, H. (1988) *The New Public Health*, Milton Keynes, Open University Press.

ASHTON, J., (ed.) (1992) *Healthy Cities*, Buckingham; O.U.P.

AUDIT COMMISSION (1992) *Homeward Bound*, London; HMSO.

BOTTOMLEY, V. (1993) 'Four Point Plan to develop Purchasing', *Department of Health Press Release*, 23rd February.

CHARLWOOD, P. (1992) 'Have we got what it takes? Developing the capacity for effective purchasing' in *Beyond the Contract Relationship*, IHSM Conference Proceedings, 5 December p. 9–10.

COOK, J. (1987) *Whose Health is it Anyway?*, London, New English Library.

CULYER, A. J. *et al.* (eds), (1990) *Competition in Healthcare*, London, Macmillan.

DELANEY, F., and MORAN, G. (1991) 'Collaboration for Health in Theory and Practice', *Health Education Journal*, vol 50 no 2, pp. 97–9.

DEPARTMENT OF HEALTH (1992) *Health of the Nation*, London, HMSO.

DEPARTMENT OF HEALTH (1989) *Working for Patients*, London, HMSO.

DEPARTMENT OF HEALTH (1990) *Contracts for Health Services: Operating Contracts* (EL(90)MB/24).

DONALDSON, L. J. (1992) 'Maintaining excellence: the preservation and development of specialised services', *BMJ*, vol 305, 21 November.

ENTHOVEN, A. C., (1985) *Reflections on the Management of the NHS*, London, Nuffield Provincial Hospitals Trust, Occasional Paper No 5.

ENTHOVEN, A. C. (1989) 'What Can Europeans Learn from Americans?', *Health Care Financing Review*, Annual Supplement p. 49–63.

FILLINGHAM, D. J. (1991) 'When Bargaining is a Life or Death Issue', *Personnel Management*, March pp. 36–9.

FOSTER, A. (1991) 'Intentions and Possibilities in the Commissioning Process', *Beyond the Contract Relationship*, IHSM Conference Proceedings, 5 December 1991 pp. 5–6.

GENERAL MEDICAL SERVICES COUNCIL (1992) *Commissioning Care: Options for GPs*, November 1992.

GIBSON, T. (1979) *People Power*, Harmondsworth, Penguin Books.

HAM, C. (1991a) 'Managed competition in theory and practice',

Internalising the market, IHSM Conference Proceedings, 25 January 1991, p. 5–7.

HAM, C. (1991b) *The New National Health Service*, Oxford, Radcliffe Medical Press.

HAM, C. and HEGINBOTHAM, C. (1991) *Purchasing Together*, London, King's Fund College.

HAM, C. (1992a) *DHA/FHSA Developments*, NAHAT Discussion Paper, October.

HAM, C. (1992b) *Locality Purchasing*, Birmingham University Discussion Paper 30.

HAM, C. (1992c) 'Learning from the experience', *Advancing the Reforms*, IHSM Conference Proceedings, 5 March 1992, pp. 9–11.

HAM, C. (1992d) *Health Policy in Britain*, London, Macmillan.

HARRISON, S., HUNTER, D. J., JOHNSTON, I. and WISTOW, G. (1989) *Competing for Health*, University of Leeds: Nuffeld Institute for Health Service Studies.

HEALTHGAIN CONFERENCE '92, *The Public as Partners: a Toolkit*.

HOGG, C. (1991) *Healthy Change*, London, Socialist Health Association.

HUNTER, D. (1993) *Rationing Dilemmas in Healthcare*, NAHAT.

ILLICH, I. (ed.) (1977a) *Disabling Professions*, London, Boyars.

ILLICH, I., (1977b) *Limits to Medicine*, Harmondsworth, Penguin.

JARILLO, J. C. (1988) 'Strategic Networks,' *Strategic Management Journal*, vol 9, p. 31–41.

JARROLD, K. (1991) in *From Hierarchies to Partnerships*, IHSM Conference Proceedings, 29 November, 1991, pp. 5–8.

JOHNSTON, R. and LAWRENCE, P. R. (1988). 'Beyond Vertical Integration — the rise of the VAP,' *Harvard Business Review*, July–August 1988, pp. 94–101.

JONES, L., LENEHAN, L. and MACLEAN, U. (1990) *Consumer Feedback for the NHS*, London, Kings Fund.

KINGS FUND COLLEGE LEARNING SET. (undated) The Commissioning Experience, Kings Fund Papers, No 6.

KLEIN and REDMAYNE. (1991) *Patterns of Priorities*, NAHAT Research Paper No 7.

MAYNARD, A. (1991) 'Will Competition Work?', *Internalising the market*, IHSM Conference proceedings, 25 January, 1991, p. 17.

MEDICAL PRACTITIONERS UNION (1992) *Alternatives to Fundholding*.

MILES, R. E. and SNOW, C. C. (1986) 'Organisations: new concepts for new forms,' *California Management Review*, Spring 1986, pp. 62–73.

MCIVER, S. (1991) *Obtaining the Views of Users of Health Services*, London, Kings Fund Centre.

MORGAN, G. (1986) *Images of Organisation*, London, Sage.

MORGAN, G. (1989) *Creative Organisation Theory*, London, Sage.

MOSS-KANTER, R. (1985) *The Change-Masters*, London, Unwin.

MOSS-KANTER, R. (1989) *When Giants Learn to Dance*, London, Unwin.

NEWCHURCH & CO. LTD. (1992) *Social Businesses: restructuring the Public Sector*, October 1992.

NHS MANAGEMENT EXECUTIVE. (1992) *Local Voices*, Leeds.

NHS MANAGEMENT EXECUTIVE. (1993) *Purchasing for Health, a Framework for Action*, Leeds.

O'DWYER, A. (1990) *Intersectoral Collaboration in the Healthy City Network*, University of Liverpool MPH Thesis.

POWLES, J. W. and GIFFORD, S. (1993) 'Health of Nations: Lessons from Victoria, Australia,' *BMJ*, vol 306, 9 January 1993.

QUINN-MILLS, D. (1991) *Rebirth of the Corporation*, Chichester, Wiley & Sons.

RIES, A. and TROUT, J. (1986) *Marketing Warfare*, London, McGraw Hill.

SCHONBERGER, R. J. (1990) *Building a Chain of Customers*, London, Guild.

SCHUMACHER, E. F. (1974) *Small is Beautiful*, London, Abacus.

SENGE, P. (1992) *The Fifth Discipline*, London, Century Business Books.

SMITH, R. *et al.* (1993) *Working together for better Community Care*, SAUS.

SMITH, A., and JACOBSEN, B., (eds) (1988) *The Nation's Health*, London; Health Education Authority.

SPEIGAL, N. *et al.* (1992) 'Managing Change in General Practice,' *BMJ*, vol 304, 25 January 1992, pp. 231–4.

TAKERT, A. R., (ed.) (1988) *Making Partners*, Utrecht, WHO.

THOMPSON G., *et al.* (eds) (1991) *Markets, Hierarchies and Networks*, Sage, London.

TOWNSEND, P., DAVIDSON, N. and WHITEHEAD, M. (1988) *Inequalities in Health*, Harmondsworth, Penguin.

WINN, L., and QUICK, A. (undated) *User Friendly Services*, London, Kings Fund Centre.

WIRRAL HEALTH AUTHORITIES (1993) *Health in Wirral*, Wirral.

WOLSTENHOLME AND DAVIDSON, (1993) 'Making a Reality of Community Care', *Primary Care Management*, vol. 3, no 4, April 1993, p. 2–4.

YOUNGER, T. (1992) *Purchasing: Observations of an American in London*, discussion paper presented 19 August 1992.

Chapter 8

THE IMPACT OF COMPETITION

by Kieron Walsh

■ INTRODUCTION

Market mechanisms and competition are central to the development of the new public sector management. At one extreme there is the privatisation of services such as water, gas and electricity, with government retaining, at most, a regulatory role, attempting to ensure that monopoly power is not exploited, and that the needs of consumers are considered. Where privatisation is not seen as appropriate or possible a range of other mechanisms are being used in order to introduce market pressure. In local government services there has been widespread competitive tendering for manual services, now to be extended to white-collar and professional services, notably housing management. In central government there has been the establishment of executive agencies and, more recently, market testing. An internal market has been introduced in the National Health Service, and in social care there is a 'mixed economy of care' with extensive provision of services by private providers. Market mechanisms are also beginning to have an effect in other sectors for example the police service and the justice system (Raine and Willson, 1993).

The range of mechanisms being used is wide. Figure 8.1 shows the various mechanisms that have been developed and the contexts in which they are used. The implications of these changes are difficult to interpret, because there has not yet been time for detailed evidence to emerge. There is, though, sufficient data to allow us to draw some tentative conclusions. This chapter summarises the evidence on the impact of competitive mechanisms in government under six headings: the financial impact of market mechanisms; the managerial and organisational effects; information and market mechanisms; service quality; accountability; and the impacts on staff and industrial relations. I then go on to consider likely future developments of competitive and market processes. I shall finish by trying to draw out some of the lessons of competition and markets as we have experienced them in the public service.

Market mechanism	Context of use
Competitive tendering/Market testing	Local government — building and highways construction and maintenance Manual services, such as refuse collection Leisure services Professional Services Housing management Central government services National Health Service — ancillary services
Private sector provision allowed in competition with public services	Building control service Inspection of schools
Contracting with the private sector	Community care
Internal trading	Local authority direct service and direct labour organisations
Devolved financial control	Local management of schools Fundholding family practitioners
Executive control/Opting out	Grant-maintained schools Trust hospitals and other health units
Purchaser/Provider split	National Health Service, social care, and more generally

Figure 8.1   Market mechanisms in the public service

■ FINANCIAL EFFECTS

Much financial benefit has been claimed from the introduction of market mechanisms in the public service, but the basis for such claims is not strong. It is difficult to make accurate assessments of the costs of services before and after changes because of the limitations of accountancy, and concerns for commercial confidentiality. The costs of the client side are difficult to determine. The increased social costs, for example of unemployment, are not known. Despite these difficulties some assessment can be made.

Research has commonly shown that savings follow from contracting out and competitive tendering (for a summary of the findings on the financial impacts of competition *see* Carnaghan and Bracewell-Milnes, 1993). Central government has generally claimed substantial savings from its own contracting out, typically of 25 per cent or more. William Waldegrave initially claimed such savings from market testing in the Civil Service, but, more recently, has reduced the claim to savings of 14 per cent. It is difficult to judge the validity of such claims since they are simply assertions, with little or no supporting evidence. In the National Health Service a National Audit Office (National Audit Office, 1987) study reported savings of about 20 per cent from competition for domestic, laundry and catering services though with increasing management costs. Domberger and his colleagues (Domberger *et al.*, 1987), in a study of cleaning in the National Health Service, found that there were cost reductions of 34 per cent where service was contracted out, and of 22 per cent where the in-house provider won. Others, too, have found that savings followed from competitive tendering in the National Health Service (Milne, 1987, Milne and McGee, 1992).

In local government the Audit Commission has found savings of 14 per cent following the tightening of the regulatory regime for highways works (Audit Commission, 1991). Academic studies have also generally found savings in local government. Domberger *et al.* (1986, 1988) and Cubbin *et al.* (1987) found savings of about 22 per cent where refuse collection was privatised. Studies of the Local Government Act 1988 have found lower savings. A *Local Government Chronicle* survey (*Local Government Chronicle*, 1990), following the first year of competition, found average savings of 5.6 per cent. A study conducted for the Department of the Environment found savings of about 6.5 per cent (Walsh and Davis, 1993). In both cases there were considerable variations from service to service and local authority to local authority. Generally, the evidence from compulsory competitive tendering is that there are savings to be made, though they are probably not as great as is sometimes claimed.

In the case of other changes there is rather less clear evidence. Neither the Financial Management Initiative (Metcalfe and Richards, 1987) in central government nor the Resource Management Initiative in the National Health Service (Packwood *et al.*, 1991) are easy to assess. The evidence is that they had limited effects that could easily be dissipated. The Next Steps Initiative and the opting out of hospitals have had a greater impact. There has been a strong emphasis on cost-cutting following the introduction of the Next Steps Agencies, and agencies claim improved efficiency through better cost-control. Managers in the National Health Service generally claim that change has improved financial management (Appleby *et al.*, 1992). Other studies have been more dubious about the financial effects, for example, the Audit Commission has argued that it is difficult to make any accurate assessment of costs before and after the introduction of market mechanisms in health (Audit Commission, 1993a, 1993b). In schools, too, assessment is difficult; headteachers claim greater efficiency but the objective evidence is limited. The Audit Commission has found that schools are, generally, managing their finances effectively, though there are examples of poor financial management (Audit Commission, 1993c).

Overall it is as well to be sceptical of the financial benefits that are claimed as following from the introduction of market mechanism. Information is difficult to gather and in many cases studies rely on assertion or on surveys of managerial perceptions. The initial cost of establishing market-based systems may be high, and savings may be offset by increased managerial costs. The safest conclusion seems to be that there are savings in some cases, but that the effects are highly variable. It may also be that savings are likely to be dissipated over the long-term (Szymanski and Wilkins, 1992). In the United States of America, where there is a longer history of the use of contracting mechanisms, recent studies have been sceptical of its value (Smith and Lipsky, 1993; Kettl, 1993). The market for public services is at an early stage and the long-term effects of competition are likely to depend upon the nature of competition for particular services. In simple, repetitive services, such as cleaning, it is easy for providers to enter the market. The effects are likely to be quite different in professional services. Markets are likely to develop more slowly, and the effects are much less predictable.

■ MANAGERIAL AND ORGANISATIONAL EFFECTS

The traditional approach to the organisation of the public service has been based upon hierarchical management systems and self-sufficiency in service provision. The management focus was internal and production-oriented, with limited focus upon, or influence by, the service user. There was a strong emphasis on size, in order to gain economies of scale and scope. Public service organisations were typically large with long hierarchies of managerial control. The introduction of market mechanisms is leading to fundamental change in this traditional organisational and managerial approach.

The integrated hierarchical approach is giving way to organisational differentiation based upon the purchaser–provider split and devolution of financial control. The purchaser side is responsible for defining the service to be delivered, letting contracts or procuring the service, and monitoring and inspecting the service actually delivered. The provider, whether inside or outside the public organisation, is responsible for delivering service within the terms specified. The patterns of purchaser–provider relationships that are emerging vary in the degree of monopoly. In some cases there are single purchasers and single providers, in others there is a much more diverse market. The patterns are illustrated in Figure 8.2.

Patterns of provision are likely to change over time, for example because of integration of purchasers, as is happening in the health service, or the entry of more providers into the market. The tendency, at the moment, is towards more monopolistic approaches,

Purchasers

		Few	*Many*
Providers	*Few*	Bilateral monopoly e.g. local authority purchasing refuse collection	Monopoly provision e.g. single hospital providing services to a range of health purchasers such as general practitioners
	Many	Monopoly purchaser e.g. Social Services Department purchasing from many residential home providers	Open market e.g. building maintenance to schools

Figure 8.2   Patterns of provision of public services

for example through co-operation between health and social care purchasers.

The markets for public services are typically 'quasi-markets', rather than competitive, private markets (Le Grand and Bartlett, 1993). It is rarely the case that the ultimate service users are customers, paying for services directly with their own money. There are normally professionals acting as purchasers on behalf of users. It may be that, over time, users will come to act more as direct purchasers or customers, but there is little sign of this at the moment. The process of choice in the public service is characterised by little in the way of consumer sovereignty. What is emerging is a network-based approach to the management of public services, with an increasingly wide range of external and quasi-autonomous internal providers. The network-based approach to management leads to increasing formalisation and internal complexity. The operation of contracts and quasi-contracts requires formal specification, systems for work ordering, invoicing and payments, detailed procedures for work recording and variation, and processes for letting and managing contracts. Formal mechanisms are emerging for the resolution of differences between purchasers and providers. Relationships that previously operated on an informal basis are being formalised in contracts and service level agreements. The market-based system has led to an increasing use of business planning, performance management and quality assurance systems. Market adjustment is replacing hierarchical control.

Market mechanisms create conflicting pressures for centralisation and decentralisation within public authorities. The devolution of financial control closer to the point of service delivery, for example to social care managers, gives more autonomy to service managers, but the need for co-ordination, allocation of resources, the establishment of strategic frameworks, and the resolution of conflicts leads to renewed centralisation. In education, for example, schools have gained greater autonomy than they had previously, but the Department for Education has strong powers over finance and the curriculum, and decision-making within schools has become more centralised in the hands of headteachers and governors. Similar patterns are apparent within the National Health Service, for example in the role of trust hospital managers.

The development of market mechanisms has led to questioning of the way that central support services, such as personnel, law and finance, operate within public organisations, particularly in local government. Central services are seen by trading units, or units with devolved financial control, as creating uncontrolled costs. Central services costs are simply recovered by being allocated to direct service accounts. The result has been the establishment of internal trading arrangements — Service Level Agreements. These agreements are quasi-contracts, stating what central services are to be provided, for what price and under what conditions. Managers with devolved control are increasingly unwilling to be tied into services and procedures over which they have little control. The result is that the organisation becomes an inter-related set of contracts rather than a managerial hierarchy.

The establishment of competitive processes leads to an increased clarity of roles within the public service, at both the political and the managerial level. A major aim of the changes is that politicians should be responsible for strategic decisions and play only a limited role in the day-to-day management of services. Providers would operate to clear performance measures, allowing politicians to control at a distance. In practice the effectiveness of market mechanisms in establishing clear separation between politicians and managers has been limited. Ministers have been unwilling to let executive agencies operate with full autonomy. Local authority politicians frequently find themselves uncomfortable with the strategic role and the purchaser–provider split. In health and education the changes have placed considerable control in the hands of headteachers and senior managers, and the role of governors and non-executive members of health bodies is unclear.

The formal clarity of the separate roles of clients and contractors, and managers and politicians is often belied by overlap and confusion in practice. It is not at all clear how the roles of purchaser and provider can be separated in practice, for example in the assessment of needs in social care. At the political level the distinction between strategy and service delivery is not always clear, particularly at times of crisis. Contracting, competition and other market mechanisms are leading to a diversification of organisational form in the public service. Private, voluntary and non-profit organisations have a more explicit place in the organisational network. External agencies, such as voluntary organisations, are having to change their form to cope with competition, becoming more commercially aware and market-oriented. They are having to operate on the basis of contracts rather than grants.

There have been a number of management buyouts, and other forms of 'externalisation'. Public organisations sometimes trade with each other. What is emerging is a gradation of attachment to the public service, varying from direct employment to one-off contracts. Boundaries between the public and the private are becoming less clear, as private and voluntary organisations carry out public duties.

The development of market mechanisms has been based upon the assumption that policy-making and strategy can be rigidly separated from service delivery. It has been a commonplace of policy studies that policy and service management are inextricably linked. In practice the introduction of market mechanisms leads to policy-making being more open and manipulable at some times than others. Before contracts are let or framework agreements established for government executive agencies, there is some freedom to make decisions. Once a contract has been let or agreement established the ability to make changes is limited, and public service organisations find themselves tied into a pattern of provision and of spending that cannot easily be varied. The establishment of market mechanisms for public services leads to a combination of flexibility and constraint. This development will have significant implications for policy planning and budget systems.

■ INFORMATION

The introduction of market mechanisms has made it clear that public service organisations commonly operate with poor information. The specification of services requires detailed information if it is to be effective, and performance monitoring must be based on sound reporting. Public service organisations have faced two major information problems in managing on a market-oriented basis. First, they have found that they lack much of the information that they need. Letting a contract, for example, requires knowledge of the work that needs to be done and the sites on which it is to be performed. Detailed knowledge of the nature of the work to be done is likely to be held mainly by those who are involved in actual service delivery. Traditional systems were able to cope with informally held information, in the heads of those who actually did the work. Markets and competition require the formalisation of information systems. Second, information systems are not adapted to the needs of managers operating in a market context. The second problem is the greater, and is enhanced by a lack of understanding of what their needs are.

The new market-based public service management requires detailed knowledge of the services that are to be provided. Strategic approaches to management require information that enables managers to be confident that service delivery actually embodies policy and organisational value. It is difficult to keep information up to date without appropriate technology; many local authorities are investigating the use of geographic information systems, which allows constant changes to be managed more effectively. The initial cost of establishing the basic nature of service is high. The letting of contracts, for example, has often required a great deal of detailed measurement of work-sites.

The control of market-based management systems in the public service depends upon the development of effective accrual and commitment accounting systems, without which it is extremely difficult to be clear on the financial position of trading accounts. In the past managers have mainly been concerned with ensuring that spending is maintained within budgets, that is, with expenditure. The management of trading accounts requires a closer knowledge of income *and* expenditure. Cash flow must be managed, so timing of income and expenditure becomes more significant. Managers need information to set and monitor performance targets, maintain a continuous cost/income comparison, identify short-term financial problems, make possible the analysis of long-term trends, obtain appropriate information for tendering, and monitor progress against plans.

In the early stages of the development of competition there was a tendency to search for comprehensive information technology solutions. This was the case, for example, after the introduction of the Local Government Planning and Land Act 1980. The attempts to introduce comprehensive solutions have often been costly failures. The most extreme case is that of Wessex Regional Health Authority. In many trading organisations the trend has been that managers have devised their own informal information systems because new or existing systems work poorly. These systems have gradually become more formalised over time. As with other aspects of management the means of managing information must be learnt.

The relatively poor performance of management information systems for the management of competitive processes has four causes. First, public service information systems are designed with public reporting in mind. They have traditionally been poorly adapted to commercially motivated management. Secondly, information systems tend to reflect the structure and power distribution of the traditional public organisation, with its departmental emphasis and central financial dominance. In part, information systems are poorly integrated because they reflect the lack of integration of the organisation itself. Thirdly, there are difficulties in information systems created by the separation of purchasers and providers, with differing values and incentives. It is often in the interests of contractors or providers to conceal information from clients or purchasers. The final reason for the failure of information systems is that there is little experience of what is needed. It takes time to learn how to manage information in the new system.

In the longer term the development of markets tends to lead to improved information systems, though with the danger that they are biased. It is a common statement of managers involved in competition that it has led to an improved knowledge of the services that they provide. It is, increasingly, leading to an investigation of the way that services can be made more responsive by incorporating better information about what service users want. The techniques for discovering user needs, though, are at an early stage of development. The danger of bias is that the system works to the measure of performance, for example that rates of return or measures of throughput become substituted for more grounded performance measures.

■ QUALITY

The introduction of competition has led to a closer focus on quality in the public service. This development is apparent first in the development of formalistic systems of performance measurement. There has been an explosion of performance indicators (Carter *et al.*, 1992). A second formalistic approach is the development of certificated quality assurance systems, involving adherence to British Standard 5750, the British Standards Institute's statement of the requirements of a quality management system. Local Government Management Board's (1993) figures show that about a quarter of local authorities have included the requirement to achieve BS 5750 in one or more of their contracts. Interest is also being shown in BS 5750 in education, social care and health, though to a much more limited degree.

The attitude to formal quality indicators and assurance systems is mixed. Indicators have been criticised as being imposed from the top down and emphasising quantitative over qualitative factors. It is particularly difficult to develop performance indicators for human services. Certificated quality assurance systems have been criticised as being costly and bureaucratic. It has also been argued that they are oriented to manufacturing industry and inappropriate for public services. On the other hand it has been argued that quality indicators and quality assurance systems are valuable in moving away from a focus on inputs and emphasising a concern for process and outputs.

The Audit Commission has argued, in its study of the role of the client in competitive tendering systems (1993d), that there should be a move towards performance- rather than method- or input-based contracts. A performance-based approach would require a focus on the clients or users, and on the benefits that they should get from service. There is some evidence that public services are beginning to develop such an approach, but it is at an early stage. In many cases it is difficult to determine what output should be, for example determining the precise nature of the output in social care. Equally, it may be difficult to be precise about how inputs and outputs are linked in professional services. The means of specifying in performance terms will take a great deal of development.

The move to competition and markets has focused attention on who it is that should determine quality. For simple products or services it is relatively easy for the consumers to make a judgement of the quality of what they receive. In such cases, for example refuse collection, the service users can fairly easily tell whether they have received the service, and complaints can be used as an effective monitoring method. In other cases the service is complex and it is difficult for the user, and perhaps even the provider, to assess quality (Walsh, 1991). This may be the case, for example, for professional services, such as legal advice. In such cases it may be that we need to rely upon third-party assessment through specialist inspectors.

There are differences over whether competition has had a detrimental or beneficial impact on quality. Critics argue that it is has resulted in a decline in quality, the government that it has improved quality. Certainly there have been some obvious quality failures, for example escapes of prisoners after the contracting out of the transfer of prisoners to court. The safest conclusion is that the introduction of competition has had a mixed impact upon quality, but that it has focused attention on service standards. Where there is failure it is more likely in the early stages of competition, immediately after a contract has been let. The move to competition has also tended to result in more uniformity of standards.

■ ACCOUNTABILITY

The introduction of market mechanisms creates the need for reconsidering processes of accountability. Salamon (1981) has argued that provision of public services through contracting out introduces a form of 'third-party government'. As Kettl (1993, p.39) argues:

> *Even as the blurring of responsibilities between the public and private sectors blurs the boundaries between them, the separate interests between each sector remain. The most important issue is whether the sharing of public and private power endangers the public interest that the government is obliged — by the Constitution, by law, and by public will — to pursue*

The introduction of a purchaser–provider split within public service organisations creates similar divisions of interest.

In traditional public service organisations those who provide are held to account on a hierarchical basis, according to a line of authority running through management to the political level. Market processes require that accountability should be built into contracts. The problem is that this may require knowledge of the likely issues with which accountability systems will have to deal before those issues are clear. It may be difficult to determine whether service failure is the result of poor specification or the activity of the contractor. In some services failure to perform may not be apparent on the surface, and inspection may be difficult. Experience in the United States of America has pointed to problems of accountability. Smith and Lipsky (1993) argue that there are problems for users in assigning responsibility between purchaser and provider. Salamon (1981, p. 260) argues that contracting places:

> *. . . federal officers in the uncomfortable position of being responsible for programs they do not really control . . . Instead of a hierarchical relationship between the federal government and its agents, therefore, what exists is a far more complex bargaining relationship in which the federal government has the weaker hand.*

The contrasting argument is that accountability is not a matter of whether there is control by elected government and staff who are responsible, but a pragmatic matter of service quality. William Waldegrave, the minister responsible for the Citizen's Charter has argued:

The key point in this argument is not whether those who run our public services are elected, but whether they are producer-responsive or consumer-responsive. Services are not necessarily made to respond to the public simply by giving citizens a democratic voice, and a distant and diffuse one at that, in their make-up. They can be made responsive by giving the public choices, or by instituting mechanisms which build in publicly approved standards and redress when they are not attained (Waldegrave, 1993, p. 13)

Choice in the market, on this argument, replaces voice in the polity as the means of ensuring accountability.

The debate over accountability raises fundamental issues about the nature of the public realm and how it operates in a world of contracts and markets. Harden (1992) argues that we need a form of 'public law contract' because of the inadequacy of private law remedies in the context of government. The issue is not so much one of whether the market is better for the service user than the traditional, politically controlled, bureaucracy, but the balance between different forms of accountability. Unless we are willing to move to much more radically individualist forms of service, it is still the case that there must be authoritative decisions about the overall allocation of resources at a collective level. Market mechanisms then work within those allocations. The present pattern of markets in the public service is operating to increase choice through markets on the micro-level. At the same time it is increasing control over the basic allocation of resources at a central level. The debate over accountability illustrates the tension between the perception of people as customers for services and as citizens.

■ STAFF AND INDUSTRIAL RELATIONS

The move to competition and markets for public services has considerable implications for staff. In some cases staff have suffered. It is the least advantaged, for example women with part-time jobs, who have typically suffered most. Competitive tendering for local authority services has led to reductions in the level of employment, pay and conditions. The main effect has been cuts in employment, often of 20 to 30 per cent or more, particularly in cleaning, refuse collection and grounds maintenance. Many trust hospitals have made significant reductions in staff and the size of the Civil Service has been reduced substantially. There has also been a change in the nature of the workforce. The number of manual workers has declined relative to the number of non-manual workers. The reason for this is that competitive processes themselves are complex and involve their own bureaucracy. The purchaser–provider split creates an element of duplication, and inspection and financial control systems can be demanding of staff time. The Audit Commission (1993b) has commented on the administrative 'paper chase' that is involved in introducing the new mechanisms in the Family Health Service Authorities. There has been much comment on the administrative costs of the new approach to the management of the National Health Service. The transaction costs of the new system can be high involving increased administrative work.

Pay and conditions have worsened for some and improved for others. Manual workers in less skilled areas of work such as the cleaning of building have, in many cases, suffered substantial pay cuts. Bonus systems have been simplified or eliminated. Hours of work have been changed. On the other hand the move to the market has often led to an improvement of the pay and conditions of senior managers. In some cases, though as yet only a minority, there has been a move towards performance-based payment systems.

Competition involves a shift of influence away from professionals and workers towards managers, as the 'right to manage' is asserted. Staff management systems are consequently being tightened. Absenteeism is being much more actively and rigorously managed. Staff are being required to work more flexibly. What seems to be emerging, if only slowly, is an organisation that consists of a core of employees, who are seen as central to the organisation, and are employed on relatively favourable terms, and a range of more peripheral employees, working in less favourable conditions.

There is more direct control of industrial relations at a decentralised level as a result of competition. Certainly national bargaining systems have continued in all public services, but their importance is beginning to decline. Thirty or so local authorities have opted out of national bargaining. Trust hospitals, opted-out schools, independent colleges and trading organisations in local authorities are all beginning to set their own pay and conditions and bargain directly with their own staff. There are strong pressures for the decentralisation of bargaining in the Civil Service.

■ FUTURE DEVELOPMENTS

We are at an early stage in the development of market principles for the management of the public service. In the Civil Service a high proportion of staff are now employed in 'Next Steps' agencies, but the degree of autonomy of those agencies is still limited, with the Treasury still exercising considerable control. The National Health Service is still in the process of establishing trusts, and adjusting the management framework to the new system. The role of the Department of Health in a more fragmented system is not yet clear. Only a small proportion of schools have as yet opted for grant-maintained status. Local authorities still control large numbers of council houses. Social Services departments have only taken the first tentative steps toward the separation of purchaser and provider and the external purchase of service. Competitive tendering in local government is only now being extended to white-collar services and housing management. Certain services, for example the Magistrates' Courts, are only now beginning to feel the impact of competitive, market-based systems of management. This is not to underestimate the level or the importance of the change, or the impact that it has had, but simply to argue that there is more change to come than we have so far experienced, unless there is a radical change of direction.

The future of the public service, presuming the continuation of trends that are already well established, has a number of characteristics. First the internal organisation of public bodies will take the form of a nexus of contracts. Each part of the organisation will have a closely specified relationship to the others, creating a complex of contract-based relationships. To take an example, the housing management contractor will provide services to the housing management client, but be a client for services from the housing maintenance contractor. Both the housing management contractor and the housing maintenance contractor will purchase from the finance department as provider. The finance department in turn will be a purchaser for computer services, and so on.

The second characteristic, going along with this separation of purchaser and provider, will be the declining role of the elected local politician. More service control and oversight is to be exercised by appointed bodies, for example in health and education (Stewart, 1993). Central government control is increased by the establishment of service standards laid down by ministers through regulation. The separation of purchaser and provider will reduce the direct influence of politicians over service provision.

Performance measurement will increase as an approach to service management. It may be that the public will become more involved in the establishment of standards at the local level, but central control is at least as likely. The ostensible advantage of performance-based approaches is that they allow control without direct involvement.

The purchaser/provider split is likely to be reviewed as public organisations learn to manage on a market basis. The initial separation, often very radical, is likely to give way to mixtures of separation and co-operation, as is increasingly happening in private sector industry (Best, 1990). There is already a change in the way that the client/contractor split operates in the local authority. In some cases direct service organisations are taking on more of what was initially the client role, through self-validating monitoring systems. The nature of client–contractor relations is likely to vary considerably from one service to another, for example the nature of the relationship will be very different in social care compared with housing.

There is likely to be increasing interest in developing more explicit market processes for the management of the public service. Vouchers, for example, have been little used, but there are signs of increasing interest in voucher systems in countries such as Sweden, which may be reflected in Britain for example in child care. There may be some increase in direct user control in health, housing and education.

Overall the public service of the future is likely to have the character of a network rather than an organisation. The line between public and private is likely to be increasingly unclear, which raises significant issues of public service ethics. The extent of provision of public services by private sector organisations will, inevitably, increase. The degree of contracting out has, so far, been limited, but there are signs of increasing interest in public sector markets.

■ LESSONS TO BE LEARNT

The public service is only beginning to learn the lessons of market-based systems of management. Indeed, the first lesson is that there is a need to improve methods of learning. The separation of purchaser and provider means that there is a greater distance between those responsible for ensuring that public services are provided, and the actual service providers. Improved learning mechanisms are particularly necessary in complex professional services such as social care, housing and health. There is also a need for better understanding of the markets for public services, that is, for better market research. There is a danger that the development of markets will divorce the public service from practice.

The second lesson is that information systems need to be improved. There is a need, for example, for better information for service costing. In the National Health Service the knowledge of unit costs is often limited. The creation of effective costing systems will take a great deal of effort. As MacKerrell (1993) says:

> *Management information systems can be extremely expensive to create and there is no one correct way, no magic formula for producing information. There is a constant temptation to invest in the next stage — the latest piece of hardware, the most up-to-date piece of hardware — but, if the outcome is not a different, better decision, then the effort may well be wasted*

Johnson and Kaplan (1987) have shown that the creation of effective information systems is as much a problem for the private as for the public sector. Organising the public service in future will increasingly be the organisation of information.

The third lesson is that strategy processes are more important than structure. The tradition, in the public service, has been for structure to dominate. Many years ago Chandler (1962) argued that strategy preceded structure. The experience of competition has shown that process also needs to precede structure. There is a need to consider how services are specified, how contracts are let and managed, and how differences are resolved. Budgeting and policy-planning systems need to be adapted to take account of competition. The danger of not thinking adequately about organisational process is that services become ossified in outdated specifications. Organisational cultures will also need to adapt to competition.

The fourth lesson is that managing through contracts and markets involves trust as much as sanctions. A punishment-based approach to the management of contracts is only likely to be efficient in simple services. In any complex service there is a need for what Macneil (1980) calls 'relational contracts', that is, for contracts that ensure effective relations between purchaser and provider over time. Relational contracts need to be based upon trust, and mechanisms are needed for the building of trust. The relational contract recognises the need for the partners to a contract to work closely together, and to maintain co-operation over time.

The fifth lesson is that competition and markets will not always lead to savings. It is not at all clear, for example, that the new approach to public service management has yielded savings in the National Health Service. Certainly there are likely to be high initial costs in establishing the systems that are necessary to manage public services. The costs of client-side management for local government services have been found to be between five and ten per cent of the value of the contract (Audit Commission, 1993d) and the costs of preparing for competition about seven per cent of contract value. Savings may only accrue in the long term. Equally problems of monopoly may also lead to long-term increases in cost. To pursue market-based approaches to management purely on financial grounds would be dangerous.

The sixth lesson is the need to be aware of the danger of corruption and inappropriate behaviour. There is little evidence of corruption having increased greatly as yet, but there is always the danger that the large amounts of money involved will prove a source of temptation. Perhaps more importantly the introduction of commercial incentives may lead to inappropriate behaviour. The commercial motivation may lead to the pursuit of 'profit' at the expense of service, especially in a context of performance-based management. There is clear evidence in a number of health and local authorities of dubious behaviour following competition. The Audit Commission also quotes examples in schools.

The seventh lesson is that the management of the client side requires skills that are underdeveloped in the public service. These skills are likely to vary from service to service, being very different in, say, refuse collection compared with health. There is a need not only for 'hard' skills, such as knowledge of contract law or inspection processes, but also for 'soft' skills such as the ability to influence providers. Client-side skills need to be developed at a number of levels, from the policy client role to the ability to monitor the day-to-day provision of service.

The eighth lesson is that there are likely to be problems in the initial management of contracts. The development of contracts and specifications is causing public service managers and politicians to review the nature of services. The learning of new ways of operating, even for simple services, is likely to take time, requiring adequate lead-in periods. There is also a need to recognise that preparation for new approaches takes a good deal of time, which may be difficult to find in a situation of financial constraint.

The ninth lesson is that there is a danger of developing systems that are excessively complex. This has been apparent in the development of systems of internal trading for central services through service level agreements. In some cases this has led to large numbers of agreements, in some cases hundreds and perhaps even thousands. Time recording systems can be excessively detailed, and lead to the breakdown of informal relations, as staff will only relate to each other when there is appropriate accounting code to cover the transaction. Similar problems are apparent in some works-ordering and invoicing systems. The danger is the replacement of traditional bureaucratic systems with a new market bureaucracy of client managers and inspectors.

The tenth lesson is that there is a need for better means of determining user needs and requirements. Contracts have, so far, been dominated by existing understandings. The development of competition provides an opportunity for a fundamental review of the nature of services. New approaches are being developed, for example locality purchasing methods in the National Health Service. Users and internal purchasers are likely to become more demanding as experience of the market grows. Systems for determining user need will be difficult to create in complex areas of service, such as social care where users may be poorly placed to define their needs.

I have focused on ten major lessons. Clearly others could be cited. The most important overall lesson of contracting is that there is a need to review the whole nature of management in the public service. Competition changes the relationship between politicians and managers, and between managers and professionals. Relationships with users may also change. Processes of accountability will need to reflect new problems of management. The understanding of the nature of public service is undergoing a fundamental change. There is an increased focus on quality and on the performance of services rather than inputs. Competition is not the only mechanism that is leading to change but it is the development that is likely to lead to the most radical reorientation.

■ CONCLUSION

The public service in Britain is only in the early stages of the major revolution that is likely to follow from the introduction of market mechanisms. There are dangers but also opportunities. As Richardson (1993) argues in the case of social care in the United States, where contracts and market mechanisms have been developing since the late 1960s:

> *Contracting in the US is beset with problems, both for voluntary organisations and government. Within the paperchase the needs of service users receive scant attention, whilst agencies struggle to provide services to more for less as funding is cut and government pushes more of the costs of running the contracting system onto contracting agencies. But contracting in the U.S. also shows that these problems can be solved, given a willingness to innovate and the political commitment to address longstanding issues . . .*   (p. 47)

If we are to be able to operate an effective market-based system in the public service then effective institutions and cultures need to be developed.

The danger is that the market, with its ostensible simplicity and efficiency, erodes the commitments and values that are needed in public service. In the private sector markets are becoming more complex, involving combinations of co-operation and competition. There is likely to be at least as much complexity in the public service. We need to understand the particular character of public service markets, based, as they are, on needs rather than wants. Citizens in public service markets are not simply customers, and this means that there is a need to develop a distinctively public approach to marketing and to managing through competitive processes.

Hirsch (1977) has argued that the market needs to be underpinned by non-market values, for example of trust, honesty and fairness, if it is to operate effectively. The danger of the market is that it creates values and incentives which make effective exchange relationships impossible. This argument applies with even more force to the use of market mechanisms in the public sector. The fundamental relationship between citizen and government, is not one of exchange but one of mutual commitment, and public services are not simply a reciprocation for the payment of taxes. The role of government is more than the effective delivery of service, and market mechanisms can, consequently, only be secondary to political mechanisms.

■ REFERENCES

APPLEBY, J., LITTLE, V., RANADE, W., ROBINSON, R. and SMITH, P. (1992) *Implementing the Reforms: A Second National Survey of District General Managers*, Birmingham, National Association of Health Authorities and Trusts.

AUDIT COMMISSION (1991) *The Impact of Competitive Tendering on Highways Maintenance*, London, HMSO.

AUDIT COMMISSION (1993a) *Their Health, Your Business: The New Role of the District Health Authority*, London, HMSO.

AUDIT COMMISSION (1993b) *Practices Make Perfect: The Role of the Family Health Services Authority*, London, HMSO.

AUDIT COMMISSION (1993c) *Adding Up the Sums: Schools' Management of their Finances*, London, HMSO.

AUDIT COMMISSION (1993d) *Realising the Benefits of Competition: The Client Role in Competition*, London, HMSO.

BEST, M. (1990) *The New Competition*, Cambridge, Polity Press.

CARNAGHAN, R. and BRACEWELL-MILNES, B. (1993) *Testing the Market: Competitive Tendering for Government Services in Britain and Abroad*, London, Institute of Economic Affairs.

CARTER, N., KLEIN, R. and DAY, P. (1992) *How Organisations Measure Success: The Use of Performance Indicators in Government*, London, Routledge.

CHANDLER, A. D. (1962) *Strategy and Structure: Chapters in the History of American Industrial Enterprise*, Cambridge, Mass, MIT Press.

CUBBIN, J., DOMBERGER, S. and MEADOWCROFT, S. (1987) 'Competitive Tendering and Refuse Collection: Identifying the Sources of Efficiency Gains', *Fiscal Studies*, vol 8, no 3, pp. 49–58.

DOMBERGER, S. MEADOWCROFT, S. and THOMPSON, D. (1986) 'Competitive Tendering and Efficiency: The Case of Refuse Collection', *Fiscal Studies*, vol 7, no 4, pp. 69–87.

DOMBERGER, S. MEADOWCROFT, S. and THOMPSON, D. (1987) 'The Impact of Competitive Tendering on the Costs of Hospital Domestic Services', *Fiscal Studies*, vol 8, no 4, pp. 39–54.

DOMBERGER, S., MEADOWCROFT, S. and THOMPSON, D. (1988) 'Competition and Efficiency Gains in Refuse Collection: A Reply', *Fiscal Studies*, vol 9, no 1, pp. 86–90.

HARDEN, I. (1992) *The Contracting State*, Buckingham, Open University Press.

HIRSCH, F. (1977) *Social Limits to Growth*, London, Routledge and Kegan Paul.

JOHNSON, H. T. and KAPLAN, K. (1987) *Relevance Lost: The Rise and Fall of Management Accounting*, Boston, Mass., Harvard Business School.

KETTL, D. F. (1993) *Sharing Power: Public Governance and Private Markets*, Washington D. C., Brookings Institution.

LE GRAND, J. and BARTLETT, W. (eds) (1993) *Quasi-Markets and Social Policy*, Basingstoke, Macmillan.

Local Government Chronicle (1990) *Supplement*, 6 July.

LOCAL GOVERNMENT MANAGEMENT BOARD (1993) *CCT Information Service: Survey Report no 7*, London, Local Government Management Board.

MACKERRELL, D. K. D. (1993) 'Contract Pricing: A Management Opportunity', in I. Tilley (ed.), *Managing the Internal Market*, London, Paul Chapman Publishing, pp. 146–60.

MACNEIL, I. (1980) *The New Social Contract*, London, Yale University Press.

METCALFE, L. and RICHARDS, S. (1987) *Improving Public Management*, London, Sage (2nd edition 1990).

MILNE, R. G. (1987) 'Competitive Tendering in the National Health Service: An Economic Analysis of the Early Implementation of HC(83)18', *Public Administration*, vol. 65, no. 2, pp. 145–60.

MILNE, R. G., and MCGEE, M. (1992) 'Competitive Tendering in the NHS: A New Look at Some Old Estimates', *Fiscal Studies*, vol. 13, no. 1, pp. 96–111.

NATIONAL AUDIT OFFICE (1987) *Competitive Tendering for Support Services in the National Health Service*, London, HMSO.

PACKWOOD, T., KEEN, J. and BUXTON, M. (1991) *Hospitals in Transition. The Resource Management Experiment*, Milton Keynes, Open University Press.

RAINE, J. and WILLSON, M. (1993) *Managing Criminal Justice*, Hemel Hempstead, Harvester Wheatsheaf.

RICHARDSON, J. (1993) *Reinventing Contracts: Transatlantic Perspectives on the Future of Contracting*, London, National Council for Voluntary Organisations.

SALAMON, L. M. (1981) 'Rethinking Public Management: Third Party Government and the Changing Forms of Government Action', *Public Policy*, vol. 29, pp. 255–75.

SMITH, S. R. and LIPSKY, M. (1993) *Non-profits for Hire: The Welfare*

State in the Age of Contracting, London, Harvard University Press.

STEWART, J. (1993) *The New Magistracy*, London, European Policy Forum.

SZYMANSKI, S. and WILKINS, S. (1992) *Cheap Rubbish? Competitive Tendering and Contracting Out in Refuse Collection — 1981–1988*, London, London Business School, Centre for Business Strategy.

WALDEGRAVE, W. (1993) *The Reality of Reform and Accountability in Today's Public Service*, London, Chartered Institute of Public Finance and Accountancy.

WALSH, K. (1991) 'Quality and Public Services', *Public Administration*, vol. 69, no. 4, pp. 503–14.

WALSH, K. and DAVIS, H. (1993) *Competition and Service: The Impact of the Local Government Act 1988*, London, HMSO.

Chapter 9

THE COMMERCIAL ENVIRONMENT

by Elizabeth Ransom and Serena Simons

■ INTRODUCTION

The public sector is not what it was. The environment in which it operates, the markets that it serves and the organisations of which it is composed have changed considerably over the last ten years and are substantially different from the way they were a generation ago. One of the major changes — and the one most discussed, praised and decried — is the increasing 'commercialisation' of public sector bodies. This broad term encompasses many different types and degrees of change, with previously nationalised monopoly industries being opened up to competition and the full force of the market at one extreme and the half-hearted adoption of business jargon at the other.

Whatever the degree of change, there has been a general shift towards greater customer focus and increased competition with the consequent adoption of commercial principles and practices. The transition, however, from a policy- or service-led culture which tolerated or even encouraged inefficient bureaucracy to a more commercial culture and external environment has sometimes proved difficult and uncomfortable. Experience has shown that, notwithstanding the many achievements and successes in adapting to new circumstances, most public sector bodies face a number of internal and external obstacles to adapting to a commercial or quasi-commercial environment.

This chapter looks at the difficulties that organisations face and that hinder effectiveness (whether inherent in the organisation or resulting from the way 'commercial forces' have been imposed), and suggests how marketing disciplines and approaches can be harnessed to help overcome them.

■ THE COMMERCIAL ENVIRONMENT

Of course the extent to which public sector bodies operate in a commercial environment varies considerably between different types of organisation and even within individual organisations, and this in turn is reflected in the type of challenges and difficulties they face. It is therefore useful to segment the public sector into broad sub-sectors reflecting their commercial position and character.

The major segments displaying distinctive characteristics in terms of commercial conditions, to which reference is made in this chapter are as follows:

- nationalised industries in a near-monopoly position which, while operating commercially, are not wholly subject to market forces due to a lack of direct competition. This segment is gradually moving out of the public sector through the government's privatisation programme, but in doing so faces particular challenges in adapting to different conditions;

- government bodies whose work has commercial applications and which operate commercially in the conventional sense, at least in part. However, government restrictions prevent them from taking an aggressive competitive stance;

- public sector organisations whose main purpose is the provision of services to the public. These organisations do not operate commercially in the strict sense of the word, but increasingly are adopting commercially derived approaches or are facing competition in some areas of their activity. This segment, which includes the health service and local authorities, is one that has often found it difficult to reconcile its social mission with the values of the marketplace;

- government departments with a high level of contact with the public but which may be seen as a necessary fact of life rather than as a service provider. This segment includes the DVLC, the Contributions Agency of the DSS and the Inland Revenue;

- other government bodies or departments whose prime activities are policy or administration and with little contact with the public.

Some of the problems in adapting to a more commercial environment are common to all segments; others stem from the particular circumstances of that segment. Such differences are indicated in the course of the text.

■ ADAPTING TO THE COMMERCIAL ENVIRONMENT: OBSTACLES AND CHALLENGES

The obstacles and challenges faced by public sector organisations in adapting to a more commercial climate fall broadly into three categories:

- those that arise from government or EC policy or other aspects of government ownership
- those related to the 'marketplace' in which the organisation operates
- those that arise from the characteristics of the organisation and the way it has developed historically

Each of these is discussed in turn.

Issues arising from legislation, policy or other features of government ownership

Very few organisations are entirely free. The interests of shareholders, the demands of bankers and general and industry specific legislation all can have a significant impact on many aspects of business. For example, many organisations in both the public and the private sector have been significantly affected by recent environmental legislation which has imposed major action programmes and correspondingly major costs on their businesses. The Financial Services Act of 1986 affected not only individual companies but led to substantial structural changes within the investment services sector. Health and safety legislation affects all organisations, and so on.

Nevertheless, public sector organisations may experience a different order of intervention from government which hinders their ability to operate in a commercial or quasi-commercial way. These include:

- *subsidies to nationalised industries.* Although not unique to nationalised industries (the agricultural sector also coming readily to mind), governments in the past — and still today in many countries — have provided often substantial subsidies to publicly owned companies. The financial difficulties of these organisations sometimes reflected global problems facing their industry, as in ship-building, for example; however such subsidies (coupled with government tolerance of mediocre management) also allowed inefficient practices to continue, allowed procrastination in tackling difficult management issues such as reorganisation or downsizing and protected companies from some of the rigours of the marketplace. The result of this was to increase the scale of the challenge, and perhaps the pain, for such companies when changes in policy required them to compete fully on commercial terms in the market.

- *investment and funding.* A major difference between public sector and private sector organisations is their access to different sources of funding. Nationalised industries and other government bodies transacting commercial business cannot normally and at their own discretion raise finance from the usual sources open to the private sector such as venture capital, the stock market, bond issues or other debt finance. This can limit their ability to develop and even run their businesses as they see fit. Most particularly, it may limit their ability to invest in the fabric of their business and to set in place the elements required for future business growth.

  The effects of such funding constraints are the same in principle as those experienced by private sector organisations who, for whatever reason, are unable or unwilling to raise additional finance which they would like: these include, most obviously, slower business growth, reduced ability to improve the quality of the product or service perhaps resulting in reduced customer satisfaction, and, at the worst, placing the company at a competitive disadvantage.

  Organisations themselves cannot overcome the lack of funding in the face of government policy or resource constraints. The challenge is to minimise the effects of insufficient funding — as any company in a similar position must do — by carefully defining priorities for investment. The use of commercial techniques such as investment appraisal and customer research to identify customer priorities can be very valuable in this process.

- *tendering procedures.* EC regulations impose strict rules on public organisations in regard to the tendering of contracts for the provision of goods or services. While in one sense obtaining — and in some cases (such as local authority Direct Service Organisations), providing — such services on the open market is the very stuff of a truly commercial environment, it is actually very different from the way most companies do business. Most companies seeking to source a service or place a contract externally will usually invite a small number of suppliers to put forward a proposal or, if a firm specification can be made, a bid for the work. These will probably include suppliers with whom the company has worked previously and others with a particular reputation in the field. In some cases the contract may simply be given to a particular supplier because the company does not wish to go through the tendering process and because it has confidence in the chosen service provider.

The process of open tender brings its difficulties. It can take an inordinate length of time to go through the process, it can require considerable staff time (and hence cost) to review the responses. For organisations putting forward tenders the challenges are equally daunting in terms of costing the contract properly, anticipating what competitors might do and devising an appropriate proposal. The cost of tendering should not be underestimated either.

Here again commercial disciplines are valuable. The clearer the brief or specification and the more it is focused on the outputs of the work, the better. In the authors' experience, there are two common weaknesses in public sector briefs: in some cases the tasks are too tightly specified, leaving no room for alternative approaches which might achieve the same objectives more effectively; in others, the brief is too loose and vague, perhaps because those responsible for issuing the invitation to tender have insufficient understanding of the requirements to do the work sought. They therefore look to the proposals to help define the tasks for them, something which is potentially highly wasteful. A good brief will focus on the objectives of the work, the applications of its outputs and identify any particular constraints, for example time and budget. The benefits are that it will help weed out unsuitable suppliers, it should lead to a better quality of response and it sets clear criteria for the evaluation of the tenders received.

- *ability to compete with the private sector.* Public sector bodies that offer services with commercial applications are encouraged to find new markets as, for example, the Meteorological Office and the Laboratory of the Government Chemist (which provides forensic science services of a similar nature to those provided by private laboratories) have done with considerable success. However, government bodies are not encouraged to be aggressive in the market, particularly in direct competition with the private sector. This, of course, is understandable, as such competition could be construed to be unfair given the advantage of public funding; nevertheless, it does limit the ability of such bodies to become fully commercial.

- *the political dimension.* Many, perhaps most, public sector bodies are in the business of preparing or executing government policy in some way or other. There is no doubt that this creates a different climate and attitude to that which exists within private sector organisations, and this is discussed further below. Suffice it to say here that the fact that accountability for the success or otherwise of the work of many civil servants lies with ministers can lead to a lack of initiative and a cynicism or lack of conviction about the durability of work done. This is a feature inherent is such organisations and can perhaps only be minimised by ensuring that the organisation's goals are carried through into the staff appraisal and development process.

The nature and characteristics of the organisation

The differences between public sector organisations and truly commercial companies are of course myriad. A key difference stems from the very purpose of the organisation itself and the way it is therefore viewed both by its own employees and by those that use its services or are affected by its activities — often, and sometimes absurdly, called 'customers' (as if, by using a word, the thing becomes a reality). This area is perhaps the greatest source of confusion and discomfort at the 'commercialising' of the public sector.

What, then, are the real differences in the nature, purpose, characteristics and style of public sector organisations that create difficulties or obstacles to adapting to a very different environment?

- *differences in organisational purpose and objecties*. Many, perhaps most, public sector bodies were established to fulfil an administrative role or to provide services on behalf of government or local government. The objectives and ethos therefore have historically been those of public service and even — to use a wholly unfashionable word — duty. This compares with the prime profit motive of business (which does not, contrary to the views of many, preclude a multitude of worthy objectives and exemplary practices). Many people attracted into working for the public sector were attracted by its social purpose and some deliberately eschewed the commercial values of the business world.

As well as the personal difficulties that individuals may have in embracing an ethos that may seem alien to them, there is a genuine dilemma in regard to the extent that 'market forces' can or should be applied to public sector organisations. The difficulties, for example, of reconciling the traditional values and practices of the health service with constraints on which drugs may be prescribed or hospitals competing for patients on price — with the consequent need to keep the cost base competitive even if this is at the expense of valuable and world-class research work — are not easily resolved.

Before addressing the practical aspects of taking on commercial disciplines or adopting a new mind set in regard to the purpose and activities of the organisation, it is clearly important to attempt to reconcile traditional perceptions of the role of the organisation with new objectives and priorities and to try and forge from this a coherent mission and organisational philosophy. It may well be that the commercial approaches being imposed are less of a contradiction than first supposed and that market disciplines can result in improved 'customer' service and improved focus, enabling it to achieve social objectives more effectively. It must equally be recognised that the creation of a commercial environment is not necessarily a panacea and can create as many problems as it solves.

- *cultural change*. The adoption of a commercial perspective and commercial practices may represent a substantial change in organisational ethos, particularly given that the personal values of those working within a traditional public sector organisation may be very different. Cultural change is almost always difficult to achieve — no wonder that it is currently one of the major growth areas of management consultancy — and particularly so if there is a deep-seated resistance to change or the need for change is not recognised by those that must bring it about.

Yet to operate successfully in a more commercial environment and to get the greatest benefit from commercial techniques, change is usually needed. This may simply be a minor refocusing or it could permeate most aspects of the organisation and its activities encompassing, for example, the focus and objectives of the organisation and individuals within it, corporate values, working practices and the range of activities undertaken.

Unfortunately, there is no easy recipe for achieving cultural change effectively and any organisation seeking to do so is well advised to plan the whole change programme carefully and bring in the help of experts to facilitate the process. Key elements are likely to include a careful definition of the future style sought, a definition of the steps required to get there (which of course implies a candid assessment of the current position and the barriers to change that exist within the organisation), the involvement of representatives from all parts of the organisation, and an active communication programme to ensure all employees understand what is expected of them and why. While there should be consultation throughout the organisation and communication must be two-way to enable issues and genuine grievances to be aired, active resistance should not be tolerated or it may damage the whole change process.

- *management commitment.* For change to be achieved in the culture or working practices of the organisation it is essential that management fully understands and is committed to the new environment. Staff must be able to see that management subscribes fully to the new values. However, resistance to change can be as strong here, and potentially more damaging, as further down the organisation.

- *staff capabilities.* While public sector organisations attract many high-calibre people, it is often the case that staff at all levels have little knowledge of and, in some cases, little aptitude for commercial approaches. Lower grade positions are often poorly paid and consequently attract workers unable to find more attractive jobs. Such people may find it difficult to adapt to a new environment.

The calibre of staff taking on marketing or other commercial responsibilities is more of an issue. With the cult of the generalist which is prevalent in civil service departments, individuals with little or no marketing experience or even training may be given marketing responsibilities, in some cases making decisions for major research projects or advertising campaigns. There is a trend towards recruiting specialists, particularly in local authorities and the health sector, and this clearly provides a means of overcoming lack of indigenous expertise. There are two risks, however. The first is the ability of public sector organisations to attract marketing and other commercial people of the highest calibre, given the lower prestige of the sector, poorer career prospects and comparatively less attractive salary packages. This problem has been eased to some extent by the effects of the recession which has forced many able marketers to look at wider career options and by the growing opportunities within the public sector. The second risk is that staff used to a more commercial environment become frustrated by the organisational culture, their inability to make things happen, achieve results and obtain the recognition they seek.

The alternative to recruiting specialist commercial staff — transferring other staff, usually generalists, into the function and supporting this with the use of external consultants — is altogether less satisfactory: it risks allowing mistakes to be made through inexperience or ignorance and it may well be both more costly and less effective.

If a more commercial approach is to be taken it is necessary to put in place the appropriate skills, even if this means recruiting from outside the organisation. It may also mean offering salaries which are higher than those of equivalently graded staff in other functions but are competitive with similar posts in commercial organisations.

The nature of the market

As stated earlier, the extent to which public sector organisations operate in a commercial environment varies significantly. The market of a nationalised industry is very different from that of a central government department which is different, in turn, from a hospital trust and so on.

The real challenge for any organisation — in the private sector as much as the public sector — is understanding the size, structure and characteristics and dynamics of the market, the requirements and expectations of customers and how these vary between different customer groups. The core techniques and processes for doing so are common to all sectors even if the markets themselves differ substantially.

So, what are the characteristics of the public sector marketplace, what particular difficulties do they pose and how might they be addressed?

- *market definition*. For most public sector organisations the 'market' is not a market in the conventional sense of the word, with its implications of customer choice, direct competition and the exchange of money or other consideration between the 'customer' and the provider of goods or services. In most cases, services are paid for indirectly through taxation, decision-making by the user is limited and there is no direct competition. Even where there is a market in the sense of paying customers and competitive services as, for example, with museums or other public amenities, the interests of other groups may need to be taken into account also and objectives may not be solely commercial.

  The market could therefore include a number of groups. Most obviously there are the users of the service and those that might potentially use it in future; there may be a group that deals with the organisation on behalf of the 'customer', as in the case of employers' payroll departments and the Inland Revenue or the Contributions Agency of the DSS. The market could also be construed to include those that fund the services but do not use them directly themselves. This most obviously applies to local authorities who may need to consider the attitudes and preferences of charge payers more widely even where a particular service has a narrow user base. And there may be other audiences which, although not part of the market, may need to be taken into account, most obviously the government which acts as parallel to shareholders in commercial organisations.

  The fact that the market might not be conventional in commercial terms need not inhibit the adoption of a more business-like approach and a greater customer focus. The process of identifying all groups that have a relationship with and expectations of the organisation remains a valid one and provides a basis for defining objectives, services and standards in relation to each group. A number of government agencies whose markets are not commercial in the conventional sense have been through this process and found it of value.

Here again, the difficulty that may be encountered is one of sufficient and appropriate resources to analyse the market, understand its requirements and adapt the organisation to meet these more effectively.

- *customer attitudes and expectations*. The customers of public sector organisations often do not see themselves as customers at all and, indeed, are not customers in the conventional sense. Their expectations of public sector organisations may be constrained by past experience and by the knowledge of the limited resources available to improve service standards. The lack of choice and their dependence on the organisation may even engender a stoic resignation. There may therefore be little incentive for the organisation to improve service standards in contrast to a 'real' market where maintaining customer satisfaction is crucial to retaining market position.

  Achieving a customer focus is therefore a greater challenge in the public sector than it is in the commercial world where it is a business imperative. Organisations have to make it part of their own ethos for its own sake (and of course to please their political masters). It is therefore admirable that so much has genuinely been achieved in this area right across the public sector.

  Many public sector bodies began with very little understanding of their customers' attitudes towards them or the services they provide, or of their preferences and requirements. Market research, often undertaken by external agencies, has proved valuable here and remains a useful tool for measuring the effectiveness of service improvements and monitoring customer satisfaction. Indeed, we would suggest that something of this kind is necessary to maintain the virtuous circle of continuous improvement, in the absence of commercial incentives.

- *competition and market forces*. Competition in the public sector is rarely comparable to that in the private sector in the sense of the organisation being one of a number offering broadly equivalent products or services. Even nationalised industries often enjoy sole supplier status for their core products. However, competition has increasingly been introduced in particular areas of the organisation's activity, for example in IT support or clerical operations. Market testing has been the major force in introducing competitive conditions and has forced affected departments to address issues surrounding productivity (and hence cost) and service quality. Marketing techniques such as competitor analysis have proved valuable here to understand the relative position, strengths and weaknesses of the in-house provider.

Nevertheless, the lack of real competition deprives most public sector organisations of the key spur to innovation and service improvement. There is no doubt that the need to achieve and maintain competitive advantage over other companies is a driving force in most businesses: in markets where competition is limited and companies' position secure, there is a tendency for organisations to become sluggish and complacent, laying themselves open to assaults by new entrants into the market.

Competitors also provide a useful point of comparison for many aspects of an organisation's activities: service quality, reputation among customers, financial performance, salary levels, staff productivity and product pricing are just some examples.

In the absence of full-blooded competition, organisations must find other ways to stimulate innovation and customer focus as these will not be forced by competitive pressure or by customer insistence. Possible methods of achieving this include comparisons with other organisations in broadly comparable fields, introducing performance measures on customer satisfaction, seeking and rewarding innovation and ideas for improvement, and managing customer expectations upwards by informing them of what they should expect. Customer charters go some way towards this but are unlikely to optimise performance on their own.

■ MEETING THESE CHALLENGES: THE ROLE OF MARKETING

We have seen that the challenges facing public sector organisations are many and diverse, and that it is not always possible to tackle them in the same way as commercial companies given that conditions are often very different. However, though responses to changing conditions in the environment are particular to the circumstances of the individual organisation, many of the same techniques and approaches can profitably be brought to bear.

Marketing techniques in particular can help organisations adapt to a new environment by providing both a better understanding of that environment and the means to respond to it more effectively. However, to be of value they must be applied properly, which means using people with experience in the field and a track record of effective marketing.

A number of marketing techniques have been touched on in the course of this chapter in relation to specific issues and are discussed in more detail elsewhere in this book. At the risk of repetition, this final section summarises the principal ways in which marketing can assist public sector bodies and suggests the conditions necessary for its effective introduction.

Key marketing techniques

- market analysis: the collection of market data and its analysis are a core task of any marketing department.

- competitor analysis to provide a thorough understanding of competitive organisations and the organisation's relative strengths, weaknesses and characteristics.

- customer research to learn more about the scale and nature of the 'market'.

- customer analysis and segmentation: understanding the customer and the differences between different customer groups lies at the heart of achieving a customer focus and increasing levels of satisfaction.

- definition of the organisation's strengths and weaknesses and the opportunities and threats within the market.

- establishment of customer service standards encompassing all factors that customers consider to be important. Such standards need to be reviewed and updated regularly.

- communications activities: a core marketing responsibility is the management and implementation of communications programmes.

Managing marketing effectively

- define the role and remit of the marketing function: the responsibilities of marketing departments differ between organisations and their role and remit therefore cannot be assumed to be understood. It is important that this is made clear not only for the benefit of those within the marketing function but for other departments with whom marketing will have dealings;

- set realistic and, where possible, quantified, objectives: these should recognise the limitations of both marketing and the organisation as well as the opportunities for development and improvement;

- senior level responsibility and support: the influence and effectiveness of any function is greatly affected by the seniority of the staff concerned. Without active management commitment, the full possibilities that a marketing focus can bring will not be realised. Even if there is not a marketing person at board level (or the equivalent), there should be a clear overall responsibility at this level;

- ensure appropriate skills and experience are in place: in addition to appropriately qualified marketing specialists, it may well be of value to provide marketing training for senior management and other key staff so that its potential contribution can be recognised and, hence, obtained;

- allocate sufficient resources: marketing activities may well represent a new area of cost or resources may need to be increased to achieve marketing objectives. Good marketing planning will help ensure that resources are effectively targeted and the best value for money obtained;

- produce, implement and monitor a marketing plan: this is both a management tool for the marketing function and a valuable process in its own right. The planning process ensures that key issues are considered, that information gaps are identified and that marketing activities are best geared to achieving the organisation's objectives.

Marketing techniques alone will not enable public sector bodies to adapt successfully to the new demands of a changing environment and changing customer and public expectations. However, they can make a valuable contribution to this process both in understanding the market and in helping address its requirements and opportunities more effectively.

Chapter 10

PREPARING FOR MARKET TESTING

by Guy Hollis and Janet Baker

■ INTRODUCTION

One of the most significant changes in public sector management since the mid-1980s has been the establishment of programmes on which public services have been exposed to competition against the private sector. The introduction of competitive tendering legislation for local authorities, was rapidly followed by similar requirements in the health service. The 1990s have seen market testing programmes and targets as an established part of programmes of change in the central government sector. Now the focus has moved once again onto local government, whilst central government programmes continue. New and second rounds of competitive tendering are being put into place for the remainder of the decade.

Market testing in the public sector, therefore, is not a new experience. Indeed some organisations have gone beyond the externally imposed requirements, to voluntarily test a wide range of their services. But as more and varied services are drawn into market testing programmes, it is important to look for common ground across the public sector, to ensure that the process is as productive as it can be. An area where mistakes and opportunities have been plentiful in the past, involves the recognition and definition of the all-important relationship between suppliers and customers. There needs to be new recognition that this relationship is no longer simply between the public sector organisation who both decides upon the service *and* delivers it, and the customer. The relationship is now extended to the 'enabling' authority (or the controlling client), the provider and the customer. We have therefore identified some of the common issues prevalent when redefining these relationships, and a number of approaches which may be of help. To do so we have drawn upon the experience of Coopers &

Lybrand in assisting clients within the public sector to prepare for market testing in the form of CCT, voluntary competition and other programmes. Our experience has identified a number of particular strands to these preparations:

- separation of client and contractor functions;
- preparation of tender strategies and documentation;
- training and structures for effective contract management;
- business planning;
- performance measurement and management.

General thoughts

The introduction of market testing in the public sector has brought to the attention of managers a number of so-called 'new' issues. An example of the most pressing of these has been the need to produce the detailed definitions of services which the public sector is providing in order to be able to procure such services from the private sector, or as a minimum to establish external benchmarks for the continued provision of such services in-house. At the same time, through market testing, expectations have been raised as to the potential to achieve positive benefits from the process, in terms of:

- reductions in the cost of services;
- assessing and ensuring the quality of service provision; and
- the potential to achieve improvements to the service.

These have not been the only cultural changes to take place as a result of market testing. It also needs to be recognised that market testing has, in some instances, brought about staff discontent, heavy workloads, and a predatory external environment. These have caused, in varying degrees, difficulties for all of those who have been concerned in the implementation of market testing. Almost inevitably, it has sometimes been difficult to balance all of these demands. To also maintain a positive approach to the recognition of customer requirements may have seemed to some an additional burden at times, but there are many examples of market testing processes where a positive and *service-focused* approach has been taken.

But we should first of all examine why this is not always the case. It has sometimes been the case that customer requirements have *not* been adequately reflected in a market test because the first step of *identifying* the customer correctly has simply not been taken. Much worse have been the cases where the manager responsible for the market test has simply *ignored* the customer, choosing to judge in isolation what the customer requires and how this might be varied. And in other cases, the *multiplicity of activities* to be undertaken in a market test has become too burdensome, and adequate time allocation for preparation, and to enable proper focus on customers, has not been given.

How then *does* the customer fit into a market test? A market test requires a number of mechanistic activities which have to be undertaken — these include an approach to potential suppliers (normally through advertisement), preparation of specifications, detailing of contract conditions, tender evaluation and negotiation. In addition, tests of the potential supplier market are often undertaken to meet external requirements — which may be encapsulated in any of the following:

- European regulations (Procurement Directives);
- national requirements (compulsory competitive tendering); or
- local regulations (market testing programmes).

A pathway needs to be found through what is fundamentally the quasi-scientific process of the market test, recognising the (often) limited resources available to the market test manager. And as important is the creation of and establishment of a capable permanent client structure. The client structure must be able to both manage the service provision in a contractual sense, *and* ensure that there is a continuous and *real* relationship with the customer for the contracted services.

We have therefore considered the role and place of the customer in a market test, in the context of the very real pressures which the test process itself may bring to bear. Three key issues have been identified which we discuss in more depth in this chapter:

- defining who the customer is for services which are to be market-tested;
- deciding how the interests of the customers will be expressed and represented on an ongoing basis in a service which is market tested; and

- choosing the mechanisms by which customer requirements will be quantified and the quality indicators for that service will be established and measured.

A final but fundamental issue for the market test team must be to ensure that innovation and responsiveness to the requirements of the customers will be nurtured, assured and even improved upon in a contractual relationship. A market test should not be allowed to be a block on continuing development and refinement of a service. And customer needs do change, and the market test and any contract must be as flexible as necessary to meet this requirement too.

In order to establish some clarity for these issues, in the potentially complex process of a market test, we have developed what we hope will provide a logical sequence of steps for managers through the customer-related issues which they face. We have set these out in five stages:

Stage 1:	Strategic issues
Stage 2:	Mechanisms for identifying customer inputs
Stage 3:	Specifying customer requirements
Stage 4:	Management options for client arrangements
Stage 5:	Preserving and ensuring innovation

Stage 1: Strategic issues

It is sometimes difficult for a market test manager to feel able to spare the time, or the manager may feel it to be beyond his or her scope, to see the wider implications or opportunities derived from market testing. In many organisations, the market test of a service will be part of a wider programme of competitive tendering. This programme may be on a phased basis over a few years (as for compulsory competitive tendering in local government) or each year's programme may consist of a number of simultaneous tests. Examples of this latter approach can be found within government departments where annual cycles of tests running in parallel have been established.

Whichever approach is in place within an organisation, there are some common results. One of these results is that a customer may be the recipient of a number of services which are under review within the market testing programme. This will be particularly the case where these customers are within the same organisation as the providers of services which are to be market tested. Therefore, customers may find themselves in the position of receiving a number of services which are subject to testing — for example, financial services, IT support, reprographic services. In some instances the managers of a service to be market tested are themselves customers of other services which are being tested, and are dependent on the recognition of their needs and price sensitivity to be properly established, if their own success in competition is not to be jeopardised.

No service manager, or organisation, should assume that a customer will be able to respond with ease to this situation. A corporate framework will need to be considered which should ensure the capability and capacity of the customer to input or be represented within a market test. And such a framework may be of equal benefit or indeed necessity, whenever there are multiple customers who receive a service from the same source, and this source is to be market tested.

Alternatively, the customer may be *external* to the organisation within which the market test is taking place. Recent examples of this have been the testing of planning services, educational support services, and social services. Whilst we shall examine in later sections of this chapter, how these customers may be involved with a market test, we shall first consider the more strategic issue:

- how does the test of *a number* of complementary service activities affect the recipient customer?

Again a framework must be put in place to ensure that multiple tests do not harm or hinder the customer unknowingly. For example, a customer who finds that two market test managers have individually (re)specified their services without co-ordination or adequate consultation, may subsequently discover a 'gap' or vacuum in service delivery.

It is therefore of great importance that an organisation considers the framework for a programme of tests from both a corporate and a customer perspective. We have set out in Table 10.1 a selection of the potential pitfalls from a customer perspective, for an organisation which does not do this.

There are a number of potential benefits to the customer also, which will be enhanced by a strategic approach to market testing.

- *gaps* in services are created
- difficulties of *costing* services whilst a number of "feeder" services are being tested
- *overburdening* of customer for information and inputs
- *uncertainty* may reach a worrying level if co-ordinated communication is not in place

Table 10.1 Potential pitfalls

- increased *clarity* of how services are interrelated
- additional *choice between* services may be facilitated
- opportunity to *comment* on relative benefits or disbenefits of a number of services is established

Table 10.2 Potential benefits

The strategic framework should therefore include a series of critical success factors which ensure that potential benefits are achieved, and pitfalls avoided. The framework should aim to support the customers of the services to be tested, but at the same time must not be so complex or rigid that the flexibility for the managers of the services which are to be market tested is unnecessarily constrained. The minimum strategic framework would therefore:

- establish the overall purpose and focus of a programme of tests;
- set out the objectives of the programme — for example, compliance with legislative requirements, improved services, increased services;
- affirm the focus on *service* delivery and customer safeguards; and
- establish the minimum requirement that the programme will be reviewed against key delivery criteria derived from the organisation's strategic objectives.

Both from a marketing point of view — in which customer awareness of your chosen message is paramount — and to achieve a good customer/service provider relationship in the future this framework should be clear and well communicated.

Stage 2: Mechanisms for customer inputs

Once the organisation has established the strategic framework for market testing, whether for multiple or single tests, the framework should be communicated to both customers and staff to ensure:

● clear understanding of the organisation's strategic objectives;

● compliance with the objectives and the review mechanisms;

● recognition of the organisation's commitment to its stated objectives; and

● an established pattern and process for the provision of information and consideration of comments and questions.

The process should therefore ensure communication both internally and externally, and sit within clear corporate statements in order to, as far as possible, 'demystify' the market test. There have been cases where this process has not been adopted, and the first customer inputs have been the result of worried staff expressing their very real concerns about their future and that of the service. A more strategic and corporate approach therefore establishes an open and responsive environment for customer and staff inputs.

The mechanism for customer inputs will vary according to the service. But a clear lead has been established within the housing management area. A local authority with a housing service going through voluntary or compulsory market testing is required to:

● establish lines of communication with all tenants;

● gain tenant inputs into the specification and contractor selection process; and

● enable a tenant body to 'opt out' of a contract which is non-performing and to establish a tenant management organisation.

We do not argue that this level of customer input is easy to achieve or to sustain. A very real problem within the housing field has been the lack of tenant associations which would form vehicles for this level of involvement. Some housing authorities are working extremely hard in such cases, to find out the alternative routes for tenant participation and to implement them. One linchpin of all of this work will most likely be regular and full tenants' newsletters, which will raise the likelihood of a market test/CCT as a future requirement many years prior to the tender process. This will be followed by open forum meetings and door-to-door question-and-answer sessions. Such actions should ensure a planned and comforting increase of awareness of the competition process and the potential outcomes from it. And this establishes a good precedent for other market test processes to follow.

The mechanisms for the identification of the requirements of customers, should as a minimum include:

- newsletter or note explaining the test, and the process to be followed, and the proposed customer involvement in this process;

- a customer questionnaire ensuring adequate information is held on the type and level of service currently being received; and the questionnaire should also enable comment on the level of satisfaction with current service levels and types;

- a representative customer 'focus' workshop to test the results of the questionnaire for reasonable analysis of responses (this or a similar group may well also have been involved in commenting on the questionnaire prior to circulation);

- feeding in of customer responses to the statement of requirement for the service which is to be tested, and therefore into the detailed specification of the service; and

- a process of sample or collective customer review of the specification.

A number of local authorities have established groups of elected Members either to act as customer review panels or to overview the process. In some instances such groups may have co-opted service customers or external 'experts'. This has often been an extremely constructive way of ensuring that:

- officers have an 'independent' view of the process and the detail;

- Members feel better able to inform and represent their constituents on matters related to the service and the market test; and

- any necessary revision to types and levels of service can be reported by Members who have a fuller understanding of the balance of customer requirements.

The final choice of mechanism will be dependent to a large degree on the scale of the service to be market tested. But a basic rule of thumb must be that the customers or a truly representative body should be:

- fully briefed to make their participation effective;
- properly canvassed to ensure validity of their inputs; and
- regularly involved and informed at key stages.

The overriding benefit will be a customer body which is not taken unaware at any subsequent changes to the providers of services, and who can also form an effective part of the process of service monitoring and review.

Stage 3: Specifying customer requirements

One key lesson from earlier rounds of market testing and competitive tendering has been the need to ensure that a specification is produced on the correct basis. That is, that a specification should reflect customer needs and wants, *not* what a service provider considers it is there to do, *nor* a service manager's view of 'what is best'. At this point, a number of different interests are likely to come together — or to clash. These interests will probably include:

- the corporate body;
- any political environments;
- service providers; and
- customers.

A logical way to commence the specification process in order to draw together these interests is to establish a 'statement of requirements'. This will establish:

- the strategic objectives of the service;
- the key performance requirements; and
- the operational parameters.

The Statement therefore establishes a clear framework and basis for the service, which can be used as a consultative document. It will also prove a useful introduction to the detailed specification within the tender documentation.

Many authorities have found that it is not easy, on a practical level, to include too many people in the writing of the specifications. It is important that a small team take control of the writing procedure itself — possibly a service deliverer and client officer. One authority has recently undertaken the process through the establishment of a pro forma, completed firstly by each section manager, and then considered across the service and by the client officer. However, there are other examples of not including customers directly, but instead through client officers and elected Members. One good example has been found in a Ministry of Defence establishment where a sample of customers were brought into workshops to discuss the specification at each stage. In a local authority, where services may be provided to a very wide populace, emphasis will again fall on the representative role of Members, perhaps a co-opted panel/committee members, and existing user groups — business forums, for example.

Most importantly, the philosophy of the specification must be to look towards customer requirements. There could therefore be clear statements for each service element of:

- the key reasons for the service;

- the customers whose requirements are to be met;

- outputs which will be required and the means of reviewing these;

- the interface and the responsibilities of the client agent, the customers, and the contractor;

- the mechanism for customer comments, requests and complaints, and how expectations will be met; and

- minimum levels of response to such inputs from customers and customer representatives.

Stage 4: Management options for client arrangements

We have already seen a number of different client management arrangements being put in place to meet the requirements of market testing within the public sector. These have ranged from fully devolved arrangements — concentrating contract management across geographic areas or groups — to highly centralised client departments or units. In some cases, a customer may agree to take on the client role for all customers, and therefore establish an overall client function. In explaining the most appropriate client management structure, there are a number of factors which should be considered. In particular, each option must be evaluated to test how well it meets the criteria of the organisation. Some of these criteria will be obvious, such as:

- cost; and
- effectiveness.

Other criteria will be more particular to the individual organisation. For example, it will be appropriate to consider factors such as:

- culture and philosophy of the organisation; and
- level of complexity of the contract.

There is no absolute right and wrong as to how to establish client arrangements. The most important issue is whether the arrangement ensures a workable contractual arrangement from both customer and contractor perspectives, without unacceptable levels of cost being introduced.

- level of capacity at customer level;
- practicality — including number of customers;
- efficiency;
- effectiveness;
- level of specific expertise required (for example, is there a need for a professional background or technical skill).

Table 10.3 Evaluation criteria

Overall, it is essential that the arrangement is as effective as possible to ensure that the best value possible is gained from the contract/service level agreement. Whatever organisational arrangement is selected, the client organisation must be able to:

- establish the cost of the current and future service

- review service levels
- design the specification and contract documentation
- prepare the specification in liaison with customers for the service
- design and manage the market test/tender process
- evaluate tenders and award the contract
- manage and review the contract
- prepare for the next market test

The organisational arrangement which is established will also need to reflect the structure of the contract itself — for example, is it a framework arrangement where customers can 'call off' directly their individual requirements? Or is there a need for a central overview/control of the amount of work purchased? We set out below two different examples of client management which have been put in place. We also examine some of the advantages and disadvantages of each.

Example 1: Small central unit with customer inputs

A number of local authorities have used the debates on enabling and competition to identify and develop a very particular form of strategic organisation, and customer-driven services. A particular example of this approach has been Berkshire County Council, where the organisation of the authority focuses on strategic management and contract management, with market testing of other services within a planned framework. A particular imperative for this authority has been to ensure that the perceived benefits of the structure are not lost by duplication of activities. This local authority, then has taken a decision to avoid any potential overlaps between client and contractor activities, minimising client costs and structures to focus on contract management. A contract for a range of services to customers external to and within the authority, has recently been placed, which is based upon this philosophy and which we explore here.

The client role for the services to be tested was established to encompass:

- contract letting;
- contract review and management;

- interface with elected Members (a role which is shared with the contractor); and

- contract payment.

The customers for the services of the contractor include individual members of the public, external groups and bodies, elected Members in their constituency role, and the Council and its committees. How then is the customer interface established and ensured, and the contract effectively managed?

The contract is based upon two key mechanisms for monitoring and review, and these are:

- reports on progress and performance which are generated by and provided by the contractor; and

- both an area-based and a centralised system of issue-specific and/or geographically focused committees.

Thus the routine information required to manage the contract is handled centrally, but customer issues are considered in a political and service environment, rather than administrative environment.

An example of how this operates is set out below:

- local service-related issues raised by the customers for the service are reported to area committees, with a report on their basis, implications, possible action and cost prepared by the contractor.

This process means that local customer issues are addressed on a local basis, by people who have a shared interest in both the area and the service. The potential disadvantage of this type of system is the number of issues which may be on such an agenda at any time.

Overall the contract is managed centrally, in terms of performance, payment and the commissioning of work. Instructions to the contractor are therefore controlled through the central client core.

Example 2: Fully devolved contract

An alternative to this level of central control and local/central customer inputs, can be found in the example of a contract recently placed within an authority which has a highly devolved management and financial structure. In this instance the contract was placed on behalf of customers using the service, within all of the authority's departments. The philosophy of the contract was to establish *direct* control between customers and the contractor, without a central 'expert' client function. Therefore the process was based upon full involvement of the customers, assisted by a (temporary) project manager from the department which was the largest consumer of the service. A steering group of customers was established and charged with:

- establishing the minimum level of their demand for the service over the life of the contract;

- reviewing and adapting a specification drafted on their behalf;

- considering the most appropriate contract mechanisms to meet their own needs — including mechanisms for commissioning of work, penalty procedures, and revisions to requirements;

- interviewing, briefing and evaluating proposed tenderers; and

- tender evaluation and post-tender negotiation.

The result was that a single contract was let by the commissioning authority, which formed an umbrella for *individual* service level agreements for each customer department with the contractor. The relationship between customer and contractor is therefore direct, supported by the contractual framework and potential for recourse within the service level agreements and beyond these to the contract itself. The contractor has three key incentives for ensuring customer requirements are met:

- the ability for the customer to buy services from alternative sources once the level of guaranteed usage that they entered into has been reached;

- the direct monitoring/enforcement power held by the customer; and

- the impact on the overall contract if any customer has grounds to use these enforcement powers — thus a failure to satisfy a single customer can jeopardise both the service level agreement with that customer and the overall contract.

The customers who feel less skilled and therefore more unsure about exercising any part of their powers, are supported on request by a nominated officer within the largest customer department. Therefore the department which has the most resources managing its part in this contract, makes available expert advice to other customers but without taking on an overall client role.

In practice a balance has to be established, to ensure that customers do not take percipient contractual action on what is a very performance/output-based contract. Recognising this potential danger, a number of potential contractors stressed their wish to establish very early contact with individual customers, and to develop a partnership approach to the establishment of the final service level agreements.

These then are two quite different approaches to introducing and including the customer within the process of a market test and the management of a subsequent contract. Each meets these challenges very well, adapting the structure to reflect:

(i)   the number of customers for the service
(ii) the practicality of a direct contractual relationship
(iii) the option of drawing in elected representatives to focus on and safeguard the needs and comments of both multiple and single customers.

Stage 5: Preserving and ensuring innovation

We commented at the beginning of this chapter that a market test is fundamentally a quasi-scientific process — there are a number of steps which must be taken and external or internal requirements to be satisfied. But anyone close to the public sector will emphasise that the needs of customers are not frozen at the point at which a specification is finally agreed. Within organisations, restructuring, budgetary pressures and other market tests may alter the shape and nature of the recipients of a contractor's services. Externally, the needs of the population to be served may be altered by changed political agendas, alterations to related services, or the altered profile of the population itself.

The market test process — in the form of the contract let — and the contractor themselves must therefore be able to meet the changing needs of the customers. It is therefore essential that the market test achieves the following:

● a tracking mechanism to identify changing customer needs;

● adapts to meet these needs;

- maintains a balance between the new and the old requirements so that no development is at the expense of the continuing demand for services.

It is easier and simpler for this awareness and responsiveness to be achieved if the original relationship which has been established by the contract has adequately reflected customer requirements. Thus the tools which, as we have seen, can be used effectively to draw up the original specifications for service, can be utilised on a continuous basis throughout the contract life:

- questionnaires circulated to customers;

- comments and complaints received about the services which customers are receiving;

- customer focus groups; and

- panels of customer representatives.

We have also seen examples where the contractor has been more directly involved in identifying changes — and is required to monitor and report on such changes by the specification and contract. For example, a contractor may be required to identify any of the following, depending on the relevance to the service which they are delivering:

---

changes in national legislation and the implications and options arising from these changes

changes in profile of the population for a service (derived from national/local information)

trends in the delivery of similar services elsewhere

key patterns from complaints/suggestions received

To ensure the effectiveness of this information, and the comprehensiveness of the client organisation's response to it, one local authority has charged a service contractor to represent the authority on the national and regional bodies of which the authority is a member. Joint surveys and working are therefore undertaken by the contractor rather than the client, to ensure that the close service and customer relationship is preserved through up to date market/service information.

Irrespective of which of these mechanisms is favoured as the most appropriate to ensure service provision on a dynamic basis, it is essential to ensure that the contract itself does not inhibit this responsiveness. Therefore the contractor must not be penalised for identifying changes — for example, financial loss should not result, unless of course it is the direct result of penalties for non-performance of the contract. Some organisations have explored schemes possible to be built into service contracts which provide incentives to contractors who in some way 'add value' to the original service requirement. Such incentives may be for cost-saving schemes which the contractor identifies or develops, or for exceeding the required performance standards (without additional cost to the client/customers). Organisations which are uncomfortable with incentive schemes which offer direct financial reward for a service that may be beyond the letter of the contract, but that could reasonably be seen as falling within the sphere of close customer focus, allow any such innovation to offset penalty points which the contractor may have gathered. Again a limitation on the acceptable parameters of this would need to be defined to ensure that a performance below a minimum standard was not ignored.

It has been noticeable that some of the most dynamic contracts, where customer requirements have driven the contractor and the contract, have been in services and organisations where the customer will at some point in the future have direct choice and purchasing power. Thus the local management of schools has made both direct service organisations and private contractors work hard to anticipate the changing responsibilities of individual schools. Within one central government department, the in-house reprographic unit identified a need to extend its opening hours by two hours a day. This was achievable without changes to staff terms and conditions — the flexibility had always been there — but anticipation of a market test saw a determined shift to reflect the demand, and purchasing power of the customer.

It would be wrong to portray all such changes as the result of competition and market testing. But in a number of areas such programmes have been a spur for service managers to think again about the environment within which they are delivering their services, and also for the customer to have a bigger part to play in defining the future.

■ CONCLUSIONS

We have considered in this chapter how the customer and customer requirements can be embodied within the process of a market test. For success, there are a number of factors which should influence the process

---

the nature of the particular service to be tested

the number and spread of customers

the level of technical knowledge that customers require

the role of customer representatives — whether they be elected representatives, tenant groups, consumer groups, or co-opted experts

---

The question of *how* to draw together the variety of views that will be gathered in a market test can be answered by establishing a clear and cogent mechanism for consultation and involvement. We would see these as including:

- customer surveys;
- representative customer groups for review and comment;
- seeking views on draft specifications and contracts;
- customer-based monitoring procedures as a significant part of overall contract management;
- requirements for the contractor to identify, report on and act upon as appropriate, internal and external changes affecting customers and the service; and
- regular repeat customer surveys both to feed the contract already running and in preparation for the next round of market testing.

PART D
Marketing in Action

Chapter 11

DIRECT MARKETING IN THE PUBLIC SECTOR

by Miles Young

The potential benefits of adopting a more targeted, measurable approach to marketing in the public sector could be huge, in terms of improved cost effectiveness, communications efficiency and accountability. In this chapter I shall explain how public sector marketers can adopt direct marketing techniques across a range of applications with reference to a number of relevant case studies.

The public sector is defined for the purpose of this chapter as being central and local government, quangos and nationalised industries.

■ MARKETING THE PUBLIC SECTOR — AN INTRODUCTION

The government and administration of a large, modern industrial society is a highly complex and involved task. It is estimated that up to 50 per cent of the United Kingdom's national income passes through government hands at some point, and that it employs nearly 30 per cent of the labour force. It consists of a wide variety of different bodies, ranging from central government, local government, quangos (quasi-autonomous non-governmental organisations), regional bodies and nationalised industries, each with its own objectives and purpose. And the issue of how this diverse public sector should best communicate with its many 'publics', whether individual, business or interested groups, must not be oversimplified.

This is an area where the fundamental principles of marketing cannot be applied in a straightforward fashion. Here the organisation has a designated job to do, often within a defined geographical area, often with a brief from the elected government of the day and ultimately from the ballot box itself. Marketing can be applied to the way in which that task is packaged and communicated, not whether it happens or not. Therefore throughout this chapter it is necessary to be mindful of the peculiar constraints that exist. Commonly used marketing terms like 'profitability' and 'exploiting' cannot gain credence here. However, there is much within the discipline of direct marketing that makes it particularly able to provide an effective and responsive means for the public sector to communicate with these key audiences. The paradox is that it is so rarely used.

■ DIRECT MARKETING DEFINED

Misconceptions about direct marketing are widespread in many areas, not just the public sector. To understand fully what this rapidly expanding discipline has to offer marketers in the public sector it is necessary first to attempt to define the scope and range of activity covered by the term.

The Institute of Direct Marketing describes it as 'a method of marketing that involves the identification of customers and prospects as individuals, gathering and analysing data to create targeted, relevant communications and develop a two-way dialogue. It can be used to deliver services, engender loyalty and develop customer relationships.'

Similarly, Ogilvy & Mather Direct's own definition encompasses the following points:

- it is an approach to marketing that considers the needs of individual prospects and customers, not mass groups

- it can create valuable relationships over time

- it encompasses any activity which does this, and is neither just a medium (e.g. direct mail) nor a channel of distribution (e.g. mail order)

This last point addresses head-on the principal misconceptions held about direct marketing. Many marketers still appear to believe that direct marketing is limited to the use of direct mail, prize draws or poorly targeted 'junk mail', and home shopping from catalogues run by the mail order giants like Littlewoods, GUS or Empire Stores. In the 1970s this was largely true.

But direct marketing in the 1990s is very different from this outmoded picture. Inbound telephone response and interactive electronic media are predicted to be big growth areas up to the year 2000 and beyond. In view of Ross Perot's 1992 US election promise of the 'electronic town hall' which would be constantly in touch with its public, these developments could go a long way to transforming communications between the public sector and its audiences in the future. The presidential campaign of that year 'will go down in history for the candidate's use of interactive media, 800 numbers, television talk shows and infomercials . . . direct response fundraising enabled the Democrats to raise more money than the Republicans (for the first time) and telemarketing was used to follow up the mailings' according to Dan Koeppel, in the American magazine *Direct* in November 1992.

It is unlikely that we are going to see a similar wholesale adoption of direct marketing techniques by political parties and elected governments in the UK in the short term, although their use of these methods is growing (see Chapter 13 for more discussion of this). But due to a number of vitally important technological, demographic, social and even political changes that have taken place through the 1980s the scope and application of direct marketing are broadening all the time and it can now be applied in a highly sophisticated, controlled and effective way to a wide range of marketing problems (see Chart 11.1). These include those faced by public sector organisations in an era when shrinking budgets, increased accountability and the need to provide better service are transforming the nature of external communications and face of marketing in this area. Indeed, the Conservative government's privatisations of the utilities, BT, gas, electricity and water, were responsible for many of the largest direct marketing campaigns of the 1980s and early 1990s.

The main conceptual leap required is to understand that direct marketing now involves the full range of media available (it has already been estimated by ITV that 28 per cent of commercial air time is covered by a direct response telephone number) and potential interactions with the market (or public) on an individual basis (see chart 11.2).

Fundamental to the development of these individual relationships over time, and the achievement of maximum benefit from the direct marketing approach, is the building and use of customer databases, and, increasingly, those committed to direct marketing are taking advantage of the decrease in the cost of the technology and the increase in the speed of processing to create flexible and valuable systems.

Chart 11.1 Changes driving the direct marketing opportunity

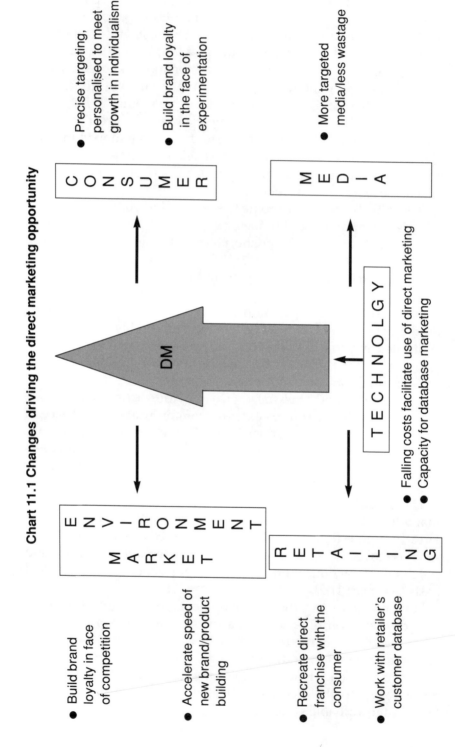

- Direct response press
- Direct response TV
- Direct response PR
- Inserts
- Door drops
- Take ones
- Direct mail
- Telephone, in- and out-bound
- Sales materials and support
- Interactive media

Chart 11.2 Scope of direct marketing

As direct marketing has become more sophisticated and targeted, so attitudes towards it have changed dramatically. A recent survey of 300 UK marketing directors conducted by the Chartered Institute of Marketing showed that the majority believed that direct marketing will grow the most over the next five years (see Chart 11.3).

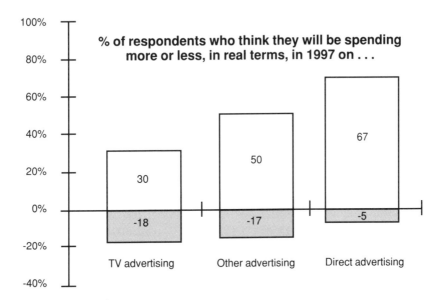

Source: Henley Centre Survey of Advertisers for the Chartered Institute of Marketing (1993)

Chart 11.3 Direct Marketing, the big winner

■ WHY THE RELUCTANCE OF PUBLIC SECTOR MARKETERS TO EMBRACE DIRECT MARKETING?

As it has been noted elsewhere in this book, the public sector has been relatively slow to adopt the better established discipline of general marketing, so it can be no surprise that the use of direct marketing in its full sense is limited to a few areas in the UK and the main success stories as to what has been achieved are largely due to the efforts of a few visionary individuals. Examples will be provided later in the chapter.

What is surprising, perhaps, is the fact that on closer examination it appears that many areas and departments within the public sector are already major users of direct marketing media and techniques without fully realising that this is what they are doing.

Local government is a huge user of direct mail for example, and central government one of the major direct response television advertisers using the Freefone 0800 and Lo-call 0345 numbers to encourage response from target audiences. The key difference is one of commitment, and the framework within which these techniques are employed. The professional direct marketer is committed to the concept of developing relationships over time and tracking the effectiveness of communications on an individual basis. In local government there is limited appreciation of the benefits of co-ordinating and targeting the written communications going out from the various departments. Amongst central government departments there is considerable concern (quite justifiable) about the acceptability of using the details of respondents from one campaign as the basis for targeting future related campaigns.

So the issue, from a professional direct marketing viewpoint at least, is why the public sector has not gone further down the direct marketing route, and is often failing to get real value from using these methods and media. To do that requires an investment in enabling marketing databases. At present, even the most advanced local authorities, like Braintree District Council which has won national and international awards for its commitment to customer service (which includes a 24-hour helpline to tenants) or Westminster, with its 'Welcome Pack' to new residents, do not have a centralised database of known information about the individuals living in the area, which can be analysed and used for more effective targeting of communications of all types. Lists and information about individuals and families are held and commonly duplicated in very separate departments. And even where the target audience

Research conducted in 1993 by Royal Mail's Electronic Services, which enables users of certain types of personalised mail to provide names and addresses on disc or down a modem for printing and despatch on customised stationery by Royal Mail, found some interesting differences in the way mail is used by local government as compared to other sectors including banking and finance, computer services, retail distribution.

The research conducted in September 1993 to a sample of 924 decision-makers, including 147 in local government found that local government:

- was the heaviest user of written communications
- was most likely to be sending mail on a daily basis
- sent 85 per cent via inhouse post (average 63 per cent)
- sent 94 per cent to internally held lists of names — minimal use of external lists
- was most concerned about the costs of mailing (and most likely to use 2nd class post)
- was least concerned about design quality of all sectors
- felt that the confidentiality of mail was the most important factor

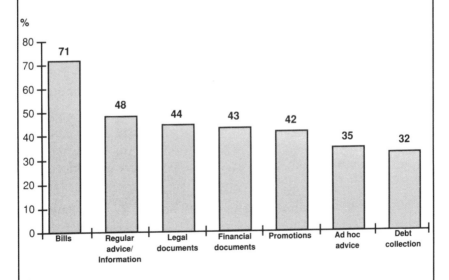

Chart 11.4 Purpose of sending letters from local government

Certainly, for the majority of the mail-users, this regular and enormous stream of letters from town hall to its public, does not constitute a marketing or promotional opportunity. It is more likely to be viewed as a necessary and vital means of communicating confidential and essential information. This was true of the statements sent out monthly by the banks — who now use them as a low-cost marketing tool for reaching targeted audiences — using selective insertion and variable messages printed on the statements themselves. This is surely a massive opportunity for local government to get a range of additional messages and offers across very cost-effectively.

consists of external groups of associations such as Citizens Advice Bureaux or Housing Associations with whom several departments may deal on a regular basis database, consolidation is rare.

However, it is in this latter area that the most advanced uses of direct marketing in the UK's public sector can already be found — the development of databases and a planned programme for their use and improvement over time to improve communications effectiveness to specific audiences. Some of these are described in some detail below — The Benefits Agency Register, the TECs, and Regional Development organisations.

It may not be that it is reluctance that has resulted in the slow adoption of direct marketing techniques — it is more likely that it is due to a profound lack of education and experience.

There seem to be three main factors involved:

● a simple lack of understanding and knowledge about the discipline, its applications and potential benefits

● the historical organisation of local authorities into separate departments with no one taking 'corporate' responsibility for all communications and viewing target audiences as a whole.

In most other market sectors experience has shown that, to be effective, the investment in a marketing database generally has to be supported at a senior corporate level, and that the benefits of being able to develop a view of individual customers across product and service areas are realised in the longer term. As more bodies in this sector accept a corporate marketing role so the environment for adopting direct marketing will inevitably improve.

- a fundamental question about the legitimacy of the use of personal data held on individuals as a result of government activity and involvement (the same concerns are not expressed about businesses) and the desire not to be seen as the electronic state-controlled 'big brother' of the Orwellian nightmare. Whilst this is not the place to debate in full the issues, many of which are still not clear due to impending EC legislation, it is certain that all direct marketers need to consider carefully the most acceptable ways of gathering and holding data on their target audiences.

◼ THE BENEFITS OF DIRECT MARKETING TO THE PUBLIC SECTOR IN THE 1990s

Given the increasing pressures on the public sector in the 1990s to change the way in which it should communicate, deal with and serve its various audiences, there will be ever strengthening reasons as to why public sector organisations should use direct marketing more actively. The Government's philosophy of ensuring that public services have both a quality and customer focus has dictated in many areas the need to focus more time and effort on identifying the needs of the public so that services can be purchased and provided to meet those needs. To do this accurately and continuously is forcing more and more local authorities to review their information technology and systems to maximise the use of information on those needs across different departments — thus providing impetus to the development of the types of systems that can be used as the foundation of a marketing database.

A marketing database can be as simple as a computerised list of customers and prospects with information about recency of response, purchase frequency, and value — proven to be the most important predictors of future response. At the other end of the spectrum it can be a highly complex relational database system holding detailed lifestyle information from questionnaires and enhanced by overlays with external profiling systems, such as Acorn or Mosaic. The key requirement is that the database enables the marketer to select a target audience on the basis of known information (see Chart 11.5).

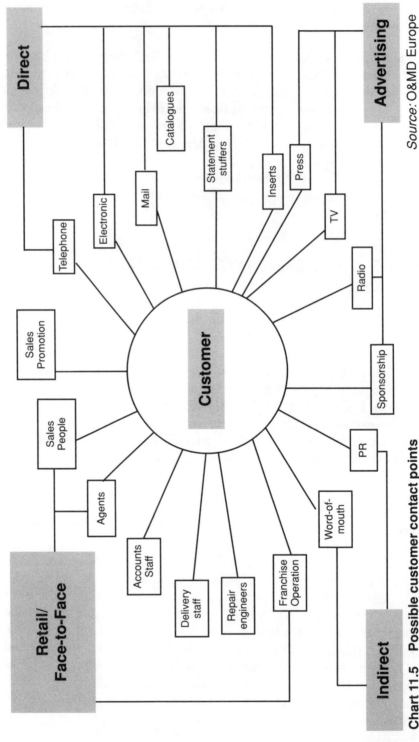

Source: O&MD Europe

Chart 11.5   Possible customer contact points

■ SPECIFIC APPLICATIONS — SPECIFIC BENEFITS

In considering the applications of direct marketing to the public sector, two fundamental divisions need to be acknowledged. Firstly these are substantial differences in dealing with individuals who collectively form 'the public', and with organisations (which could include businesses, voluntary organisations or government-sponsored associations).

Secondly, and often closely related to this, there are differences in type of the underlying objective for each particular communication, i.e. in terms recently coined by a worldwide O&MD task force looking at how direct marketing can be used to mobilise public opinion, whether it is 'grass roots' aimed at communicating to, and motivating large segments of the public, or 'grass tips' aimed at key influencers, such as businesses or tightly defined target audiences who will in turn mobilise the 'grass roots'.

Similarly, a decisive factor is whether the objective is to impart information (as with many Government campaigns) or to galvanise response and action.

Thus the range of applications reviewed and illustrated here can be defined on a four-way matrix.

OBJECTIVE TYPE	COMMITMENT	ACTION	INFORMATION
TARGET AUDIENCE	DEFINED/SMALL	MEDIUM	LARGE (NATIONAL)
MEDIA RANGE	CONTROLLED (DIRECT MAIL/ TELEPHONE)	PUBLISHED (NEWSPAPERS/ MAGAZINES	BROADCAST (TV/RADIO)
RESPONSE LEVELS REQUIRED	HIGH %		LOW %

Chart 11.6   Matrix of applications

Clearly the spectrum of possible uses of direct marketing is wide and varies by type of organisation. The objective in this section is to provide a basic framework within which the applicability of direct marketing can be assessed and to describe case studies where it has been used successfully to solve communications problems in the public sector.

In many ways, there are advantages to being relatively late developers in the direct-marketing discipline. Much has been learnt through the use of advanced research techniques in the past decade about how to avoid some of the more obvious negatives associated with direct marketing techniques and media — indiscriminate use of lists and customer files, for one thing, over-emphasis on the response rates rather than the total advertising impact of a communication for another.

■ USING DIRECT MARKETING TO TALK TO INDIVIDUALS

First, the application will be explained in terms of what can be achieved, the types of media and methods that can be employed, and where possible a specific case study will be described — some selected from the US and Europe, but the majority reflecting practice in the UK.

Education/information provision

This relates to the use of direct marketing techniques to disseminate information to a wide variety of publics, depending on the objectives/target audience. Objectives could range from mobilising support to education or simple information provision. Whilst the audience may subsequently change or modify their actions as a result, the key objective is to get the information into the hands of the right people. This can be done in two ways — by targeting specific individuals or by inviting response and thus making the target audience 'self-identifying'.

The specific benefits of direct marketing in this type of application is that it enables the user to target information most precisely, and therefore cost-effectively and measure the effectiveness of the campaign. However, in some instances where the target audience is extensive, as in our first example, direct marketing still offers many benefits in the amount and complexity of information that can be communicated.

Case study 1: US AIDS launch (1987)

This is a particularly interesting case since the campaign to raise awareness of the growing AIDS problem in 1987 was targeted at two groups — the 'grass tips' of organisations involved in the health and medical community, religious leaders, existing activists in the AIDS area, specific and ethnic minorities, and the 'grass roots'. Every household in the US was mailed by the Surgeon General.

The objective of the first stage of the campaign was:

- to generate third-party support from organisations who could influence attitudes and response to the main household mailing, and could be in the front line to deal with queries
- to deflect any criticism of the main mailing
- to ensure positive reception of the mailing

The programme developed by the American Centre for Disease Control involved:

- focus groups during development of the mailing to ensure the message worked
- meetings with a wide range of organisations
- a series of community town forums on AIDS immediately prior to the mailing covering twenty-eight cities in thirty-one days
- advance mailings to 'influencers'
- support with press conferences at national and local level

The results were monitored through extensive tracking research following the 100 million household mailings:

- 82 per cent read at least part, 66 per cent discussed it with friends and family
- Adult readership achieved 86.9 million in June 1988
- 250,000 prompted calls to an AIDS Information hotline

Case study 2: Disability living allowance (1992)

The Central Office of Information acts as an internal consultancy available to all central government departments in the area of external communications. Working with the Department of Social Security it developed a highly effective direct response television and press campaign to ensure that disabled people in the UK were informed of the benefits and allowances they are entitled to claim to help them live and work.

Objectives: to achieve a high level of response from an estimated 900,000 target audience who could qualify for the allowance. The budget was established as £2 million.

Methods: A TV direct response campaign was developed by advertising agency BMP, featuring a hard-hitting appeal by rock star Ian Dury, and offering a free 0800 telephone response service, backed up by a national press campaign.

Experience at the COI had shown that local rate 0345 numbers generally produce a more qualified response than the free 0800 although it does depend on objectives. In this case it was important to encourage all possible candidates for the benefit to call, and therefore the price barrier was removed.

Results: Response substantially exceeded the anticipated number, and a second telephone bureau had to be involved in handling the extra response.

In accordance with COI practice, a sample of respondents was followed up with research calls to find out whether they had received the literature requested.

The overall response to the campaign in terms of increased claiming by those entitled to the new allowances was considered to be highly satisfactory by the DSS.

Creating participation

Targeting information to specific groups can be used to encourage individuals to participate actively in activities at a local level. Taking the concept of targeting audiences a step further, this method requires the ability to identify the best 'prospects' and then to communicate with them in a motivating way.

The first step is to generate a qualified list which can then be the basis of a regular communication programme which should be focused on a specific offer or activity that can be measured. Some of the tried and tested techniques of direct marketing have been proving highly effective in this area — membership cards, special offers, discount or bonus schemes for regular use and so on.

Case study 3: London Borough of Sutton (Current scheme in progress)

The London Borough of Sutton have developed a leisure discount card which has been highly successful in increasing actual use of the sports services in the Borough.

Objective: To identify existing and potential users of leisure and sports facilities and generate higher levels of use over time

Target audience: Young individuals and families interested in sports activities of all kinds

Methods used: A variety of recruitment techniques were tested, including leaflets in dispensers at sports facilities, inserts in other council communications with integral reply card, and targeted direct mail to selections from the Borough's nascent marketing database. An inbound telephone service was offered (using a standard number) to answer enquiries about the scheme.

The most cost-effective source of names was the dispensers on site at the sports facilities, or 'take ones' as they are dubbed by American Express who also find them their most cost-effective source of new members.

Results: Over 7000 registered for the card at a highly acceptable cost per response, with a resulting measurable increase in use by those registered with the card.

Sutton are currently upgrading the offer with the launch of a new fitness suite and are looking at ways of using new technology in the future to monitor card usage more accurately. They plan to extend their promotional activities and mail a large proportion of the Borough's households with the leisure card offer.

A further extension of this type of application could be into the consultative process where specific publics are asked for their opinion on different development options. It has been proved again and again that people love to be asked for their opinion on almost every topic, hence the continuing success of postal questionnaires (often achieving between 15–40 per cent response). This was used to good effect by the Department of the Environment in the consultative exercise on London — Making the best better.

Interactive information provision

Increasingly direct marketing is being used to initiate and continue a two-way dialogue between customers and company — not just a one-off campaign or a one-way flow from organisation to customer. The introduction of telephone-based information services is central to encouraging this dialogue, with more and more use of freefone and local rate telephone numbers to reduce callers' concerns about cost. Recent years have seen the advent of customer care lines in the UK for well-known and respected brands, such as Kelloggs, Flora, Persil and Burger King. However the UK is well behind the US in this respect — a recent survey by telemarketing consultants Leiderman and Roncoroni found that only 8 per cent of packaged goods in the UK bore a telephone number. In the US this figure is more like 80 per cent.

What is certain is that the British public are now more willing to pick up the telephone to gain access to goods and services of all kinds, and that as their experience of professional services grows, so their expectations of the level of telephone service will increase. Figures from Target Group Index, a continuous research survey of 24,000 adults in the UK, found that nearly 35 per cent of individuals had responded to advertising by telephone in the last year, and that 30 per cent had used their telephone to call a business or a shop in the last week.

Number of calls	%	Any calls by social class	%	Any calls by age	%
None	53.97	AB	44.11	18–24	37.8
1–4	23.37	C1	39.73	25–34	42.12
5–9	5.92	C2	34.06	35–44	41.17
10–14	2.89	D	28.32	45–54	40.14
15+	2.65	E	22.1	55–64	30.33
				65+	20.53

Source: TGI 1993

Chart 11.7   Use of the telephone to respond to advertisements in the past twelve months by the UK population

The principle of offering telephone information services, linked into data gathering and database systems is one that applies to the public sector, albeit with a more complex and detailed range of information to impart. With the availability of user-friendly text retrieval systems, readily accessible to telephone operators through flexible Windows-based software, this no longer presents an insurmountable problem.

Case study 4: InterCity Telebusiness Centre (1993)

In November 1993 InterCity launched a new centralised call centre in Newcastle using an 0800 freefone number to encourage customers to book in advance. At present tickets are dispatched to travellers by post, but in future an advanced reservation system will enable them to pick up tickets from any one of 440 stations.

The principal objective for establishing a centralised facility is to encourage people to travel by rail by making it easier for customers to purchase tickets. Unlike airlines where 70 per cent of tickets are booked by third parties (such as travel agents), InterCity found that 80 per cent of their business is booked direct, but that many people experienced difficulty with making advance bookings.

InterCity started with an experimental facility in Reading that was geared to running an Apex service (where tickets had to be booked seven days in advance) due to the need to send out tickets by post. This proved successful, but did not address the needs of many InterCity travellers who wanted to book for the next day.

Research on the pilot showed that the use of freefone was encouraging people to call, with a 15 per cent increase in new business, and that customers responded favourably to the concept of one-stop shopping for rail travel.

The new facility which cost £1.5 million to set up in Newcastle has state-of-the-art telephone and database systems to maximise efficiency, encourage cross-selling and gathering of relevant customer information. With a new electronic ticketing system currently being developed as part of a European initiative its customers will be able to collect their tickets from any one of 440 stations in the UK immediately after booking.

The investment is clearly enormous but InterCity believe it is the way to develop customer relationships by improving service and ease of access, and will eventually form the basis for them to cross-sell a range of products and service to InterCity customers.

Complaint handling

Being able to encourage and effectively handle complaints by telephone has been shown to improve dramatically customer loyalty across a number of market sectors.

Technical Assistance Research Programmes (TARP) have researched millions of customers on behalf of clients world-wide. Their results are dramatic and well worth considering by any public sector body concerned about their image and long-term attitudes amongst users.

Prompt and effective handling of complaints is shown to engender more loyalty amongst those who complain, than amongst those who have no cause for complaint.

It was also found that prompt and efficient call handling is essential to achieve positive results — perhaps this is why this

Customer Segment	Brand loyalty
Experienced no problem	87%
Satisfied complainant	92%
Mollified complainant	43%
Dissatisfied complainant	23%
Non-complainant	41%

Source: TARP 1992

Chart 11.8   Automobile industry example

approach has been slow to take off in the UK across all sectors despite the strong evidence as to its benefits. The Government's own Charter initiatives have been brave in this respect since by raising expectations, they have exposed themselves to stronger criticism if complaints are not effectively dealt with. Many public sector organisations and all the privatised utilities now have service standards or customer charters against which complaints can be made.

There is some discussion as to how this activity fits into direct marketing — again it is dependent on adopting a conceptual framework. From a direct marketers viewpoint all direct contact can fit into the development and enhancement of long-term relationships. In our view, there are many wasted opportunities where this link between customer service and the marketing database is not made.

Case study 5: Braintree District Council (1991 onwards)

Braintree District Council have gained two Charter Marks for excellent service in both their housing and planning services, an Investors in People Award, and Total Quality awards. Their basic philosophy has been to do everything better — not just attempt to do one or two things really well. In a series of customer care initiatives which have involved cross-departmental teams working together to develop systems and communications they have established the following:

- 24-hour live operator telephone service, to offer help, register and deal with complaints

- open access public question time at committees in three different locations within the community

- regular surveys and panels to monitor attitudes, experience of service, and so on

- quarterly newspaper to all residents in the area

Through commitment to these measures across all areas and at the highest level, Braintree have regularly achieved outstandingly high measures of customer satisfaction amongst their public — emphasising the importance of effective two-way communication in developing loyalty and positive image.

Generating income and promoting payment options

A major task of many public sector bodies, particularly the 500 or so principal local authorities, is to raise funds. In the case of local authorities maximising the yield from the Council tax is a key priority.

As the survey conducted by the Royal Mail's Electronic Data Interchange services showed (see Chart 11.4 on page 207) the bulk of regular communications from local authorities are financial in nature — either bills or reminders. However there is little evidence that many of these have been assessed in the light of response maximisation techniques learnt by direct marketers over years of testing different options and various incentives in mass mailings on behalf of the Consumer Association's Which magazine, charities such as the Royal National Life Boat institution, etc.

It is more likely to find a 'direct marketing' approach to these problems at a national level. As noted previously, an extension of this application has been the use of direct marketing to sell shares in the newly privatised industries — which constituted several of the largest direct marketing campaigns of the 1980s and was enormously successful if the levels of over-subscription for the BT, Gas and Electricity campaigns can be taken as a useful indicator.

Case study 6: Netherlands TV tax campaign

Targeted at an estimated 400,000 non-TV tax payers, many of whom were young families in urban areas, a multimedia campaign was developed with a strong message as to the consequences of not paying — threatening the punishment through hefty fines.

There were six consecutive and planned stages:

i)   Public relations activity at the time when the campaign was being discussed in parliament

ii)   Commercials on TV and radio offering response numbers
iii)   Direct mail to a list that was derived from a match of telephone subscriber lists and lists of TV tax payers — to identify those with a telephone who had not paid the tax. The mailing offered a simple response device for those who do not have a television set and a compelling licence application form for those that had a TV but no licence
iv)   A reminder mailing was sent to non-respondents
v)   Non-respondents to the mailing were then 'telemarketed' with outbound calls (far more cost-effective than sending round inspectors at this stage)
vi)   The remaining few were then targeted for a personal visit

The results of the first stage of the campaign have been extremely encouraging — already over a third have paid up, with response generated by the various stages as follows:

Direct mail   47 per cent
Reminder mailing   21 per cent
Telemarketing   65 per cent

This shows that an integrated multimedia campaign, properly thought through and executed, can be enormously successful even where the 'offer' is essentially negative.

Maximising tourism

The ability of direct marketing to generate enquiries from potential tourists has long been recognised by the national tourist boards, but increasingly also by regional and more local tourism managers. The English Tourist Board has realised the income potential of the list of enquirers and actual holidaymakers that it has generated over the years through direct response advertising, and their list is now available for rental on the open market.

Experience has shown, however, that in an aspirational area like holidays it is easy to generate large volumes of enquiries that may take some years actually to convert into business. A cost equation has to be considered in terms of how long it is cost-effective to store names on a database and send them expensively printed brochures. The British Tourist Authority gets over this problem in its international promotions of the UK as a destination by only embarking on campaigns that have 50 per cent funding from a partner such as British Airways, or Forte Hotels. These deals are often negotiated on their behalf by Ogilvy & Mather who handle the world-wide BTA account.

Case study 7: Welsh Tourist Board (1992 onwards)

Closer to home the Welsh Tourist Board has a marketing problem, not unlike that experienced by many popular destinations — the desire to attract a more upmarket and affluent tourist population without alienating a core of loyal C1, C2 and D caravan and holiday camp users. The issue of the perceptions by the upmarket groups of Wales as a holiday destination is regularly researched and specifically addressed in TV and poster advertising campaigns — this year featuring famous Welsh stars such as Tom Jones and Anthony Hopkins. The direct marketing follows up with a combination of activities:

- telephone and reader response mechanisms for brochure enquiries

- direct mail to segments of the database selected by correlation to high-value geodemographic types (ACORN from CACI in this case) — such as those who live in postcodes with high penetration of 'families of five, driving Volvos, living in middle-class suburbs'

- inserts in consumer magazines and selected door-to-door distribution (also Acorn targeted) to generate further brochure enquiries

Several years of commitment to direct marketing, shared by the Welsh Office by whom the annual budgets are financed has resulted in the development of a large potential customer database — 1.5 million names. Research has shown that up to 45 per cent of people requesting the annual brochure eventually will holiday in Wales — however, the size of the database is now considered too large, and the current aim is to find cost-effective ways of cleaning and refining it down to a core of well-qualified prospects.

Recruitment

Not perhaps a mainstream direct marketing category, but an activity that has benefited from the knowledge and use of direct response techniques has been the many successful recruitment campaigns run by the Central Office of Information and the Government on behalf of specific public sector bodies, for example, bus drivers for London Transport, nurses, recruits for the Army, Navy and Royal Air Force, and the longest-running direct response recruitment campaign in this area — the Territorial Army, where telephone response on a freefone number has been handled for over eight years by the Bristol-based agency Contact 24.

The British Army have developed a highly innovative way of dealing with the problem of receiving a large number of under-age enquiries to their recruitment advertising. These respondents receive a mail pack inviting them to participate in a specially designed Challenger scheme with local cadet forces to help them develop their skills and keep up their interest in the Army until they are old enough to join up.

■ DIRECT MARKETING TO ORGANISATIONS IN THE PUBLIC SECTOR

The ways in which public sector bodies have developed their communications with businesses and organisations, for example those in the voluntary sector, provide examples of relatively advanced applications of direct marketing, particularly in the development of marketing databases that are used to target, monitor and control communications with more easily and tightly defined target audiences.

Lead generation

Due to the complexity of selling to businesses and developing effective working relationships with them, much business-to-business direct marketing involves an initial stage of lead generation, if only to identify the best prospects for a more targeted follow-up by direct mail, telephone or indeed a salesforce. Much activity from the public sector to businesses has been about 'hand raising', getting the best prospects for a particular service to identify themselves. This reflects the shortage of really high-quality qualified lists on the market, and for many organisations is the first step in building the all-important targeted database of prospects and customers. Much of government activity aimed at businesses at a national and local level is about maximising participation in schemes of various kinds, and requiring active involvement and commitment to the relationship over time. It is vital that resources are focused on talking to the right people to ensure that results are achieved — and lead generation is a vital first step.

There have been many initiatives by the Government to promote the importance of training to British business over the last decade, and the agencies and bodies promoting the training have metamorphosed several times to reflect changing market conditions and needs. One campaign that proved highly successful in this area was developed in the late 1980s by Ogilvy & Mather Direct.

Case study 8: Business Growth Training (1990)

Business Growth Training offered five types of training to British companies through the government-backed Training Agency. Initial campaigns which had concentrated on a two-stage approach to lead generation had proved to be relatively expensive and not wide-ranging enough in terms of generating awareness amongst the target audience who had been targeted at work. Ogilvy & Mather Direct were asked by the COI and their clients, the DTI, to develop a new campaign.

The objectives were clear — firstly to raise awareness of Business Growth Training and, secondly, to reduce cost per lead.

The target audience was defined as being managing directors and senior executives of small to medium-sized businesses (5–500 employees), many of whom had a low perception of the need for training in their businesses.

Amongst other media it was decided to use inserts in Sunday supplement magazines, since inserts often prove to be highly cost-effective in lead generation, and could reach the target audience in a more relaxed and receptive mode as consumers.

The results of the campaign run in the Sunday Times and the Mail on Sunday's You Magazine were very positive. Cost per response was reduced by 30–60 per cent and research showed that awareness of the insert was very high. Vitally important, the demand for training experienced at Area Training Office level also increased significantly during this period.

Targeted information provision

As noted above, the real long-term benefits of direct marketing can only be achieved by commitment to a marketing database. There are few really good examples of how this has worked for public sector organisations, but this one clear example of how a committed approach has paid dividends in reducing unnecessary wastage, increasing participation, and developing good will with the target audience, stands out.

Case study 9: The Benefits Agency Publicity Register (1993)

Since 1990 the Central Office of Information's direct marketing team has been working initially with the Department of Social Security and latterly with the Benefits Agency to develop a highly sophisticated database of information about the large number of voluntary and third-party organisations who need to receive and disseminate information about DSS benefits. The objectives of the database were threefold:

- to reduce wastage — previously all material was being 'mass mailed' to all advisors in this area, without any information as to its relevance to the advisory body's work and customers — resulting in many advisors being swamped and unable to deal effectively with the material received or deal effectively with the material that was relevant to them

- to develop a more professional two-way relationship with advisors who were seen as key to effective communication of benefits and entitlements from the DSS, thus the need for them to be more selective, more responsive and helpful

- to maximise the effectiveness of future communications both in reaching the end audience and in achieving more targeted support from the advisory network operating in this area

Using an external database bureau to provide a flexible, relational system not readily achievable within the DSS, a database of some 84,000 advisory organisations has now been built. This records the type of organisation under 70 main categories (which range from GPs, Citizens Advice Bureaux, social workers, to charities and so on), individual contacts within each organisation (as often different individuals are responsible for different areas of advice), a highly sophisticated 'walk in profile' which records the types of people that will come into any particular organisation in seven key categories relevant to the BA (currently covering about half the database)

Names were initially gathered of data from response to previous direct marketing campaigns carried out by COI on behalf of the Departments of Health and Social Security, and then proactive enhancement through selected external list sources, mailed to generate awareness and interest in being on the Register. Detailed questionnaires were completed by a high proportion of recipients to register areas of interest and operation and to ensure more targeted communications in future. Membership cards are sent out to respondents with a local rate telephone number for members to update their records, order further copies of the catalogue or add themselves to the file. Additionally the entire Register is mailed with an annual catalogue of all literature available, and then targeted on the basis of known information for specific campaigns, by the Benefits Agency and other government departments with the emphasis now being on the advisors to register interest and request more information, rather than bulk mailing leaflets in the first place. Members are asked to nominate colleagues or other organisations for inclusion on the Register.

The BA are very pleased with the results of the investment made in developing the Register to date. Response rates are high and feedback indicates that good will amongst the organisations has improved, with a real appreciation of the benefits of more targeted and relevant information. The organisations are more receptive to government materials received and more likely to participate actively in their dissemination to their contacts than before — a recent campaign in support of Drugs and Solvents Abuse information, which drew heavily on the Register, has exceeded anticipated response levels from advisors.

A quarterly newsletter is currently being considered as a means of keeping the advisor base up to date, and the COI believe it has been their most successful database marketing programme to date, one that can serve as a model to other government departments.

Encouraging participation

As with individuals, many public sector campaigns to businesses have as their principal objective the need to encourage participation in a specific scheme or programme. In marketing to organisations such campaigns can have a clear focus and a tightly defined target audience which facilitates cost-effective use of direct marketing methods and media.

*Case study 10: Designs for a trophy for the Citizen's Charter
'Charter Mark' by schools (1992)*

In another COI-managed campaign, this time on behalf of the
Citizen's Charter team in the Government, O&M Direct were asked
to develop targeted communications to encourage students
between the ages of 14 to 18 to design a trophy that would be
awarded to up to 50 organisations who won the Governments'
Charter Mark for achieving stated standards of service to the public.

The objective was actually to persuade schools and their students
to participate in the competition. This was incentivised with a prize
for the winning student and his or her school.

The campaign entailed a mailing to secondary schools, including
a poster that could be put up, as well as entry forms and briefs for
both students and teachers. This was supported by press ads in the
educational supplements of national quality papers with a response
device so that teachers not targeted by the initial mailing could also
send off for the full information pack.

The results exceeded anticipated response, with entry levels of more
entrants than expected and designs of an exceptionally high standard.

Seminar/trade fair attendance

A widespread and common application of direct marketing to
businesses by the public sector is generating attendance at events
— this has been widely used by the DTI in promoting various
initiatives, by regional development boards, and by national
governments looking to promote inward investment. The total
expenditure on direct marketing in Spain in 1992 is estimated to
have grown by 30 per cent as a result of the two world events
staged there in that year — the Barcelona Olympics and Expo '92
in Seville.

Case study 11: Expo '92 (1991/2)

Ogilvy & Mather Direct Europe, headed by the Madrid office, were
appointed by the Spanish government, to develop an overall
communication strategy, with the specific measurable objective of
generating 18 million visitors to the Expo in 1992.

The principal target market was defined as being the travel trade,
specifically European tour operators, to encourage them to include
the Expo as a destination.

A database of key contacts was developed totalling 976 people (remembering that in most European countries 80 per cent of the package holiday market is accounted for by five top operators), and they were invited by mail and telephone follow-up to attend a presentation, as a result of this campaign 51 per cent of the target audience actually attended a presentation.

In parallel a combined awareness and direct response press advertising campaign was developed targeted to the travel trade and designed to influence world-wide opinion leaders.

This appeared in 29 countries and was adapted in 11 different languages, with an offer of further information in 7 languages. Over 70,000 responses were received and a tracking study showed that spontaneous recall of Expo'92 amongst the target audience was 42 per cent after the campaign — higher than for the Olympics or Eurodisney! This demonstrates the potential effectiveness of a dual purpose approach to press advertising if it is properly conducted.

The results achieved by this carefully orchestrated international campaign were more than satisfactory with all major operators including Expo amongst their destinations and the target of 18 million visitors achieved.

Developing partnerships

Many organisations in the public sector will never have access to budgets of the kind available to a government department or a national campaign, but at a local level have to concentrate limited resources on maximising effective communication to business audiences that they will have to deal with regularly over a period of time. Database and direct marketing are tailor-made for this situation — identifying and communicating with quite tightly defined groups — whether limited by geography, size or sector.

■ SOME GUIDELINES FOR THE EFFECTIVE USE OF DIRECT MARKETING

Despite these many excellent examples of how direct marketing has been used cost-effectively in so many areas to consumers, organisations and businesses, as noted earlier, the take-up of direct marketing in the public sector remains very low. The main obstacles appear to be those highlighted above, a lack of understanding and knowledge of the methods and benefits of direct marketing. But perhaps direct marketers themselves are also partly to blame. It is one of the most scientific disciplines within marketing, and despite its relative youth (only really being well established in the UK since the late 1970s) it has already shrouded itself in the mystique of jargon and complex terminology for what is, in fact, just applied commonsense.

This over-complication, as well as the concern about the use of personal data and the building of databases, may have put off many potential users in the public sector. But, rationally there are no obvious barriers against the public sector entering into this rewarding, cost-effective and increasingly acceptable method of marketing. Here are five key questions as a checklist for embarking on direct marketing to help ensure that you gain the benefits that a targeted, measurable, and interactive approach has to offer the public sector.

1 Can you use it in a targeted and controlled way?

A good starting point is to ask whether you can identify a particular group for a specific campaign, since it is with such a defined audience that very specific objectives can be established for a test campaign, a budget set and a range of activities tested. Most newcomers to direct marketing tend to start with smaller, more controlled activities to one segment or sector, and expand from there on the basis of intital success. The groups could be identified on a list (either internal or externally held), defined by a geographic area, or perhaps be reachable through very specific media or magazines (i.e. the voluntary sector).

It is important to set clear, measurable objectives against which you can decide whether the campaign has succeeded or not. These also provide the basis for deciding how much you can afford to spend on a campaign.

2 How can you introduce interaction and encourage response?

Whilst talking about using offers may sound contradictory in the public sector, it is well worth understanding the need to motivate people to respond to a communication. Direct marketers understand this implicitly and will always look for a way to package a proposition and add value to the respondent. Setting deadlines, offering discounts, and simplifying response should all pay dividends. From all that has been said about the growth and acceptance of the telephone as a response device, and a way of getting information, this should be part of your plans if you can deliver a reasonable service. If not, it is possible to subcontract answering services to high-quality practitioners.

In the case studies, the Benefits Agency provided a membership card, Sutton offered a discount, and in the case of InterCity the motivation is created by offering better service nationwide.

3   Have you understood the communications needs of your target audience?

Good direct marketing, like any communication, requires that the perspective of the recipient is considered. Is their current level of knowledge known? Have they participated before? Can their needs be precisely addressed? Ideally market research in the form of focus groups or interviews should precede all campaigns, although this is not always possible and sometimes too expensive to contemplate for a small programme.

Research on customer databases in other sectors shows that in order to develop a fruitful long-term relationship it is necessary that direct marketing communications received are perceived as relevant, potentially interesting and part of a planned programme. People do not want to be mass-mailed with irrelevant communications, since this will devalue the relationship they have with the organisation. Therefore research can pay dividends in ensuring that what is communicated to various target audiences works on all levels, not just in generating response and action from a minority.

4   Can you learn something to improve future results?

Testing out the effect of different elements of the campaign is vital to learning what will work best in the future. Tests can include basics like targeting, or which media to use, as well as executional factors like offers, creative approach, and so on. Commitment to direct marketing requires long-term testing and the ability to improve results continually over time.

The first step for most newcomers to the discipline is to establish systems to enable them to measure response accurately in terms of telephone calls received, coupons returned and other expressions of interest which in this sector may result in people walking into the town hall. Once this is done, you will be able to analyse precisely the effect of a campaign, and over time develop the ability to test different approaches against each other.

Testing has proved that the single most important element in determining levels of response is the effectiveness of targeting. These test results from a mailing programme by Ogilvy & Mather Direct in the 1980s show the effect of different elements on response.

■	List (targeting)	x6
■	Offer	x3
■	Timing	x2.5
■	Creative	x1.35
■	Response mechanism	x1.2

Source: O&M Direct

Chart 11.9   Communication effectiveness — targeting

It is clear from this chart that whom you are reaching is the most important factor, six times more important than response mechanism, and three times more important than timing. Even if you have a brilliant creative concept, if it is not reaching the right people, it will not work!

5   Will you be able to build and enhance your database of information for analysis and targeting in the future?

Everything we have been talking about points to the importance of adopting a databased approach to communications: the importance of targeting for results; the need to understand your target audience and communicate effectively over time; the requirement to understand their perspective and offer meaningful benefits and offers to motivate participation and action.

The database should become the foundation on which these activities can be carried out, and now marketers in all sectors are realising the widespread applications and benefits of developing what are commonly called customer information systems — not only in marketing terms, but in delivering fast, accurate and effective customer service and in planning resource allocation for the future, developing new products and services, and so on.

The technology is increasingly available at a decreased cost, and many organisations in this sector would do well to review systems developments with marketing requirements in mind, since a flexible, relational system that can take data from different sources and provide analysis should help in the quest to deliver better service quality within a reduced budgetary framework.

■ CONCLUSION

Direct marketing and the public sector have not been natural bedfellows, though the discipline has much to offer. The key to its future exploitation is to understand the nature of the public sector itself. The huge developments which are driving the change from provider culture to service culture in this sector means that interactive communication between the organisation and its customer will increase; and direct marketing must inevitably play a larger role as it does so.

■ REFERENCES

BIRD, D. (1993) *Commonsense Direct Marketing*, London, Kogan Page.

INSTITUTE OF DIRECT MARKETING (1993) *The Practitioner's Guide to Direct Marketing*.

CHARTERED INSTITUTE OF MARKETING AND THE HENLEY CENTRE FOR FORECASTING (1993) *Metamorphosis in Marketing*.

OGILVY & MATHER DIRECT EUROPE (1991) *Identifying and Keeping Customers in the Single Market*, London.

Chapter 12

ACHIEVING EFFECTIVE ADVERTISING

by Gene Wonnacott

■ THE CHANGING FACE OF LOCAL GOVERNMENT ADVERTISING

Public sector advertising during the mid-1980s and early 1990s saw dramatic changes from its traditional base within the area of recruitment advertising. Authorities have become more aware of the benefits of good advertising in terms of both value for money and image. There is also a marked change in the way in which local councils have adopted a more professional approach to the entire subject of advertising and their relationships with the advertising industry.

For many years the public sector has given a low priority to its advertising. Recruitment advertising is a perfect example of this, with very little consideration being given to good copywriting, design, layout or media selection. In the main, copy was just repeats of previous advertisements with changes in closing dates and salaries in publications which had always been used, and everything else was left to the advertising agency to finish.

In the 1980s the public sector was a big spender on advertising, with an estimated total expenditure in 1985 of approximately £500 million, covering all areas of advertising. A typical breakdown of spending at that time for a shire county was 60 per cent on recruitment advertising, 40 per cent on areas like public notices and tourism. Of this figure about 60 per cent was spent with the regional press and 40 per cent with the national media.

In the early 1990s local authorities are still a major spender on advertising, with the estimated expenditure for the 130 authorities who are members of the National Association of Public Service Advertisers for the year 1992/93 being in the region of £32 million. There has been a major change in the actual areas where the money is being spent, recruitment showing a continuing downward trend and more being spent on leisure, tourism, public notices and general awareness advertising.

Public sector advertising began to show improvements in the late 1970s with local authorities experiencing difficulties in recruiting in certain key areas of employment. Although the answer at that time was the use of bigger advertisements and the introduction of graphics, at least it showed that some thought was being given to the subject and that advertising could have its advantages. This system of bigger and better advertising is best illustrated by the increase in health service advertising at that time, so much so that the Department of Health took steps to reduce this level of expenditure.

A further step in changing the attitude of authorities towards its advertising was the need to obtain better value for money in all its areas of activities. Councils for the first time looked at exactly where their money was going, what was being obtained for that level of expenditure and the services provided. Typical annual local authority advertising spend in the early 1980s was, rural shire county £600,000, Scottish regional council £1 million, metropolitan borough £425,000, London borough £750,000, Midland-based shire county £750,000. One northern-based city council was spending £600,000 with just one publication.

The need to look at its expenditure in greater detail highlighted for a number of authorities the urgent need to examine methods of improving their advertising performance and ways of achieving better value for money from this operation.

Councils at the same time became very concious of the need to promote their own image and the importance of adopting a favourable corporate identity. At last the foundations were beginning to be laid for the public sector to become efficient advertisers.

The early 1980s saw the introduction by a then small number of councils of in-house advertising units, dedicated to providing the departments of their authority with all the services previously provided by a commercial advertising agency.

■ THE NATIONAL ASSOCIATION OF PUBLIC SERVICE ADVERTISERS

In November 1984 seven such authorities met with the intention of exchanging information and ideas on the running and future development of local authority in-house advertising units. This forum grew into the National Association of Public Service

Advertisers (NAPSA), which by 1994 had expanded to a total membership of 130 councils representing all tiers of local government in England, Scotland and Wales.

Out of its total membership today, 35 NAPSA members operate in-house advertising agencies, all with full agency recognition from the Periodical Publishers Association. The Association has developed into an organisation offering full support to public sector advertisers in the vital areas of staff training, regular meetings with other local authorities, contact with both national and local media and commercial advertising agencies. All of which has been instrumental in local government becoming more professional in all its advertising activities.

Even those member authorities which work with agencies in the private sector have benefited from the initiatives introduced by NAPSA — especially with regard to staff training and direct contact with the media. The annual three-day NAPSA training course in basic advertising skills for public sector employees is always over-subscribed.

An important development of the in-house agency concept was the establishment of 'consortium' arrangements with other authorities, in that one authority acts in the role of advertising agency for other councils which are perhaps not large enough to introduce their own similar schemes. This system is at present operated by five in-house agencies, with one situated in the south-west operating on behalf of fifteen other councils.

Similarly, with the recent development of colleges of further education becoming independent establishments and the introduction of local management of schools many in-house agencies have found themselves in direct competition with agencies in the private sector for their business — with the authority agency winning the majority of accounts.

■ THE SELLING OF ADVERTISING SPACE AND COUNCIL-OWNED PUBLICATIONS

Recent years have seen the in-house agency become like any commercial advertising agency offering exactly the same service to its departments and other clients. Also, a number of authorities have appointed experienced advertising staff from both the agency and media to senior posts within the in-house operation, ensuring the professionalism of the agency.

Coinciding with this new approach to advertising by the public sector was the development of advertising sales, an important area for income generation by any authority. This includes the selling of advertising space to the private sector in such diverse items as council-owned newspapers and publications, including job vacancy lists and tourism guides, general information leaflets, internal telephone directories, library tickets and even salary advice slips. This form of income generation is becoming more and more important to all local authorities, with many councils achieving impressive annual sales figures. In many instances this activity of selling is undertaken within the in-house advertising agency.

Corporate identity plays an essential role in public sector advertising, with many authorities working to strict guidelines on exactly how their advertising should appear in print. A number of councils have produced corporate identity advertising manuals which detail their exact requirements when orders are placed. These manuals are used by individual departments when preparing copy and copies are lodged with their main media to ensure that all those involved in the preparation and publication of advertisements are aware of what is required.

Not only does it ensure that an authority's advertisement corresponds to the corporate identity ruling but by specifying type sizes and faces the final printed size of the advertisement is known before the order is placed — ensuring that value for money is achieved.

With directives from the Audit Commission that councils must make themselves more cost-effective many have set up small sales teams to gain additional income while at the same time promoting themselves and the service which the authority provides. It has to be remembered that advertising sales are not to compete with other similar business ventures; they should not be solely a source of making money. The object is to finance publications which disseminate information to the public.

There are three primary ways in which a local authority can proceed with an advertising sales venture; hire a private company to sell on behalf of the authority on a commission basis; let a private company sell some of the space with the authority selling the remainder themselves; or bring the entire operation in-house.

The selling of advertising space should not be confused with that undertaken by certain private companies which produce guidebooks and other publications and carry out the entire operation themselves, giving the authority an agreed number of free copies in return for an endorsement of the project.

In costing any such venture it is advisable that all overheads are taken into account, including such items as office rent, heat, light, telephone, etc. These matters need to be built into the cost analysis so that a correct financial appraisal can be made.

Although it is quite possible to make each publication cost-effective through advertising sales there is a further element worth considering. That is, the selling of the publication to increase revenue. A good example of this might be an industrial directory. The advertisers pay to be included in one section and a selling price is then placed on the publication. It is often advisable to have a price on such publications, as not only will it bring extra revenue but it also has a dampening effect on distribution.

Other important areas to look at if producing your publication in-house and selling your own advertising are printing and reproduction. Examine the market for your publication, promotional costs, point of sale material (if applicable), copyrights (including photographs and maps, authors), copy collection and billing and accounting.

Another area which can involve the authority in the selling of advertising space is that of the council-owned newspaper. This needs to be handled differently from a guide book or directory. Before launching a civic newspaper it will be necessary to obtain approval for a realistic budget, which must cover the cost of printing and distribution as well as of journalistic expertise.

Not every printer is capable of producing a tabloid newspaper and enquiries should be made to find the names of companies that can provide such a service. Distribution can be either through the Post Office's household delivery service, or through a private distribution company.

The key to the success of a civic newspaper is to find a production editor who will be responsible for the sub-editing of the copy, layout and liaising with the printers. Not many authorities will be able to find this facility in-house and most will be required to buy this service in. A great deal of thought should go into finding out the prospective editors' background and experience before they take control of the authority's newspaper.

■ VALUE FOR MONEY

Value for money in advertising is essential to any local authority. However, commissions and discounts are only part of the saving which can be achieved. Copywriting, style selection and composing can all generate substantial savings.

The most significant cost savings can be achieved by adopting a more professional approach to media selection. We have all heard about some of the methods used in deciding in which particular publication an advertisement should appear; 'we used it before'; 'I read it'; 'it is the cheapest'; 'put in enough publications and we are bound to be successful'.

Poor media selection is both costly and inefficient and the most sophisticated advertisement will fail if the media selection is flawed. Media selection must be based upon factual response and not just 'gut feeling'.

So what is needed to set up an effective analysis system? The most important thing is to get prompt, accurate information. In the case of recruitment advertising this could entail a simple questionnaire to be completed by the recruiter asking for the number of applicants, interviewees and starters against the relevant media.

The information then needs analysing and processing. Software packages are available which will analyse the response information and show clearly the most effective media in terms of response and cost.

Response analysis is essential when authorities are faced with advertising for those vacancies which traditionally have proved difficult to fill. Social services have a number of examples of such posts. Fortunately there are a number of publications aimed at this particular market but it is important to identify the media which is read by your target audience.

In many instances it is not purely the case of advertising the vacancy; the authority must also sell itself not only as offering an efficient care service, with the right career prospects, but also as an area/location in which the possible applicant would like to work and live. An example of this was the major problem faced by one local authority trying to recruit care staff following nationwide publicity over a number of alleged child abuse cases. In this instance the advertising of job vacancies adopted a two-prong marketing approach; after identifying the right media and target readership, the advertising copy had to sell both the job and the authority.

A similar case, following publicity over the level of care provided by a council resulted in advertisements appearing with the headline

'We are prepared to show our dirty washing in public'. Both cases illustrate the value of advertising being an important marketing tool.

There is a debate about which part of the response analysis is the most important — the number and cost per applicant, interviewee or starter? All this information is essential to ensure effective media selection. We can see trends developing that suggest that the media which produces the greatest number of applicants usually produces the most interviewees and starters. It can be argued that the numbers and cost per interviewee are the most important figure as whatever happens in the recruitment cycle after that stage is entirely dependent on the authority — not on the advertisement in the chosen media. Response analysis shows quite clearly where the responses are not coming from.

The figures used are based on the number of completed application forms received and it is interesting to note the differences between the number of initial enquiries and completed applications. Where there is a big difference there is very likely an urgent need for investigation.

Response analysis is essential information for any authority if effective media selection is to be achieved. It is certainly not a 'once only' exercise. It has to be carried out on a regular basis — at least at three-monthly intervals — and the trends analysed. Media selection decisions can then be taken with confidence and non-effective media deleted from your schedules.

■ THE ADVERTISING AGENCY

As mentioned earlier in this chapter the majority of local authorities use the services of a commercial agency for the placement of its advertising with the media. Currently there is no statutory obligation for authorities to seek competitive tenders for advertising services. A number of councils, do, however, employ this method when appointing an advertising agency. However, like many aspects of advertising, what works with one council may not be the best route for others.

It is sensible to set up a User Group which is constituted from all departments with a major advertising spend; smaller departments should also be represented. The authority's Purchasing Department should be involved in an advisory capacity to assist in writing the tender and to play a major role in assessing the response. Does your authority want a full service agency agreement with all the hidden costs that this may entail? do you want flexibility to pay for only the services you require? will the tender cover all advertising? If you agree on terms with an agency do you sign a document tying you to these terms for a fixed period? These are the questions that need to be answered early on.

What does your authority want? — for example regular pick-ups of copy, all advertising to be trade set, the agency to be required to write copy regularly, what information will you as the client require about spend, and how often will this information be needed, etc.

Questions can be phrased appropriately on a tender document to cover all these and many other points. Do not forget that the agencies will need to know something about you — for instance your total spend, spend by different types of publication, i.e. trade, regional, local and national media, and some indication of spend in some of the more regularly used titles. In addition, they will need to know if they are dealing with a central point within the authority or with a number of different departments as individual clients.

You must be clear about the cost of the service which you require. This does not solely mean discounts, if any, that are to be returned by the agency to you. It should cover such aspects as lay-out, border styles, type faces, etc. Returned commission and discounts are really just an added bonus. Agencies do need to make a profit in order to service your account to the level which you require. If they make little or no profit because they are returning large sums to you do not expect a high standard of service to be provided.

You must decide whether the tender is to be advertised widely or if you will supply the document on a limited circulation basis to the agencies you know. This latter action is possibly the best way forward. You should consider the benefit and/or shortcomings of using local agencies, regional agencies or those just based in London. In addition, will the size of the agency, however it is measured, be important?

Should you decide to advertise your tender widely be prepared for a large number of requests for the document. Competition for clients between agencies is strong, which can only benefit the client at the end of the day. If you require the agencies to carry out a particular task at their presentations to your authority then allow them sufficient time for preparation.

Do not invite a large number of agencies to present. Not only does it cost their time and effort it also costs yours. The whole idea of asking a company to tender is for you to be able to draw up a shortlist of those who should be considered, ideally no more than four companies should reach the final presentation stage. Be certain to find out if they will charge for work undertaken for the presentation if they are unsuccessful.

Allow sufficient time for the process to work — if you are working to a deadline by which the tender must be let then allow a minimum of four weeks between telling the agency they have been successful in their bid and the date when you expect them to commence working for you. Agencies will always tell you that they can take over from an existing agency overnight — however, development time for procedural matters and enough time for both parties to get to know each other is vital.

After the tender has been let, continually monitor and review not only the effectiveness of the agency but also whether your authority is fulfilling its part of the deal. Good communication and trust between agency and client are essential.

■ THE IN-HOUSE ADVERTISING AGENCY

Appointing an advertising agency is a big step for any local authority, but an even bigger step is the decision to bring all your advertising in-house and establish your own agency. The initial consideration is your authority's advertising spend. Following discussions between NAPSA and the Periodical Publishers Association it was agreed that no applications for agency recognition by a local authority with an advertising spend of less than £300,000 per annum would be considered.

If an authority can meet this basic criterion then it must ask itself the question 'Why In-House.'

The considerations will include:

Cost savings — the opportunity to make very real savings is there, through the revenue brought in by negotiated volume discounts and by commissions paid by the media. When authorities are dealing with a commercial advertising agency only a small percentage of commissions is returned to the client.

Speed of reaction — In any advertising situation an in-house team can provide quick answers to both client and media on a wide range of questions. Their answers are immediate in the majority of cases and in others take only minutes. The reason for this is:

Knowledge of the authority — an in-house agency has a far better knowledge of the authority and the way in which it operates within the general sphere of business. In addition to this members of the agency know individuals better than any external agency can, and they have a better understanding of the policy of the council.

Control and advice — generally an in-house agency has no particular reason to encourage its clients to spend more than is really necessary on their advertising. There is room for greater control of possible resource wastage when it is possible to give quick advice on media choice and cost to the decision-making manager. This is only possible when the specialist knowledge is in-house, because members of the team are more likely to ask searching questions of a line manager than an account executive with an external agency would.

Once the decision is made to go in-house it is essential for the authority to discuss the plans with all possible client departments to ascertain their exact advertising requirements and to gauge the possible workload which has to be undertaken by the agency. Discussions should also take place with the local media to let them know what is happening and ensure their involvement in the project from day one. At this stage preliminary reference to the Periodical Publishers Association should commence with regard to submitting an application for agency recognition. At the same time your existing external agency should be consulted to ensure a smooth change-over of operation. In 1993 a unique partnership was initiated by the appointment by a local authority of a commercial agency to assist in the establishment of an in-house advertising agency — this was a six-month initial contract.

In general all advertising originates within individual departments, with orders being sent to the agency accompanied by the appropriate order form and instructions. If any changes are needed at this stage they will be carried out in consultation with the client department. Advice on publication date, media choice and layout is readily available from the authority's own agency.

Most in-house units operate on a system of direct debiting of the client departments for advertising place. This means that each department still maintains full control over their advertising budgets. Experience has shown that it is not feasible for an in-house unit to hold the authority's entire advertising budget.

Income to the in-house agency is derived through one of two tried and tested methods. The in-house agency whilst recharging departments retains a percentage of the discount or commission which has been obtained on the particular advertisement, passing the greater part back to the client, or, it makes an agreed service charge to departments in return for allowing all savings achieved by the agency to be handed back to the client.

The majority of in-house agencies now use fully computerised advertising systems. This includes placement of orders, provisional costings, payments to the media, departmental recharges, budgeting and response analysis. There are two main software packages in use by local authorities, one produced by a commercial company and one developed in-house by a NAPSA member authority.

An interesting development over recent years has been the appointment of advertising managers by a few authorities who were already using the services of commercial advertising agencies. This post offers the benefit of a 'centralised' system for those not wishing to set up their own in-house operation. The advertising manager is responsible for all liaison between the authority and agency, negotiating terms and discounts, providing a central point for queries from the agency and media, giving advertising advice to departments and offering a training provision for employees.

■ NEW TRENDS IN LOCAL GOVERNMENT ADVERTISING

Over the last decade local government advertising has changed dramatically. The changes range from the very basic areas of recruitment advertising, from a more competitive approach in what was a shortage market in particular skills, to the present trend of reduced advertising spend on recruitment and increased levels of other forms of public sector advertising.

Local authority advertising is moving more and more into realms of 'marketing advertising'. A district council recently decided that action was needed to encourage greater use of its community halls. It was decided to launch a two-week advertising campaign in the local free newspaper. This resulted in two full-page advertisements simply showing an empty hall and a list of its possible uses. The layout and copy of this advertisement won a national advertising award for the authority in the category of 'the Best Advertisement of Benefit to the Local Community'. An increase in use and enquiries about the eight halls being promoted was also reported. The entire exercise achieved the aim of raising the awareness of the community of this facility offered by the local authority.

A further example is that of a county council wishing to improve the take-up of school meals at a particular education establishment.

Following discussion with staff at the school it was decided that the marketing answer to this was leaflet distribution in selected parts of the school's catchment area.

Specially commissioned artwork produced an attractive four-page colour leaflet which depicted sample menus of meals available from the school canteen together with nutritional details and examples of prices. It was decided to make use of the distribution service offered by the local free newspaper which enables the advertisers to select individual areas, even streets, of the target area. This campaign resulted in a 7 per cent increase in the number of pupils taking school meals.

Authorities are facing further changes in the very near future, with the need to publish Performance Indicators in local media commencing in 1994, proposed local government reorganisation and compulsory competitive tendering. With regard to Performance Indicators, NAPSA have recently had the opportunity of working with the Institute of Public Relations (Local Government Group) and the Audit Commission on the production of an information book on good public relations and advertising practice with regard to making this material available to the public. This booklet was distributed by the Audit Commission together with their own official publication instructions.

A further new development is the publication and adoption of a code of good advertising practice for local authority in-house agencies jointly produced by local government advertisers and the Periodical Publishers Association.

It was felt that with the increase in the number of in-house agencies, which in itself was gratifying from the point of view of keeping greater controls on the spending of public money, there were points which needed to be emphasised concerning the way in which in-house agencies conducted their business in relation to those publications which are members of the Periodical Publishers Association.

In order to deserve the revenue from commission to which PPA agency recognition entitles such agencies it was felt that certain criteria should be enforced. The Code of Practice covers such areas as booking of space, official orders, full, clear and concise information to the media, contact names and telephone numbers, good copywriting, the quality of copy submitted and the provision of camera-ready artwork. Authorities are also requested to ensure that the media are made fully aware of their policy on corporate identity and are supplied with bromides of the logo to be used.

The code also includes sections on the payment of accounts and procedures for dealing with complaints and invoice queries. Further areas covered are the dissemination of media information to the relevant departments of the authority and relations with media representatives and telephone sales staff.

The media, both local and national, are aware of the many problems facing local government and are quite prepared to work with local authorities in general, or, in the case of regional newspapers, with their local councils to assist wherever they can. The media have been strong supporters of NAPSA since its formation in 1984, offering assistance in the form of training facilities and an input into regular training programmes. Such help is encouraged and builds a closer working relationship between the authority and the press.

Many members of the media have long supported the growing advertising professionalism within the public sector and have been known to say that the in-house agencies are in terms of services provided, prompt payment of accounts, support of the media and general working relationships the equal of any commercial advertising agency.

■ EUROPEAN ADVERTISING

Another area in which local government advertising is becoming gradually involved is European advertising. A number of authorities already had experience of advertising in Europe, although with little luck to date. This is an area which will need research if it is to be successful. Recruitment advertising within the Republic of Ireland is well established, especially in the areas of health, nursing and social services.

The whole subject of European advertising is extemely wide and varied. The National Association of Public Service Advertisers has, in conjunction with the Local Government Management Board initiated a European Awareness programme looking at European media, the equivalence of qualifications, movement of labour, skills availability and shortages within the member states of the European Union. The programme also contains input from the European Commission on employees' rights and equal opportunities. An important element of the training scheme is a working knowledge of local and regional government within Europe.

NAPSA have already established close working links with commercial advertising agencies, media and local government in member states. Part of this initiative was two study trips examining public sector advertising, marketing and the advertising industry in the Republic of Ireland.

■ CONCLUSION

Advertising is a science, and it is becoming more necessary for local government to adopt a more professional approach to this entire area. It is no longer a job which any member of staff can do in addition to any other duties he or she may have.

Your advertisements are an essential part of the marketing process of your authority. Through them many will judge your image, especially local readership — do your advertisements, whether they be recruitment, general information or public notices, project the desired image of your authority.

It is important that layout, design, copywriting and corporate identity all display efficiency and effectiveness and build on the public concept of the council. Similarly low costs should not have any bearing on where advertising is placed. Making unnecessary copy or layout changes just for the sake of saving money is also a false economy.

Advertising is an essential part of the marketing process and is an area which is slowly, but very necessarily, improving. The 'hit and miss' principle of advertising used by local government is becoming far more professional.

There is help available to all local authorities wishing to improve their advertising performance. Any advertising agency will suggest improvements in all areas. They do not just exist to place your advertisements for you; the media, both local and national, or NAPSA, can offer assistance.

To judge how good your advertising is place yourself in the reader's position — is your advertisement conveying the right message?

Chapter 13

POLITICAL MARKETING IN BRITAIN

by Nicholas O'Shaughnessy and Dominic Wring

■ INTRODUCTION

Late twentieth-century British politics has witnessed the evolution of mass media-centred electoral races. Technological advance has helped national party headquarters control their regional support networks and influence the mainly London-based British media, particularly the broadcasting organisations. One of the consequences of this shift from the more personalised, community-centred style of campaigning has been the evolution of an arguably more presidential, image-conscious electoral race: a move many have bitterly resented (*see* Foley, 1992). Since 1945 political campaigns, like marketing strategies in general, have developed beyond the standardised radio broadcast and poster offensive to embrace the opportunities presented by both television and advertising. Consequently the major party organisations have instituted committees and procedures to deal in public relations exercises and liaise with print and television journalists. Juxtaposed to these developments, parties are increasingly seeking to communicate directly with their potential supporters and, as a consequence, embrace marketing technologies in a bid to do this effectively.

The concept of political marketing

In a now famous article, Kotler and Levy developed the idea that marketing should seek to embrace a sphere of interest beyond the profit-orientated business paradigm (Kotler and Levy, 1969). Some academics such as Lazer (1969) gave credence to the broadening thesis whilst others, particularly Luck (1969), maintained marketing should pursue its preoccupations within the field of commerce.

Kotler and Levy rebutted the purist and hitherto dominant concept of marketing as a function of commerce by developing the argument that the subject could desirably embrace a wider remit: ' . . . the crux of marketing lies in a general idea of exchange rather than the narrower idea of market transactions'.

In particular it was argued that marketing could conceivably be applied to numerous non-profit organisations seeking to manage their relations with the public. Examples of organisations given included libraries, hospitals, the police service as well as political candidates. Subsequent discussion of the marketing concept has sought to validate this broader area of interest (*see* Hunt, 1976 and O'Levy and Iredale, 1976).

In developing the broadening thesis, Kotler and Zaltman (1972) utilised the term 'social marketing' to describe that group of activities relating to non-profit organisations' management of exchange relations with their publics (*see also* Kotler and Roberto (1989) for a more recent review or this concept). Social marketing embraces a number of activities, including an area of political interest. Several texts have sought to explain and develop political marketing as a theoretical concept (Reid, 1988; Niffenegger, 1989; and O'Shaugnnessy, 1990).

Market orientation can be seen as the crucial measure by which a political marketing exercise can be distinguished from its antecedent, the propaganda campaign. Propaganda is an entity which exhibits little formal concept of information exchange, such as in the form of opinion polling, between politician and publics and principally seeks to coerce its audiences towards the acceptance of the communicators' belief   (Jowett and O'Donnell, 1986; and Qualter, 1985). Several authors have sought to develop marketing models of political competition in a bid to delineate and illuminate the aggregate parts that make up a campaign strategy. In applying marketing to politics, some have sought to analyse campaigns with reference to the traditional '4Ps' model, with emphasis placed on the management of the marketing mix consisting of price, product, promotion and place (Farrell and Wortmann, 1987). Butler and Collins (1994) adopt a different approach, placing emphasis on the specific process aspects of political campaigns and the way they differ from mainstream commercial marketing practices. Aside from these issues of strategy, Smith and Saunders (1990) highlight the importance of opinion research in the modernisation of political marketing in Britain. In seeking to highlight the similarity of modern political campaigns to service marketing, Martin Harrop

(1990) sums up the significance of the phenomenon by identifying and defining the impact that marketing has had on recent British electioneering practices:

It represents a qualitative change in the nature of 'state of the art' campaigns: a move from tactics to strategy, from promotion to marketing, and from issues to agendas.

■ THE EVOLUTION OF POLITICAL MARKETING CAMPAIGNS

Compared to other countries, American politics offer the most dramatic insight into the development of the political marketing phenomenon. The United States was the first to witness the emergence of full-time political consultants, not just in the sense of the professional lobbyist on Capitol Hill, but in the form of specialist marketing advisers able to help prospective candidates for elected office in all aspects of campaign techniques and strategies (Sabato, 1981). The whole marketing professionalisation of United States' politics has been well documented in several studies (for example *see*: Kelley Jr, 1956; Nimmo, 1970; R. Agranoff, 1981 and Luntz, 1988). Significantly a new body of literature is beginning to examine the evolution of political marketing in other countries (Bowler and Farrell, 1992). Recent contacts between the Washington and London-based parties' election specialists have not only heightened and renewed British interest in US electioneering techniques but reinforce the possibility that American state-of-the-art technology may play a greater role in Westminster elections of the future[1]. It is worth considering some of the key developments in political marketing, namely televised advertising, direct mail and opinion polling. Each of these has been pioneered and continues to be developed in the United States' constant cycle of elections in races for anything from a post on the local council to the ultimate prize of the presidency. Not surprisingly major innovations and most interest in techniques both tend to focus on the more important American electoral races. The fact that the United States plays host to so many campaigns, particularly compared with Britain, helps

---

[1]   During the American presidential elections of 1992 senior Conservative official Sir John Lacey visited Washington to advise the Republicans. Labour consultant Philip Gould helped with the Clinton campaign effort.

explain why it has been at the fore in the development of political marketing. The resulting novel campaign ideas and methods are now awaited with much interest by a growing audience of non-American consultants.

The television spot

The televised political advert, or 'spot' (so called because of its thirty- or sixty-second duration) gained major public notoriety during the successful presidential election of 1952 (Clark, 1986). There had been previous political adverts, masquerading as films, such as those launched against the Democratic candidate, Upton Sinclair, in the 1936 Californian elections for state governor (Davies, 1992). However, the use of spots by Republican candidate Ike Eisenhower's campaign team in 1952 was one of the first serious attempts to craft and use advertising in a presidential election. Significantly the race for the presidency is the only wholly national campaign in the cycle of American elections and the adverts can hope to capture a massive audience. Consequently campaign consultants Alfred Hollender and Rosser Reeves advised General Eisenhower that the successful incorporation and awareness of the potential of televised spots could help mobilise and engage the interest of the electorate (Clark, p. 415). The adverts which followed have become an important part of political campaign history. In them the future president was filmed answering questions asked by an aide in a studio. The same questions were then recited by carefully selected people who best represented ordinary members of the public. The resulting footage was edited together in order to present a false image of spontaneity on the part of the candidate. The subsequent adverts had the right impact making Eisenhower look calm and statesmanlike, particularly when contrasted with his presidential rival, the Democrat Adlai Stevenson. The episode helped to popularise both the use of spots and the idea of promoting candidates' images, not just their professed policies. Since these early days of political advertising the genre has developed into a well documented art form of its own (Jamieson, 1992a).

The Eisenhower campaign was a modest attempt by later standards. In particular it lacked the venom that has since characterised political advertising. The most famous negative advert in political history, often referred to as 'Daisy', was a simple conception which implied tragic consequences for humankind if Americans failed to support the Democratic presidential candidate,

Lyndon Johnson, in his re-election bid of 1964. The ad featured a girl picking a flower in a field, then suddenly the countdown and explosion of a large bomb: the spot ended 'Vote Johnson like your life depended on it'. The film provoked furore from the opposition Goldwater campaign and guaranteed massive publicity and repeats on primetime television for an ad which was only networked once or twice (Davies, p. 43). The advert's creator, Tony Schwartz, not only succeeded in helping re-elect a president but also helped promote the use of the spot as a tool for crafting negative images.

One of the most infamous recent examples of negative political advertising was run by a group supporting the Republican candidate, George Bush, in his campaign for president in 1988 (Jamieson, 1992b). The spot in question featured a serious offender, Willie Horton, who had been temporarily let out of prison on a scheme run by the State of Massachusetts. On release, the man proceeded to commit further serious crimes for which he was arrested. Michael Dukakis, the Democratic party candidate and Governor of Massachusetts, was blamed for this 'liberal' parole (or 'furlough' as it is commonly known) scheme and, by implication, indirectly labelled as responsible for Horton's crimes. The ad provoked fierce controversy not least because by using the image of Horton, a black American, the Republicans were accused of 'playing the race card'. Nevertheless, the impact of the adverts, and the ensuing television debates which aired the crime issues raised by the spot, were highly damaging to the morale of the Dukakis campaign. Even in the era of advanced political marketing strategies, the Democrats were unable to rebuke these attacks effectively. Dukakis' own worthy but intellectual response to the Horton spot was perceived as an ineffective counter-attack given the predominance of soundbite politics (Davies, p. 195). The subsequent 1992 Democratic campaign learnt these painful lessons with the result that their candidate, Bill Clinton, managed to rebut Bush's attacks and ultimately defeat him.

The Horton episode helps illustrate the way in which the work of the political marketers can become the centre of public scrutiny at the expense of the issues. Britain witnessed this development with the saga of 'Jennifer's Ear' which exploded in the middle of the 1992 campaign and dominated television and paper coverage of the election for three days (Butler and Kavanagh, 1992). In the main, Britain and other countries' party broadcasting is markedly different from the United States in that political parties and candidates cannot buy airtime on the radio or television. Each of the major (and some minor) British political parties receives a state subsidy in kind with the allocation of several free Party Election Broadcasts (PEBs) of five or ten minutes each (Harrison, 1992). It is noticeable that PEBs' length tends to militate against their making the same kind of impact as the spots, their more commercially styled American equivalents. However, attempts have been made to drop the traditional British politicians' face-to-camera appeals in exchange for more punchy and challenging conventional product advertising formats. A good example of this kind of PEB copy were the films written for the Conservatives by Jeremy Sinclair, a creative director of the London advertising agency Saatchi and Saatchi, in the run-up to the 1979 election.

Direct mail

Direct mail has been a major feature of American campaigns since the 1952 presidential race. It now serves as both a fund-raising mechanism and a tool of targeting segments of the electorate with candidate communications (Godwin, 1988). Its comparative neglect in British politics is surprising, especially given the pioneering usages made in the late 1920s by Joseph Ball, Director of Publicity for the Conservative Party (Pinto-Duschinsky, 1981).

Political direct marketing in the form of massive mailshots provides candidates, especially those rich enough, with an invaluable piece of campaign apparatus. One particular American campaign which helped build a base of support through the use of direct mail was that of the radical right motivated by Richard Viguerie (Crawford, 1980). Viguerie's and others' collective initiatives helped renovate and revitalise a whole sphere of political activity by targeting potential conservative supporters through this persuasive and intimate medium. The campaign work started in earnest in the mid-70s. By the beginning of the 1980s, Viguerie could claim some success given the ascendancy of the radical right in the guise of the Reagan presidency and the attendant coalition of conservative interest groups.

British parties began to use direct mail on a significant scale from the early 1980s onwards. Soon after its launch in 1981, the Social Democratic Party hired American consultants Craver, Matthews and Smith: their first test mailings yielded 45,000 donors; Craver himself promised that in Britain fewer mailings would contain language that was 'more under-stated, with somewhat less hyperbole' (cited in O'Shaughnessy, 1990). Since then the political parties, particularly the Conservatives, have targeted potential supporters with direct mail appeals (Swaddle, 1989). The run-up to the 1992 election campaign witnessed a large-scale use of the targeted mailshot — in particular Labour began the year by targeting thousands of voters living in the parliamentary constituencies the party had to win to form a government (*Mail on Sunday*, 1992). Furthermore there was evidence to suggest that parties, especially the Conservatives, were adopting another form of direct marketing — the telephone canvass — as a serious method of political communication, particularly when trying to reach an ageing population (Butler and Kavanagh, p. 239).

Opinion research

Market research has a long history of involvement in modern American politics. Despite pioneering work by George Gallup in the United States, political polling suffered several setbacks in its early development. Notably the 1936 *Readers' Digest* survey of voting intentions which failed to predict Democratic President Roosevelt's re-election proved a major embarrassment. This was primarily because the massive sample of ten million was based on lists of automobile and telephone owners, who were disproportionately from the wealthy classes and thus polled as Republican — the Democrats won by a landslide. The next major setback came with the 1948 disaster when polls failed to predict Harry S. Truman's presidential election victory (Teer and Spence, p. 14). Since then political candidates have sought to exploit the possibilities offered by market research. Pollsters are continuing to develop sophisticated techniques in a bid to investigate the mood of the voters, particularly those segments of the electorate who have the greatest propensity to change their voting intentions during a campaign. Most political candidates and parties still pursue research on the traditional demographic lines of views on issues dissected by class, sex, age, race and other factors. Recently psychographic research has begun to gain more prominence with the intent of trying to isolate the value structures of the population that underlie the political stances they adopt (Kleinman, 1987). Basic psychographic research discriminates segments not by any combination of demographic variables but by a type of character profile which defines groups such as the mainstream 'belongers' and elite opinion-forming 'achievers'. British parties, who have used some form of professional demographic research since the 1950s, have begun to develop an interest in psychographics. Whilst Bob Worcester used attitudinal profiling for Labour in the middle of the 1970s, the debate about the techniques gained notoriety in the 1987 election. During that campaign the Conservative organisation appeared divided into three competing camps. It later transpired that the Tory leader Margaret Thatcher had been unhappy with some of the demographic polling taken by the party advertising agents, Saatchi and Saatchi. The polls in question were largely critical of Thatcher and her style of leadership. Significantly the prime minister arranged for the more positive psychographic survey results from another supportive agency, Young and Rubicam, to be publicised within the party (Tyler, 1987). Since then a particular aspect of polling, the focus group, has mushroomed as the parties' bid to make an in-depth investigation of uncommitted voters' thoughts and values[2]. Significantly British parties have also taken to hiring some of the most eminent American consultants in the field of polling — in particular former Reagan adviser Richard Wirthlin had a brief contract with Conservative Central Office just prior to Mrs Thatcher's resignation (Butler and Kavanagh, p. 36).

■ THE IMPORTANCE OF POLITICAL MARKETING IN BRITISH POLITICS

The growth in the use of marketing methods in British campaigns does not follow an even path of development. Rather the pattern is one of uneven stages, with strategic innovations in campaign marketing often followed by either political ineptitude, inertia or a lack of resources at subsequent elections. Arguably the 1992 election marks a watershed in terms of the major and some of the minor parties' commitment to at least basic marketing strategies utilising polished advertising and some form of market research programme. In order to trace the antecedents of modern political marketing in Britain it is necessary to consider the major innovations in electioneering.

---

2   The BBC Vote Race and Channel 4 News programmes both used focus group techniques to monitor changes in public opinion during the 1992 election campaign.

The evolution of marketing practices in British campaigns

Prior to the second world war, there were limited press advertising campaigns, notably the Liberals' pioneering efforts in the 1929 election campaign (Harrop, 1990). Several of the parties were conscious of the need for careful attention to detail in publicising their cause, a trend that was developed in the postwar period, particularly during the 1959 election campaign. Since 1948 the Conservatives had retained the services of Colman, Prentice and Varley (Lord Windlesham, 1966, p. 35). The most famous and public expression of this creative campaigning came with the long campaign of 1957–9 which culminated in the successful re-election of Harold Macmillan. The campaign provoked opposition fury in the House of Commons with Labour MP Alice Bacon attacking the Conservatives' 'alien' style of electioneering (Rose, 1967). The most famous poster 'Life's Better Under the Conservatives, Don't Let Labour Ruin It' was a distillation of 'You've never had it so good', a phrase widely attributed to Macmillan in describing the prosperity of the era. Notably there were innovations in Labour party campaigns — some of which were labelled 'slick'. This trend was most graphically illustrated in the style of broadcasts adopted by the party under the direction of an advisory committee headed by Tony Benn (Labour Party, 1959). The developments in the Labour party were reinforced in the following election. The 1964 campaign also marked the end of thirteen years of Conservative rule and heralded an era of electoral success for their principal opponents. The Labour campaign utilised market research and advertising in its ultimately successful attempts to promote the party, and in particular the image of the leader, Harold Wilson. Wilson promoted the idea of 'a white heat of technology' as a campaign theme (Fielding, 1993). The theme was reminiscent of the idea of change that had underpinned the 'New Frontier' invoked by John F. Kennedy in his successful race for the US presidency in 1960.

Brendan Bruce identifies the Conservative campaign of 1970 as one of the most innovative in terms of the application of marketing techniques to electioneering (Bruce, 1992). The campaign made extensive use of advertising and was one of the first to use opinion polling to focus on segmenting the electorate and in particular potential target groups of voters with weak partisan attachments. The chief consultant to the successful Conservative leader Ted Heath, Barry Day, identified one of the key target segments to be the working-class wives of Labour-voting trades unionists (Day, 1982). As a consequence of the research findings, commercial style Party Election Broadcasts were designed to appeal to this particular (and large) group of women voters. Arguably this was one of the factors which helped the Conservatives to their unexpected victory. Ironically despite this enterprising use of polling on the part of a party, the 1970 election proved an embarassing one for the polling profession as a whole who, in the main, failed to predict the correct result (Butler and Pinto-Duschinsky, 1970). After the election there were complaints that Wilson had ran an aloof campaign, ignorant of the needs of the party and poor in comparison to the upbeat effort of 1964 (Alexander and Watkins, 1970). One of the few memorable pieces of the Labour campaign consisted of a piece of knocking copy in the form of an advert featuring 'Yesterday's Men'. The advert, a picture of six miniature models representing the Tory leadership, was widely criticised as too negative by commentators on both left and right of the political spectrum, highlighting a cultural hostility to negative image manufacture. After their defeat the controversy came back to haunt the party when the name of the advert was used as the title of a BBC documentary by David Dimbleby on the fate of the Labour leadership (Tracey, 1977).

Enter Thatcher

Margaret Thatcher and the Conservative party scored a notable success in winning the 1979 election by a comfortable margin. The victory was aided by one of the most memorable political campaigns in modern history. It also highlighted the important role an advertising agency, in this case Saatchi and Saatchi, could play in popularising and promoting political messages. The 1979 campaign initiated a decade of major success for both politician and advertising agency in their respective fields — factors which hardly militated against the idea that political advertising was an important and integral part of electioneering in Britain (Kleinman, 1987). In contrast the Labour campaign was comparatively downbeat and demoralised according to one of the senior consultants who worked for the party. Significantly sections of the central organisation resented the influence of professional consultants in terms of campaign strategy and implementation (Delaney, 1982). The prevaling image of 1979 was of memorable images and slogans, including the classic Tory poster 'Labour isn't working'. Another significant development was that the consultants, in this case working on the Conservative campaign, began to receive public credit for their efforts.

In the subsequent election of 1983 the major parties' campaigns were markedly different. The smooth-running Conservative effort, again orchestrated by the Saatchi brothers, is sometimes thought of as an example of the flawless campaign. In truth the political environment of the time strongly implied a Conservative re-election victory, particularly given an evenly divided opposition and an electoral system which favours 'winner takes all'. Nevertheless the Tory campaign was technically efficient with great consideration paid to providing television with flattering pictures of the prime minister on the campaign trail. The Conservative campaign was in stark contrast to the efforts of the opposition. The Labour campaign, though formally employing the services of Johnny Wright's advertising agency, was dogged by inertia, indecision and demoralisation (Mitchell, 1983). Similarly the Alliance campaign proved strategically problematic in terms of attempting to convey a uniform message whilst operating with a dual leadership and two separate party organisations (Butler and Kavanagh, 1984). The essence of the 1983 Conservative effort, masterminded by the then Tory Party Chairman Cecil Parkinson, was captured in a subsequent BBC documentary by Michael Cockerell. The film was simply called 'The Marketing of Margaret' and sought to analyse the way political marketing devices had been developed and had impacted on British politics (see Cockerell's analysis, 1983). It was public recognition that the phenomenon had arrived on the scene.

The 1987 campaign

The 1983 Conservative campaign has been described as a copybook campaign, the 1987 Labour campaign as tactically advanced but strategically flawed. 1987 bore witness to the increasingly commercial texture of electoral campaigns in Britain: both parties operated at this level and the influence of the United States was evident. But perhaps the election also highlighted just how superficial the marketing concept entertained by British parties actually was, limited to some impressive individual pieces of propaganda.

It is a commonplace view of the 1987 election that the Tories fought a mediocre campaign and, late in the day, redeemed it by a ferocious assault on their opponents. Labour's attack was inspired and eventually aroused their opponents from terminal complacence. The Tories' efforts faltered on 'wobbly Thursday' but, with little time to polling-day, a quick-fire press advertising campaign dredging up slogans from the 1950s helped them to a comfortable win in the election. In fact, the Tories had three different advertising agencies working for them — each more or less sponsored by a different minister (namely William Whitelaw, Norman Tebbit and Lord Young): senior party figures, in seeking to increase their influence over the campaign, saw the sponsorship of an agency and its position as power sources. Lord Beloff said 'Many loyal Conservatives may well wish a plague on both [i.e. two of the ad agencies involved in the fracas]', and the editor of the *Sunday Telegraph* asked: 'Surely the great Conservative Party is not about to tear itself asunder over an issue so quintessentially vulgar and trivial as to whether to employ one advertising agency or another?' (cited in O'Shaughnessy, 1990. For alternative perspectives on the in-fight that dogged the Tory Campaign see Tyler, 1987; Kleinman, 1987 and Sharkey 1989).

In this election the Labour Party famously created an American-style film bio under the aegis of Hugh Hudson, director of *Chariots of Fire*. It helped highlight the extent to which Labour had renewed and reinvigorated their campaign machinery in the aftermath of the 1983 defeat. The party did not formally employ an advertising agency on the campaign, preferring to rely on a group of marketing volunteers collectively known as the Shadow Communications' Agency who worked with Labour's Campaigns and Communications Director, Peter Mandelson (Hughes and Wintour, 1990). Whilst the campaign was judged a success by the media pundits, the election still resulted in a further term for the Conservatives. Leading Labour party politician Gerald Kaufman, in assessing the campaign, points to the central 'facade' of the campaign: over-reliance on innovative advertising and communications could not disguise what he (and by implication, the public) believed was a lack of coherence in the party's overall political offering[3]. This argument raises the issue of the extent to which political parties do, and can hope to, profitably utilise commercial derived marketing concepts in the pursuit of their goals. Furthermore, such a question raises the whole issue of organisational politics and the accountability of the marketers to the various formal committees as well as to the factions and groups within the parties. Most dramatically the Conservative campaign of 1987 helps illustrate the potential conflicts that can arise over marketing strategy.

---

3   Interviewed on LWT's documentary series, 'Kinnock', broadcast on ITV, August 1993.

The election of 1992

The 1992 General Election was in all its essentials a condensed consumer product marketing campaign, with the consequent invasion by marketing's techniques and ethos into realms hitherto the preserve of traditional modes of parliamentary persuasion. Both parties drew inspiration from the world of consumer product advertising. Party political broadcasts contained commercials which were advertisement-like in conception and length, with for example children (who are frequently used to sell 'family'-type products, which is what a party political programme ultimately is). The 'vox populi' method was another hoary technique borrowed from advertising. All of the parties, especially the Liberal Democrats, used it. The aim is to give a product populist credentials, to create a bandwagon effect, and in business it is highly related to the strategic goals of product launch/revival/product modification. Buyer uncertainty in these cases is high, therefore the aim is reassurance which can best be supplied by images of peer group support.

The 1992 campaign was widely derided in the media as being both boring and devoid of substantial political debate. Some of the criticisms focused on the impact of marketing, arguing that the main parties, having converged in terms of manifesto commitments, had become overwhelmingly image-conscious at the expense of the issues — a criticism regularly levelled at participants in American electoral contests (Gaber, 1992). It is noteworthy that all three major parties retained the services of advertising advisers and gave careful consideration to the planning and execution of their strategies[4]. The influence of professional expertise on the conduct of the campaign is further underlined by the fact that even the environmentalist Green party used an advertising agency, Leagas Shaffron, in the production of a visually arresting Party Election Broadcast complete with a repackaged leadership team. The only party putting up a large slate of candidates to make an issue of the drift to image-conscious politics, the splinter Liberal party, failed to make much impact in their campaign[5]. It is also worth underlining the fact that in political

---

[4]   The Conservatives used Saatchi and Saatchi, Labour the Shadow Communications Agency and the Liberal Democrats were serviced by TBWA. See *Marketing,* 9 April 1992.

[5]   The Liberal Party consists of a rump who refused to join their former colleagues in merging with SDP to form the Liberal Democrats. The Party's appeal for a return to issue-based politics was not widely heeded by any of its rivals.

advertising spending power does not necessarily correlate with vote share: the Natural Law Party spent nearly as much money as the Liberal Democrats but got a paltry amount of support at the polls (Butler and Kavanagh, 1992, pp. 242–3).

The major party campaigns made extensive use of market research, advertising and public relations' expertise in planning and executing their campaigns. The Conservative party campaign focused heavily on what was widely regarded as its key asset, the image of its relatively new leader, John Major. His presence in the campaign was a continuous reminder that the government was offering a revitalised product to the nation (Butler and Kavanagh, 1992, p.149). Major was also helped by the inevitable personalisation of the campaign, particularly given that his main opponent, Neil Kinnock, had a nine-year long record as Labour leader for his enemies to attack. The other major Conservative themes which tied in with research findings placed emphasis on their Labour opponents' image as what the Americans refer to as a 'tax and spend' party. The tax issue was remorselessly exploited by the Conservatives who linked it to the advertising slogan 'You Can't Trust Labour' and more specifically to the leadership of Kinnock. Kinnock was the subject of a classic attack campaign and formed the subject of one Tory Party Election Broadcast which gave a detailed account of the Labour leader and his political past, clearly questioning his judgement and long-held ideological commitment to democratic socialism (Butler and Kavanagh, 1992, p.176). The broadcast was reminiscent of an 1984 Reagan attack on his Democratic opponent, Walter Mondale (Hall Jamieson, 1992a). With the dissolution of the centre parties' Alliance, a new merged party, the Liberal Democrats, fought the campaign. The party, conscious that its agenda was often unclear to the public, sought to develop a positioning strategy built on a core offering. It heavily promoted itself as a more original and dynamic political alternative to the 'two old parties'. In doing this it succeeded in popularising the image of its leader, Paddy Ashdown, and differentiating its manifesto with a commitment to raising income tax to pay for an increased education budget.

The fairly aggressive Conservative campaign was tame by the standards of the print media (Harrop and Scammell, 1992). Whilst British broadcasters have strived to maintain a neutral position in respect of election coverage, the press (especially the high-circulation tabloids) have traditionally made vitriolic attacks on the Conservatives' opponents, particularly the Labour party (Curran and Seaton, 1985). The tabloids regularly provided the opportunity for the Conservative party to present a more considered approach whilst the press descended to what is often referred to as negative campaigning. Thus parties in Britain, especially the Conservatives, can often rely on nominally independent media sources to serve up vitriolic attacks without fear of an electoral backlash against slanging tactics. This highlights a significant difference with the United States where the national newspaper is not in such a strong position in the media market. Perhaps it is one reason why so many American presidential candidates (or their nominally 'independent' supporters' groups) take out paid television commercials to attack their opponents. Throughout the course of the British general election several tabloid newspapers ran numerous stories questioning the integrity and even the sanity of leading Labour politicians (McKie, 1992). The largest-selling (and Rupert Murdoch-owned) newspaper, the *Sun*, ran several frontpages resembling adverts designed to undermine Kinnock's credibility (Butler and Kavanagh, 1992, p.187).

At the end of the election there was a great deal of speculation that the tabloids' interventions had been critical.[6] Whatever the truth of the matter, it was certain that the anti-Labour press campaign enabled the Conservatives to concentrate their own in-house advertising on a narrower strategic focus. One advantage of this was that the Tories' straightforward approach did not fall victim to the kind of media introspection that befell the Labour campaign over one of its filmed attacks on the Government's health record. The Party Election Broadcast in question, 'Mandy' (or 'Jennifer's Ear' as it became known), sought to draw attention to the problem of hospital waiting lists. However the impact of the film was seriously impaired when interest turned to the alleged case on which the broadcast was based (Harrison, 1992, pp. 163–4). Consequently there was an ensuing debate over the ethics of the broadcast in which one of Labour's strongest issues, health, was largely made redundant. Stylistic and aggressive advertising techniques had presented Labour with a useful but potentially embarassing campaign tool.

---

6   Labour leader Neil Kinnock and the Conservative peer Lord Mac Alpine both agreed the role of the press had been vital in shaping the final result (See the *Independant*, 1992).

■ THE INFLUENCE AND ETHICS OF POLITICAL MARKETING.

How influential is political marketing?

In the United States political advertising gains more attention than television product advertising, with a 79 per cent as opposed to 20 per cent viewer recall (Sabato, 1981). Those most involved in an election are least influenced; but the apathetic are affected. Again, viewing habit is important. The attitudes of heavy viewers, those with lower income and education, were found to be more influenced than those of light viewers (Rothschild, 1978). Not surprisingly, the heavy viewer who does not feel involved is most susceptible of all. Soley and Reid claim that political advertising's impact on voters is as great as that of party and tenure (Soley and Read, 1981), and another analysis suggests that voter turn-out is proportional to the amount of advertising in that election (Humke, Schmitt and Grupp, 1975). An additional useful fact is that voters seem not to distinguish between television advertising and television news (Attwood and Sanders, 1975).

According to R. J. Johnson, however, political communications did influence the way some people voted in the British election of 1983; but surveys claimed that less than 2 per cent of all voters in 1987 believed they were influenced by press advertising or posters: the head of political research at opinion pollsters MORI pointed out that Party Political Broadcasts had a 50 per cent desertion rate (O'Shaughnessy, 1990).

But in Britain there are no squadrons of brief thirty-second commercials; the average prospective parliamentary candidate will spend around £5000, the contenders for the US Senate more like £5 million. These figures suggest the influence of political marketing in a climate without restraint, but they do not measure its impact. Perhaps this is anyway an impossible demand. How can the influence of marketing or marketing-related elements be disentangled from other elements of political communication such as journalistic mediation? And even if researchers try to do these things under laboratory conditions, or using survey methods, how really representative are their results? They might for example have induced artificially high levels of attention to the political message in their subjects (their peers might not have begun to concentrate on the campaign until the final weeks).

Two points, however, should be noted. The effects of political marketing may indeed be seldom more than marginal, but then elections are sometimes about margins. A close-run election could be decisively influenced by marketing-related components. Secondly, political advertising does by-pass the interrogation of the media and presents an idealised image of personalities and programme.

Criticisms of political marketing

Political marketing has had of course many critics in Britain, and such disdain arises from the rejection by social elites of all marketing, which they equate with sly manipulation: thus Carlyle's remonstrance about the advertising gimmicks of a London hatter and his belief that 'build a better mousetrap and the world will beat a path to your door'.

Many in Britain thought the rise of marketing would cleanse British politics of any intellectual pretensions it had hitherto possessed. Thus in 1986 the *New Statesman* asked:

> *How far does* image *making determine* policy *making? How far has our political process become captive to the demands of television, to the shaping of audience?*   (*New Statesman*, 22 August 1986)

Sir Alfred Sherman (1987), in an insightful piece, echoed the same idea: speaking of Kinnock, he said, 'If only he could create new policies in the image of his image — it was seriously argued — victory might yet have been within his grasp. Because political parties interact, the devaluation of ideas in one must affect their status in all' (Sherman, 1987). He believed that marketing was almost irrelevant to the rise and continuing popularity of Thatcherism:

> *Ideas were crucial: the skills of the hairdresser, the TV commercials producer or the night-club review compere were marginal.*

This point is valid. Communications can become a substitute for policy and disguise the vacuity of ideas: the press are beguiled by this, so that the focus of campaigns becomes not who has the best policies but who has the best campaign style.

Sherman's theme has been echoed by others. For Greg Philo 'Labour thus began to vacate the crucial territory of how the population understood their own history. They did it in favour of a philosophy appropriate only to influencing short term consumer purchases', falling for a 'shallow science of imagistics' (Philo, 1993). Herein, however, lies important confusion. Firstly, it is by no means clear that 'exposing' the Tory economic record would have taken Labour any further. That is anyway what Labour did to some extent: the question really lies in how different interpretations were affixed to the related phenomena of mass unemployment and manufacturing attrition. The Tories simply managed to present this as necessary, even symptomatic of growth into a service-based economy. Secondly, there is confusion as to the definition of marketing. It is more than the 'shallow science of imagistics': marketing is product as well as communication.

These and other critics have usually managed to miss the key points that ought to be raised in such a debate. Firstly, there is confusion as to the very definition of marketing itself, which is invariably equated with overtly manipulative advertising. Next, public critics, such as Lord Beloff in the 1987 campaign, doubt that it has any practical value at all.

Much of this debate is missing the point. Firstly, it is difficult to argue this in terms of theoretical abstractions. The point is not 'marketing' but surely 'what particular kind of marketing' — the laudatory biography, invented story, vox populi, talking head, negative attack: each sets in motion a different kind of ethical debate. Then, it is necessary to distinguish and not confuse the pragmatic debate, where marketing is strong, from the ethical debate, where it is on much less firm territory.

First, the ethics. Political marketing annexes the methods of commercial advocacy and is therefore dishonest inasmuch as selectivity of facts is misleading: though this is the advocacy of the barrister. But it does, as we have described, have divisive potential due to its stress on targeted media and messages rather than those which are shared by the community. It takes the focus away from debate. Political messages do not emerge from a process of exchange: they blare out at us without the maturing confluence of argument.

Political marketing has advanced internationally and is now the guiding paradigm in elections throughout the world. For instance in the 1987 Korean elections observers noticed the attention given to televised candidate spots and presentation: 'The emphasis on style has done little to elevate the level of serious debate on issues among voters' (Hewitt, Bradley and Faraso, 1987). Thus the question of how the rise of political marketing affects the nature of our democratic tradition is not a parochial one, not for the British alone. Does it lead to a blander and more evasive kind of politics that magnifies rather than transcends democracy's habituation to the short-term panacea and quackery?

Political marketing has tended to follow the conventions of consumer marketing rather than develop a richly independent genre of its own. This linkage has become increasingly apparent but may give rise to a hidden and unintended message — that politics is just a product like any other and voters should approach it as they would any consumer choice. Thus Labour's 'Jennifer's Ear' advertisement in 1992 was a synthesis of many postures of consumer advertising — the contrasting experience of two similar families, the worried mother and suffering daughter, the cloying sentimentality and the unfolding of a story without dialogue or commentary but with music and sound. The 1993 election in Canada perhaps illustrates some of the consequences of this new political consumerism. There are several legitimate interpretations of the Canadian result, including the tensions of regionalism, but it would also appear to imply nothing less than the translation of the consumerist ethos to politics. Once political loyalties were inherited. Now voters, at least Canadian ones, would appear to be practising the consumerism that the politicians have preached.

The international advance of these marketing approaches creates a new kind of world order in democracies and emerging democracies, where debate plays a secondary role to marketing and image management. Yet most political theorists — Weil for instance — have viewed debate as being the core of the democratic process, not mediability and image management.

So the consequences will be:

a) Short-termism in policy, already the besetting sin of democracy.
b) A serious distraction of the attention of legislators (and a different kind of legislator?).
c) A cycle of promise and disappointment which will greatly increase the cynicism of voters.
d) Value in politics will be defined subjectively from the market's viewpoint. This conflicts with the Burkean idea of proactivity of political leadership, as politicians cease to lead in a slavish adherence to headline and opinion poll. Yet John Stuart Mill stressed that under democracy people do not govern but choose their governors.
e) In America at least, the production of 'professional campaigners and amateur presidents'.

Another fear is that political marketing could become a vehicle for demagoguery. Ross Perot — a plausible salesman of simplistic dogmas — could via purchased advertising simply buy a credible presidential candidacy in the 1992 race; in Italy a political ingénue, Silvio Berlusconi, flooded his own television stations with persuasive advertising during his successful campaign for national office in 1994; and supporters of George Bush committed a serious breach of democratic convention with the 1988 Willie Horton commercial and its racist subtext. But America is a mature democracy: how much more vulnerable to such methods are the new ones? In the 1993 elections for the Russian parliament, the bigotry of extreme nationalist leader Vladimir Zhirinovsky, raw and unlovely in print, became witty, animated and seductive on television: the style dazzled, and transcended the malodorous substance.

So much for the ethical problems political marketing brings to the surface. What about the practical usefulness? Against the obvious utility of the marketing approach to politics, we should also set certain critical weaknesses. Some of these are the inherent limitations of marketing as a philosophy — its stress for example on satisfying objective consumer wants as defined by market research, namely opinion polling, when what is needed is imaginative interpretation of their unrecognised, inarticulate desires. Another danger is that products can be oversold and thus alienate the consumer.

A particular problem with the genre — at least in the British context — was laid bare by the 1992 General Election. For this raised a very fundamental question: are people actively resistant to political marketing, or is it that traditional marketing ideas need to be urgently reshaped to meet the sensitivities of political situations? Labour's campaign was technically much superior and there are certainly other examples of heavily merchandised campaigns that failed spectacularly. In a recent presidential campaign in Peru, the slick advertising of the losing candidate reinforced perceptions that he was rich and out of touch. British voters, like consumers in general, do not like to admit to being influenced by razzmatazz. Consequently when Labour leaders succeeded in a polished presentation of themselves, with the dull footage edited out, it was perhaps too good to be true and maybe raised fears of a hidden agenda. A more subtle interpretation would have succeeded in disguising the propagandist intent, as all good propaganda does. Most electors resent the sense that they are being overtly manipulated and when they saw the exercise, not the content, being praised, their suspicions rose. This point links in with the most controversial news event of the 1992 general election, namely the huge row over the Labour broadcast which exploded in the middle of the campaign. The ensuing rancorous and self-indulgent debate could not have helped to dampen public suspicion as to the credibility of the competing politicians. Arguably, the image of Labour suffered most given that it was the challenger. Offering an image of competence to govern as opposed to actual recent experience in office, Labour suffered when this, in the form of the credibility of a piece of counter-productive campaign communication, became the focus of public concern as opposed to the record of the Conservative government.

■ CONCLUSIONS

The past and present

In 1945 Clement Attlee was praised for an apparently modest campaign which contrasted sharply with that of his principal opponent, Winston Churchill. In that election the Labour leader and future Prime Minister was accompanied by a single journalist from the sympathetic *Herald* newspaper, and his wife who acted as his chauffeuse for the duration of the campaign. Nearly fifty years later, in 1992, John Major was widely applauded for his preparedness to emulate Attlee and the old-fashioned style of campaigning on the stump. Indeed Major's soap-box appearances in places such as Luton attracted widespread media interest as well as vociferous protests from hecklers and egg throwers. On the face of it, the two Prime Ministers' campaigns were similar. The key difference lies in spontaneity; whilst the Attlee campaign developed from day to day, the Major appearances can be seen as part of an attempt to invigorate the campaign through offering television a good story. The Conservative Prime Minister was not so much talking to the crowd in the street as developing an image of himself for the mass of the viewing public at home. In modern elections there is obvious room for unexpected developments but the advent of marketing and public relations specialists limits the opportunity for unforeseen hitches.

The future

The rise and growth of political marketing professionals is an indication that the world of politics believes marketing can offer aspiring candidates and parties an easier route to office. Perhaps the real story of British political marketing has still to be realised in terms of what might happen if funds were more readily available to pay for electoral campaigns (and not solely for the national parliament).

■ REFERENCES

AGRANOFF, R. (ed.) (1976) *The New Style in Election Campaigns*, Boston, Holbrook Press

ALEXANDER, A. and WATKINS, A. (1970) *The Making of the Prime Minister*, London, Macdonald Unit 77

ATTWOOD, L. E. and SANDERS, K. R. (1975) 'Perception of Information Sources and Likelihood of Split Ticket Voting,' *Journalism Quartlerly*, Autumn.

BOWLER, S. and FARRELL, D. (eds) (1992) *Electoral Strategies and Political Marketing*, Basingstoke, Macmillan.

BRUCE, B. (1992) *Images of Power*, London, Kogan Page

BUTLER, D. and KAVANAGH, D. (1984) *The British General Election of 1983*, London, Macmillan

BUTLER, D. and KAVANAGH, D. (1992) *The British General Election of 1992*, London, Macmillan

BUTLER, D. and PINTO-DUSCHINSKY, M. (1970) *The British General Election of 1970*, London, Macmillan

BUTLER, P. and COLLINS, N. (1994) 'Political Marketing Structure and Process', *European Journal of Marketing*, 28:1.

CLARK, E. (1986) *The Want Makers*, Sevenoaks, Coronet

COCKERELL, M. (1983) 'The Marketing of Margaret', *The Listener*, 16 June.

CRAWFORD, A. (1980) *Thunder on the Right*, New York, Pantheon Books.

CURRAN, J. and SEATON, J. (1985) *Power without Responsibility*, London, Methuen.

DAVIES, P. J. (1992) *Elections USA*, Manchester, Manchester University Press

DAY, B. (1992) 'The Politics of Communication and the Communication of Politics' in Worcester, R. and Harrop M. (eds),

DELANEY, T. (1982) 'Labour's Advertising Campaign' in Worcester, R. and Harrop, M.

FARRELL, D. and WORTMANN, M. (1987) 'Party Strategies in the electoral market: Political marketing in West Germany, Britain and Ireland', *European Journal of Political Research*, vol 15, pp. 297–318.

FIELDING, S. (1993) 'The Evolution of Wilsonism' in Coopey, R. *et al* (eds) *The Wilson Governments 1964–70* London, Pinter.

FOLEY, M. (1992) *The Rise of the British Presidency*, Manchester, Manchester University Press

GABER, I. (1992) What was the message? *Tribune*, 8 May

GODWIN, R. K. (1988) *One Billion Dollars of Influence: the Direct Marketing of Politics*, New Jersey, Chatham House

HALL JAMIESON, K. (1992a) *Packaging the Presidency: A History and Criticisim of Presidential Campaign Advertising*, New York, Oxford University Press

HALL JAMIESON, K. (1992b) *Dirty Politics*, New York, *Oxford University Press*

HARROP, M. (1990) 'Political Marketing', *Parliamentary Affairs*, vol, 43, no 3.

HARROP, M. and SCAMMELL, M. (1992) *'A Tabloid War'* in Butler, D. and Kavanagh, D. (eds).

HEWITT, B., BRADLEY, M. and FARASO, K. (1987) 'Enter the Image Makers', *Newsweek*, 14 Dec.

HUGHES, C. and WINTOUR, P. (1990) *Labour Rebuilt*, London, Fourth Estate

HUMKE, R. G., SCHMITT, R. L. and GRUPP, S. J. (1975) 'Candidates Issues and Party in Newspaper Political Advertisements', *Journalism Quarterley*, Autumn

HUNT, S. D. (1976) 'The Nature and Scope of Marketing' *Journal of Marketing*, vol 40, no 1.

Independent (1992) 14 April

JOWETT, G. and O'DONNELL. V. (1986) *Propaganda and Persuasion*, Newbury Park, Sage

KELLEY JNR, S. (1956) *Professional Public Relations and Political Power*, Baltimore, Johns Hopkins Press.

KLEINMAN, P. (1987) 'Did Psychographics win the Election?', *Admap*, Sept.

KOTLER, P. and LEVY, S (1969) 'Broadening the concept of marketing', *Journal of Marketing*, vol 33, no 1.

KOTLER, P. and ZALTMAN, G. (1972) 'Social Marketing: An approach to planned social change', *Journal of Marketing*, vol 35, no 3.

KOTLER, P. and ROBERTO, E. (1989) *Social Marketing: Strategies for changing public behaviour*, New York, Free Press

Labour Party (1959) General Election Report to the National Executive Committe, 22 Oct.

LAZER, W. (1969) 'Marketing's changing social responsibilities' *Journal of Marketing*, vol 33, no 1.

LUCK, D. (1969) 'Broadening the concept of marketing: Too far' Journal of Marketing, vol 33, no 3

LUNTZ, F. (1988) *Candidates, Consultants and Campaigns,* Oxford, Basil Blackwell.

MCKIE, D. (1992) '"Fact is Free Comment is Sacred" or "Was it the Sun wot won it?"' paper presented at the Political Studies Association Conference, September

Mail On Sunday (1992) 5 Jan

MITCHELL, A. (1983) *Four Years in the Death of the Labour Party,* London, Methuen.

New Statesman (1986) 'The War of the Agencies', 22 August

NIFFENEGGER, P. (1989) 'Strategies for Success from the Political Marketers', *Journal of Consumer Marketing,* vol 6, no 1.

NIMMO, D. (1970) *The Political Persuaders,* Englewood Cliffs, Prentie-Hall.

O'SHAUGHNESSY, N. (1990) *The Phenomenon of Political Marketing,* Basingstoke, Macmillan.

PINTO-DUSCHINSKY, M. (1981) *British Political Finance 1830–1980* Washington DC, American Enterprise Institute.

PHILO, G. (1993) 'Political Advertising Popular Beliefs and the 1992 General Election', *Media, Culture and Society,* 15

QUALTER, T. (1985) *Opinion Control in the Democracies,* New York, St Martin's Press.

REID, D. (1988) 'Marketing the Political Product', *European Journal of Marketing,* Vol 22 no 9.

ROSE, R. (1967) *Influencing Voters,* London, Faber & Faber.

ROTHSCHILD, M. (1978) 'Political Advertising: A Neglected Policy Issue in Marketing', *Journal of Marketing Research* 15: 1.

SABATO, L. (1981) *The Rise of Political Consultants,* New York, Basic Books.

SHARKEY, J. (1989) 'Saatchies and the 1987 election'; in Crewe, I. and Harrop, M. (eds) *Political Communication in the 1987 Election,* Cambridge, Cambridge University Press.

SHERMAN, Sir Alfred (1987) 'The Ad-man Cometh', *The Guardian,* June.

SMITH, G. and SAUNDERS, J. (1990) 'The Application of Marketing to British Polities', *Journal of Marketing Management,* vol 5, no 3.

SOLEY, L. S. and READ, L. N. (1981) 'Promotional Expenditure in US Congressional Elections', *Journal of Public Policy and Marketing,* 1.

SWADDLE, K. (1988) 'Hi-Tech Elections: Technology and the Development of Electioneering since 1945', *Contemporary Record,* Spring 1985.

TEER, F. and SPENCE, J. (1972) *Political Opinion Polls*, London, Hutchinson.

TRACEY, M. (1977) 'Yesterday's Men — a case study in political communication' in Curran, J. *et al.* (eds) *Mass Communication and Society*, London, Edward Arnold

TYLER, R. (1987) *Campaign: The Selling of the Prime Minister*, London, Grafton.

WINDLESHAM, LORD (1966) *Communication and Political Power*, London, Jonathan Cape.

WORCESTER, R. and HARROP, M (eds) (1982) *Political Communication: the General Election of 1979*, London, George Allen & Unwin.

Chapter 14

CASE STUDY: HEALTHWISE AND SOCIAL MARKETING

by James Kay

■ BACKGROUND

Social marketing is the application of marketing principles and techniques to social action objectives. The use of radio advertising in 'quit smoking' campaigns and the production and distribution of local authority newspapers are both examples of social marketing strategies.

The interest by public sector agencies in social marketing predates the introduction of internal markets to health and local authority sectors. As the drive to internal markets has developed so the interest in social marketing has grown. Within Merseyside and Cheshire one agency has specialised in the application of social marketing techniques and strategies in the health field.

Healthwise is a regional health information service (RHIS) with offices in the centre of Liverpool. It provides health information to the population of the Mersey Regional Health Authority (MRHA). The MRHA covers the metropolitan counties of Merseyside and the county of Cheshire. With 2.4 million inhabitants it is the second smallest of the fourteen health regions after East Anglia. Plans are now (1994) underway to merge the MRHA and the North West RHA as part of the latest batch of NHS reforms.

The Mersey region is widely perceived as the test bed and launch pad for many of the recent health service reforms. Its chairman, Sir Donald Wilson, is a powerful proponent of the 'internal market', and its last two regional general managers are currently Chief Executives of the NHS in England and Wales and in Scotland respectively.

Healthwise is an independent provider RHIS and is contracted to the MRHA to provide ten freefone helplines running seven days a week giving the public and professionals a wide range of health information. It was originally set up as an AIDS prevention service but quickly expanded its role to include many issues linked to AIDS such as sexual health, drug and alcohol abuse. Callers to the freefones were offered information about AIDS and linked issues together with details of the whole range of helping services offered by the NHS, voluntary agencies and other specialist services.

■ THE PATIENTS' CHARTER

When the Patients' Charter was launched in April 1992, Healthwise was well placed to expand its role and become a general health information provider. Under the terms of the Patients' Charter the patient is now entitled to a wide range of information about health and health care. Information must be available on issues such as hospital waiting times and the standards of healthcare offered by hospitals, health centres and other providers. Information should also be available on the nature of illnesses and treatments, the rights of healthcare consumers, the complaints systems of healthcare providers and the services offered by voluntary and self-help groups.

To help provide this information to patients a network of RHISs has now been established, one for each health region. Healthwise is one of the most successful of these taking more calls than any other three regions put together. The current call rate is over 60,000 calls a year.

Its services were expanded on 1 April 1993 to include the role of providing information about community care. Information on the rights, standards and complaints systems of social services departments, residential homes and other providers of care in the community have now been added to the Healthwise databases.

In April 1994 the service was expanded again to include data on fitness, exercise and sporting organisations. The aim is to build Healthwise into the most authoritative source possible of the widest range of health information to the general public.

■ EMPOWERMENT AS A CORE VALUE

The philosophy of the new market-driven NHS is one in which patients' expectations are an important driving force for change. Patients are being encouraged to find out about their rights and to protest vigorously if they do not get them. The adoption of the

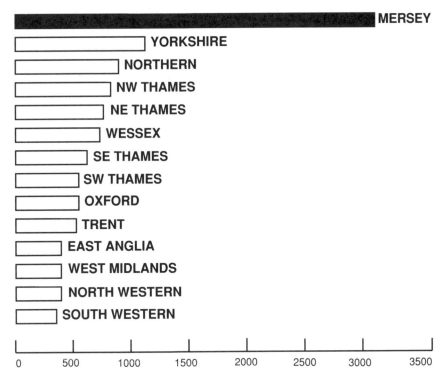

Graph 14.1   RHISs calls per million — 26.1.93–30.4.93

Patients' Charter is a public commitment to improving the quality and efficiency of care in the NHS. Its clear aim was to empower patients — to put the NHS customer at the centre of operations.

If patients are to become more articulate and powerful within the system — identifying inadequacies and complaining about them until something is done — then they will need help.

The health system has been based in the past on a system of relying on the doctor to know best. Doctors have been trained to exude expertise and self-confidence. The professional disciplines and rituals of medicine are designed to bolster the public and self-perception of doctors as an elite. Challenging the views and opinions of doctors can seem almost sacrilegious.

To make matters worse being ill undermines self-confidence and is often accompanied by debilitating and distressing symptoms such as nausea and vomiting. Surrounded by white coats — lying on your back in an alien environment and feeling awful — these are the worst possible conditions for being assertive about your needs.

The RHISs have a critical role to play in the process of patient empowerment. They are there to help the patients become more aware about their rights — what standards of healthcare have they a right to expect? And what can they do if the system does not live up to its promises? The freefone telephone service is important. Callers can contact the service at a time convenient to them and in private. All calls are treated confidentially and names are never asked for unless the caller wants leaflets or other information to be posted out to him or her.

An anonymous telephone service is much easier to use than speaking up, face to face. Many patients feel that they will be thought foolish or troublesome for asking awkward or silly questions. Much of the work of an RHIS consists of affirming to people that their concerns are important and valid — that they do indeed have a right to know. Often the caller just needs some encouragement to go back to the doctor and ask more questions. Sometimes patients are helped to prepare for this by writing questions down on a piece of paper. On some occasions the doctors have behaved badly and a complaint or even the option of changing doctors might be explored.

■ WHO KNOWS ABOUT THE RHISs?

If the RHISs are to work — then first of all the patients, the users of the services, must know that they exist. As this is an entirely new service they will also need to have a clear idea of what the service does — how it works — what it can do for them. This is a service for the whole community. It has the task of telling new residents in town where they can get emergency dental care at teatime on a Saturday night. It has the task of telling a distraught father where he can get advice from an expert on how to cope with his son's heroin addiction. It has the task of advising on where the shortest waiting time is for hip replacement.

The RHIS wants to work with young and old, with men and women, with health service users from all social classes and all ethnic groups. It wants to tell the community about a whole range of new services and new ways of seeing existing services. It wants to challenge deep-seated views and prejudices about how things are done and how they should be done in the sometimes emotive and political world of healthcare. It tries to empower patients to see that doctor does not always know best — and that holding such a view is not disloyal in any way but a necessary part of taking a more active and effective role in one's own healthcare and its improvement. These are formidable tasks.

In the rest of this article some of the marketing methods which Healthwise has used to raise its profile amongst its target audiences will be described.

■ THE LAUNCH CAMPAIGN AND USING PAID ADVERTISING

During the launch of the service in 1990 we were lucky to have the support of the Department of Health's publicity section who were running a series of regional activities designed to raise awareness of drug misuse in the community. The Mersey region was chosen as one of the three pilot regions and a central fund made available for paid advertising. The aims were to give out positive messages about helping services available for those suffering the consequences of drug misuse and also to promote the Healthwise service.

A central slogan was devised, 'Taking Drugs Seriously', and bus shelters, bus exteriors and hoardings covered with specially designed posters. In addition a three-month long radio advertising campaign was put together using young voices talking in a DJ chatter style about the new Healthwise service. The aim was to appeal to a young audience through the radio adverts and to their parents through the poster campaign.

The campaign was devised using a London-based advertising agency and was carefully researched using pre- and post-interviews with young people. The interviews were conducted on the streets in Liverpool and Birkenhead. The quantitative work was backed up by small focus groups of teenage 'rave' attenders recruited from outside music and clothes shops. These small discussion groups focused on the 'topic guide', a prepared set of questions which prompted a more in-depth discussion of the campaign and how it was perceived by the youngsters.

Finally there were also focus groups with drug injectors who were picked up by a snowballing technique beginning with existing clients of local drug services. The impact of the campaign was also measured by the rates of calls to the service from different age groups and by recording the topics raised by callers.

The findings were interesting and quite complex. The first thing we learned about was costs. Although all of the costs were met out of a central government budget we monitored them closely to learn about which methods might be followed up in further regional campaigns. Paid advertising is extremely expensive. The whole campaign came in at not far off £100,000. Of this about a third went on radio advertising, a third on the poster campaigns and the balance on bus side adverts, market research, leaflets and other publicity materials and on agency fees.

Overall the campaign worked to raise awareness of the service to some degree in the key age groups. Analysis of the calls taken by Healthwise by age group showed that in the period of this campaign the overwhelming majority of our callers were teenagers enquiring about drug issues. They also showed a massive increase in the numbers of calls overall, and this was clearly prompted by the campaign.

However, when we interviewed random samples of the youth population on the streets we got a different picture. Although there was general awareness of the issues raised and the fact that there had been a campaign about drugs, most young people remained unaware of the Healthwise service.

The focus group work gave some further hints about the impact of the campaign. Young drug experimenters in the 'rave' dance drug scene thought the radio campaign was important but not targeted at them. They didn't have drug problems — they enjoyed their drug use — had jobs — weren't 'junkies'.

The drug injectors also thought the campaign was important — but not targeted at them. It was clearly designed for the young drug experimenters — those who used dance drugs on the party scene.

So both groups thought the campaign was for the other group. It seems we had fallen between two stools. Those we attracted to the service were predominantly 'not yet users' — young people who were interested about drugs and wanted to know more but who were probably not yet using the drugs.

We learned from the campaign the following lessons:

1. Local commercial radio is an effective tool for communicating with young people — but expensive to use for paid advertising. We learned later to use other 'social action broadcasting' methods which were much cheaper.
2. Targeting of campaigns is difficult — it is very easy to miss the target group and even a small miss is 'as good as a mile'. In our later activity we worked much harder to involve the young people themselves in the planning and copywriting activity.

3. The poster campaign was not effective — we could not find any evidence of its impact. We have not used this style of publicity since although a later campaign used small bus interior adverts very effectively (*see page 283*).

4 The market research element although not cheap was critical. Without the independent research we should have misread the campaign results. Our call rates gave us the impression of total success — the research showed a much more complex picture.

5. Advertising agencies have skill and expertise in their domain but they need to be given very clear briefing. On the complex issue of drug misuse they needed to be persuaded not to use some approaches to communications which experience of drug education has shown to be ineffective. Even when funds are available an external agency may not be worthwhile. The creative input from them is real but only a very small proportion of their work.

Creative media work

Once the initial launch period was over we settled down to raising steadily the profile of the service. An important strategy was that of constant pro-active media work. We learned to distinguish between our task and that of the often reactive work of a local authority or health authority press office. Most of the time the press officer is reacting to potentially critical stories and trying to dampen down hostile coverage. Their work is very fast, responding in minutes or hours rather than over days or weeks.

Our work is more pro-active, developing longer news pieces and features and aiming to raise awareness often of complex issues. Our objectives include those of stimulating a specific response — pick up the phone, ask for a leaflet or information kit, make an appointment, have a check-up, etc.

Using photographs effectively

We have learned to use photographs and photo opportunities with local celebrities as a way of raising the profile of the service. Together with local specialist agencies we have worked with football teams, snooker and cycling champions and TV personalities.

When using photographs we have found that commissioning our own photographs from an existing press photographer increases the cost efficiency of our work enormously. We have achieved front page coverage with the help of a good photograph. Without the photograph the story would have disappeared onto page five or six of the paper. The picture catches the eye and pulls the story onto page one of a local paper. The impact is much greater. The extra £70 to £100 it costs to call out a photographer is repaid many times over by the increased impact from the story.

There are several benefits from using a press photographer who is already well known to picture editors from the local media. Firstly he or she will be geared up to working quickly. Often pictures need to be turned round in a few hours. We have found that the best photographers for this quick work can be those who also do sports work. They will have taken photographs at a football match that a few hours later are being printed in the sports editions of local papers.

They will also be able to advise you on what sort of shot will most appeal to the picture editors of your local papers. They may even be able to take the photographs in and drop them right onto the desks of the picture editor. Although you may be able to find a cheaper local photographer they will not be able to give you this quality of service.

Writing cost-effective news releases

We learned to use the media more creatively in support of our service. At first we just wrote news releases about events and activities we were involved in and fired them out to all the local and regional media. Those interested in the story would contact us and maybe run a story.

After a while we realised that much of the potential coverage was not being achieved because our work lacked focus. We began to target specific papers and/or journalists. We began to tailor stories to local angles. The story would be written by us and then adapted to the local area. In each case there was a local picture to go with the story — 'Volunteers from the Southport and Formby area seen here . . .' etc. In every case the tag line for us is the phone number and opening hours of our service.

We learned to follow up stories with a phone call — 'Have you received the news release — are you planning a piece on it?' We discovered that newspaper offices are remarkably inefficient places where stories are often lost, misplaced or filed under the wrong heading. In one instance eight out of twelve newspapers lost a fax we had sent out highlighting a new service. Six of them ran the story after we had refaxed it. Even where the paper has received the story and is not planning a story you can gain valuable information about why they are not covering your work: maybe your releases are written in the wrong style, or perhaps there is a different journalist you could contact. Journalists can be very secretive and reluctant to share information with each other. If you want to have maximum impact, following up news releases with a phone call is essential.

Almost anything is news

We learned that most stories carried in newspapers are worked up from a very flimsy base. It is fairly easy to generate 'Good news' stories. A visit to your organisation by a dignitary or specialist can be a news vehicle: 'Dr Smith seen here with Anytown's Director of Public Health . . . whilst visiting the pioneering Downtown service'. Attendance at a training course or visiting another service or agency is 'a fact-finding mission . . . by staff from Anytown's new Downtown service'.

Common themes in this type of work are those of innovation ('new', 'pioneering', etc.) and local relevance. If the stories can be backed up with photographs they are even more likely to be covered.

Targeting and impact

We learned that some issues are much more likely to generate responses from the sections of the population they most affect. Thus a feature on menopause targeting Southport resulted in a high level of responses from middle aged women wanting to know more about hormone replacement therapy (HRT) (*see Graph 14.2 overleaf*). Requests to GPs for HRT went up as a response.

Advertising — narrow vs broadcasting

An important lesson learned was that of the difference between broadcasting and narrowcasting. Most of the highly visible advertising which is done on television, radio and on advertising hoardings is broadcasting. It is a sort of shotgun approach which blasts away at whole populations. Everyone who rides past a hoarding or sees a TV advert will be exposed to it even if only for a

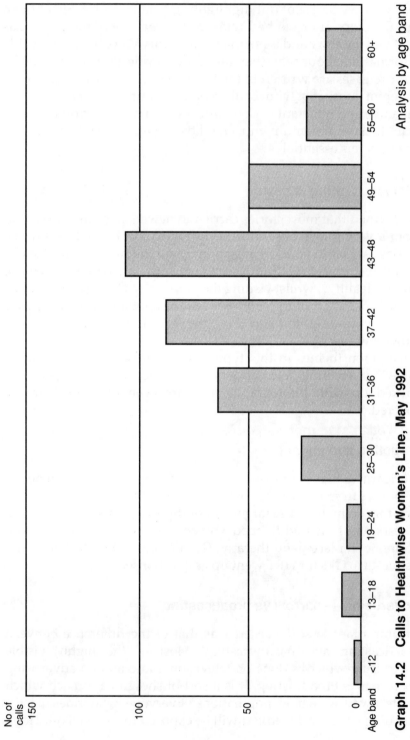

Graph 14.2   Calls to Healthwise Women's Line, May 1992

second or two. The emphasis in the design of such broadcasting is usually on high-impact, short messages with a simple call to action or sometimes just aiming to raise awareness of a product or service. Recognisable and transferrable icons and images have to be used which are then typically repeated at the point of sale. It is assumed that only a very small proportion of those at whom the message is aimed will be moved to action by it although a large number may become aware of it.

Broadcasting is expensive. Television adverts cost tens or even hundreds of thousands of pounds. Radio adverts costs thousands and sometimes tens of thousands of pounds. Hoardings cost many thousands and high-profile 'supersites' will cost tens of thousands in a campaign of any weight. In practice these costs take them beyond the budget of most public sector institutions except on the rarest of occasions.

Our experience is that even where such funds might be available they are better spent on narrowcasting. This is an approach using a variety of media which targets the audience more precisely. The media are themselves cheaper to use but more importantly they are a much more reliable hit on a more tightly defined population. Before moving on to describe narrowcasting it might be worth making the point that even where broadcasting is affordable and is effective it carries further problems in its wake.

A TV campaign that was too effective

In 1992 during the month of November there was a European Drug Prevention Week. This was led by the UK where John Major held the Presidency of the European Community. A host of high-profile activities were designed to focus public attention on the problems of drug misuse. As part of these activities Healthwise was commissioned to provide a free fone helpline back-up to services in Newcastle. They planned a promotional campaign for a week and after much lobbying managed to secure high-profile television coverage of the campaign together with our free fone number.

When we analysed the response to their campaign we were delighted. Over 1,000 calls on drug issues came in from Newcastle during that week. We sent out hundreds of factpacks on local services to Newcastle residents. It was only a month or so later when we received data from BT on the numbers of those who had tried and failed to get through that we realised what had actually happened.

Although over a thousand callers had got through, over 17,000 tried and failed to get through. Of these 12,000 tried on just one day! It is likely that most of these call came within an hour or so. Even when we allow for the fact that many of the 12,000 would have been the same callers ringing many times the picture is unsatisfactory. What this means is that on that day there were many more customers who had their expectations raised of a service that they could not subsequently use than customers who were successful. About 200 did get through on that Saturday and received a good service. This means that the large majority of our potential customers for our service on that day went away unhappy.

We had five lines in operation throughout that week. We now have ten lines but in order to meet the sort of demand that television adverts can generate we would need many more lines every time an advert went out. There are ways of devising services to meet this demand but they are quite expensive. This difficulty of devising a service which can cope with wildly fluctuating demand is another reason why many agencies will get better benefits from a narrowcasting approach which produces a steadier, lower level response over a longer time period.

Examples of narrowcasting techniques we have used in Healthwise include placing adverts in GP surgeries, dentists, opticians and pharmacists, etc, and placing adverts on the back of public toilet doors in locations frequented by specific sub-groups, e.g. in gyms and health clubs. Another narrower-casting technique has been placing adverts on the interiors of buses and inside taxis.

In all these cases the audience for the adverts is defined more tightly than with broadcasting techniques. Thus we know who goes to GP surgeries and we know that women, children and the elderly are more frequent users of buses. We know that many young people use taxis to get home after a night out. The audience is relatively captive for at least a few minutes — e.g. looking at the back of a toilet door. In the case of buses and taxis the audience's attention is held perhaps for a longer period of up to half an hour.

The relatively captive nature of the audience means that longer messages can be carried than is possible with broadcasting techniques. Some examples of these approaches are shown below.

The bus interiors campaign

In Merseyside as in many other areas there is a single bus company which runs across most of the county. Merseybus has about 1,000 buses with garages across Liverpool, Wirral, Sefton and St Helens and Knowsley. Adverts placed on the inside of buses are read by hundreds of thousands of commuters, shoppers and schoolchildren everyday.

The aim of the campaign was to raise the profile of Healthwise as a service offering health information on a wide range of topics. We designed an advert which carries our distinctive blue and white logo and the Healthwise owl. In each case a series of health questions are followed by the tagline 'Healthwise answers all health questions — ring 0880 66 55 44'. The questions cover issues such as:

'How long should you have to wait for an ambulance?'
'Your son is on drugs — who can you talk to?'
'What is schizophrenia?'
'Do dentists do home visits?'
'Does breast cancer run in the family?'

Within a month of starting the bus campaign, calls were coming in which had been prompted by it. Within three months it was the second largest source of new callers to the service.

Compared to other forms of advertising the bus interiors are relatively inexpensive. The campaign above cost about £3,000. The rate of response is much more gradual and manageable for the service. The adverts were only commissioned for an initial three-month period but benefit from a stay-up period that lasts until the space is resold. In some cases this can be as long as a year.

Condom cabs

At the end of 1993 we planned a campaign to encourage greater use of condoms by young party-goers over the Christmas period. Sexual health is one of the priority areas identified by the Government in the Health of the Nation strategy launched in 1993. This strategy and its targets for health gain have been given to regional and district health authorities. They have all devised local targets for health gain on issues such as heart disease, strokes, accidents, cancer prevention, mental health and sexual health.

Within the Mersey region the sexual health targets are particularly important because the region has a high rate of teenage pregnancies.

The region is fortunate, however, to have a very low rate of HIV positive persons. HIV is the virus which can lead to AIDS. High teen-pregnancy rates can be reduced and low HIV+ rates sustained if more young people are encouraged to think about condoms and other forms of contraception.

A local 'Condom cabs' campaign was devised and piloted within the Wirral area of Merseyside. Private hire taxi companies were approached and asked to carry condom packs in the backs of taxis working in the evenings and at weekends. Very many young people, going home after a night out will use taxis. This is just the time when thoughts turn to romance. Whilst the young people are going home their attention is caught by imaginatively designed packages hanging over the back of the front seat and holding free condoms and safe sex advice.

Each cab carrying the material also has a window sticker with the slogan — 'This cab has safety built in — Condom Cabs'. The cab drivers hand out plastic contact cards with the phone number, name and contact details for Healthwise printed on them. The cards also have details of the cab companies on the reverse side. This means that passengers now have two reasons to keep the cards: one side gives them details of the Healthwise free fone health information service, the other side of the card gives them the phone number of their local cab company. The plastic-coated card is designed for long life.

The costs of the Condom Cabs campaign have been met out of regional budgets. The long-term aim is to get the cab companies to pay for at least a proportion of the contact cards costs. We believe they will do so once we have shown the system works, because they already have to print their own cards. The new cards have a longer life and are more likely to be kept by passengers because they contain more useful information. It is a win/win set-up between Healthwise and the cab company.

■ DRAWING THE EXPERIENCE TOGETHER INTO STRUCTURED LOCAL CAMPAIGNS

Healthwise is now moving into a new form of health promotion campaign using social marketing techniques. Pulling together the experience from the first few years of our activity we have devised more structured local campaigns. The first campaign of this sort was undertaken in St Helens and Knowsley. This campaign is described in more detail below.

The District Health Authority

St Helens and Knowsley District Health Authority has two main areas, each with its own culture and character. St Helens is a Lancashire town, many of whose inhabitants have a strong Lancashire accent and are known to call a spade a shovel rather than a two-handed digging implement! The local rugby league side, 'The Saints', have almost folk hero status in the town.

Knowsley includes overspill estates from Liverpool such as Kirkby and many of its residents have Liverpudlian, 'scouse' accents, and if they like sport at all, will probably support either Everton or Liverpool football clubs.

Both parts of the district have relatively affluent semi-rural and rural areas. Overall the district has some of the highest levels of unemployment and social deprivation within the Mersey region which is also one of the regions with the worst economic indicators. Levels of heart disease are very high in the district as are smoking levels, alcohol consumption, etc.

The population of St Helens and Knowsley is 14 per cent of the region's population. In an analysis of the calls taken by Healthwise over its first year as a Patient's Charter Health information service it was discovered that less than 4 per cent of these came from St Helens and Knowsley.

After contact with key staff from the district a local campaign was put together. Overall the target was to raise the call rate to at least 12 per cent of the total calls taken from within the region. The campaign extends for a full year and a variety of campaign methods were used. One of the objectives is to contrast the different marketing strategies and evaluate their relative cost effectiveness.

The focus of the campaign

Although the aim was to raise the profile of Healthwise as a source of support and information for local residents it was also agreed to use the campaign as a way of focusing public interest on some of the key health gain priorities for the health authority. Two priority areas chosen after consultation with health authority staff were those of heart disease and screening for breast cancer.

Heart disease rates within the district are some of the highest in the UK and take-up levels for breast cancer screening were disappointingly low. The campaign materials and methods were designed to reflect these two priorities.

The process of the campaign

The campaign was a joint initiative between Healthwise and the district health authority. A series of meetings were held to make sure that all the key people were networked in for maximum impact. Those involved at a local level in the campaign included the Director of Public Health, the Local Health gain co-ordinator, staff from the Health Promotion Unit, local authority staff from the Environmental Health Department and Leisure Services Department and practice managers from GP surgeries across the region.

Throughout this process there was a continuous pressure to maintain an action orientation through the consultation. All the parties had had previous experience of consultation turning into sterile talking shops which went on and on. By agreeing on tight action deadlines from the outset this talking shop trap was avoided. This was a critical achievement given the many agencies involved and the relative complexity of the campaign.

The content of the campaign

A 'Healthy Heart Kit' was compiled to give out through the free fone helpline. The kit was assembled using readily available literature on issues such as Coping with Angina and dietary advice using advice sheets from the manufacturer of Flora and leaflets from the British Heart Foundation.

The kit was promoted in specially redesigned bus interior adverts which supplemented the region-wide campaign. Buses from the local garages carried Healthwise adverts in the same style as the regional campaign but with a special focus on heart disease. Questions in the adverts included:

'When is it a good time to kiss a stranger?'
'He doesn't smoke, he doesn't drink and isn't fat – so why did he have a heart attack?'
'What does climbing up the stairs have to do with your sex life after a heart attack?'
'When is it all right to thump someone?'

The taglines to this campaign were:

'For the answers to these questions and a free 'Healthy Heart Kit' phone Healthwise free on 0800 . . .' and 'Healthwise answers all health questions.'

Local worker

A part-time staff member was recruited to work with local GPs and primary health care teams. Her job was to go round all the GP waiting areas, dentists, opticians, etc, put up Healthwise posters, leave our plastic contact cards for people to take home with them and explain to local staff what the campaign was about. We had discovered that posters and leaflets disseminated by post were often left in drawers or cupboards. Even where they had been put up on display they were very quickly covered up by later posters from other organisations. In no time at all the average waiting area is festooned with all sorts of posters in a confusing mess. It can be almost impossible to pick up from such a notice-board the message that you need.

This key worker has a rota of places to visit and usually has to reposition the posters and restock supplies of the contact cards. This seemingly mundane activity has had a dramatic effect on the local awareness of our service.

Convenience advertising

A further strand of the campaign has been the placing in women's toilets of a series of posters which ask three questions about breast screening. The questions are asked in posters displayed in the toilet area near the hand-basins and driers. The answers to these questions are given in posters displayed on the back of the toilet doors.

Again the colour scheme and taglines reflect those used in other parts of the campaign. Toilet door advertising has been used effectively in many parts of the world to communicate complex messages on issues which are difficult to raise in more public settings. Women who would not wish to be seen closely reading an advertisement about breast cancer screening in a public place will do so far more comfortably in the privacy of a toilet cubicle. The placing of the adverts within women's toilet areas also overcomes the problem of graffiti risk from immature men and boys.

The strategy involves far more than just putting up adverts on the backs of toilet doors. A maintenance worker visits the site every fifteen days, notes any graffiti or damage to the posters and repositions or replaces as necessary. Reports are made on the response to the message as evidenced in graffiti or damage and this is compared to other campaigns and activities.

The impact of the campaign so far

When the campaign was first planned in April 1993 the call rate from St Helen's and Knowsley was 3.8 per cent. The target was to achieve at least 12 per cent by the end of the campaign. The campaign was launched in September and by the end of November the call rate had reached 12.8 per cent. A series of initiatives using local celebrities and the local media will be launched early in 1994 and other local meeting places such as hairdressers are to be included in local leaflet drops. It is clear that the campaign is already a considerable success and will exceed its targets *(see Graph 14.3)*.

■ CONCLUSIONS AND LESSONS FROM OUR MARKETING WORK

The lessons we have learned come from our own experience and some of them may not transfer easily to other settings. Despite this we think that some of the lessons have a wide application across the public sector and across particularly the field of health promotion. I have summarised some of these into bullet points.

General points

- As in other activities most of the impact from marketing comes from perspiration not inspiration. Careful, thorough planning and execution produces results.

- The most effective promotional work is done by those at the sharp end — in our case those who answer the phones. More than a quarter of our callers are those who have used us before or who have been recommended to use us by friends or relatives.

- Promotional work needs to be both awareness-raising and locally focused, leading to specific action on key objectives.

- Responses from campaigns can give misleading results unless matched by carefully controlled market research.

Advertising points

- Advertising agencies and other creative experts need to be used with care and may not be necessary. There is a need for

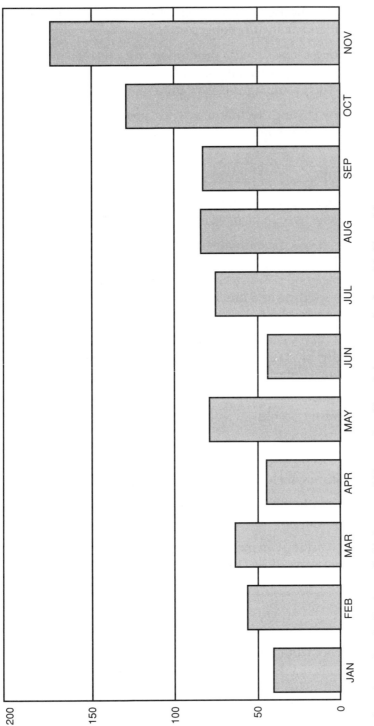

Graph 14.3   Calls from St Helens and Knowsley Month by month, Jan. 93–Nov. 93

more 'in-house' creative expertise available to the public sector and at an affordable price.

- Broadcast, mass media promotion will raise the profile of the service but it is usually short-lived. The workload produced from such campaigns is very difficult to handle.

- Narrowcasting techniques will produce responses from specific populations and usually in manageable numbers.

Media points

- Targeted and continuous media promotion work can be very cost-effective. To be most effective in media work:

  target specific journalists and media
  follow up news releases
  write good news stories about innovation and achievement
  use sporting and other celebrities
  use press photographers

- Local commercial radio is an effective tool for communicating directly to young people. BBC local radio will talk to older audiences effectively.

Organisational points

- Every contact point for the public within the health system needs to be systematically covered with low-level, low-cost literature which is designed to be kept on the person.

- Apparently mundane work such as regularly tidying notice-boards can produce substantial impact.

- Joint working can increase impact or produce talking shops — the key to avoiding talking shops is an action focus and serious commitment to deadlines.

Endnote

Readers who would like to know more about the work of the regional health information services can contact the author, James Kay, at Healthwise, 9 Slater Street, Liverpool L1 4BW 051 707 2262 and/or visit Healthwise.

Chapter 15

MARKETING AND ECONOMIC DEVELOPMENT: THE CAMBRIDGESHIRE UNIT'S APPROACH

by Keith Haarhoff

■ INTRODUCTION: HISTORY AND STATUS OF ECONOMIC DEVELOPMENT, NATIONALLY AND LOCALLY

Economic development in its current form is a very new business. Traditionally, virtually the only areas to engage in industrial promotion were the New Towns and the Assisted Areas (through their Regional Development Organisations). The key requirement was the management of government funding as an agent of Regional Policy, and this predisposed the organisations to establish contacts with major manufacturing employers to replace the sunset industries of coal, shipbuilding, automotives and steel. When the Invest in Britain Bureau was created, it too was an instrument of Regional Policy. Until recently, there was little need to develop the mechanisms and mandate to deal with differentiated, sophisticated and small company economies such as those in the south and east of the UK. DTI East was founded in 1989 to cover the six-county region; in those five years, it has passed nearly 300 enquiries on to the local Economic Development Agencies (50 per cent from US, 20 per cent from EU, 10 per cent from Japan), but only five of these have resulted in an investment in the region.

The success of the traditional organisation must be measured against this orientation, as illustrated in Figure 15.1. In DTI terms, the South-east and East is the area from the Wash to the Solent via Oxford, with 40 per cent of UK GDP and 33 per cent of UK population. The overall level of foreign investment in the UK as a proportion of the EU shows an excellent record, and, while the major problems were in the north, west and extremities of the country, the mechanisms appear to have worked well. But Cambridgeshire's male unemployment rate is now not far below the national rate (10 per cent vs 13 per cent), and there are pockets like Peterborough and Wisbech at 15 per cent. We are having to develop new mechanisms to deal with the marketing of these new economies in collaboration with the DTI and other agencies.

The competition is well organised. When *Business in the Community* reviewed European practice, they discovered that competition was not limited to the well-established Chambers of Commerce in France, where (for example) the Caen Chamber founded and operates Brittany Ferries and runs the airport. Continental Europe had perfected a whole new approach to economic development and business support: their approach involved

- development of powerful regional development bodies with 'critical mass'

- creation of a partnership framework for economic development

- developing a common purpose and partnership

- ability to invest in infrastructure and flexibility in the use of resources

- achieving a private sector stake in local success
(Coopers & Lybrand, 1992)

Europeans have a considerable advantage in the relative strength of the Chambers; 'Hamburg has a population of 1.6 million and 80,000 Chamber subscribers. . . . Birmingham, with a slightly smaller population (1.1 million) has only 5,300 Chamber members' (ibid.). As we shall see, Birmingham is, in spite of this, one of the better organised community action programmes. Other examples in the study included Limburg, Catalonia and Lombardia.

The Cambridgeshire Unit is one of the very few such agencies to be established in a part of the UK which is not the target for government regional development policy through either the New Towns Commission (as with Peterborough, Milton Keynes and Corby) or Regional Selective Assistance (as in the cases of the north-east or north-west of the country). The Unit (and others which have followed it) is entirely staffed with people from marketing backgrounds in the private sector. Thus Cambridgeshire has provided a perfect opportunity to apply the techniques of pure

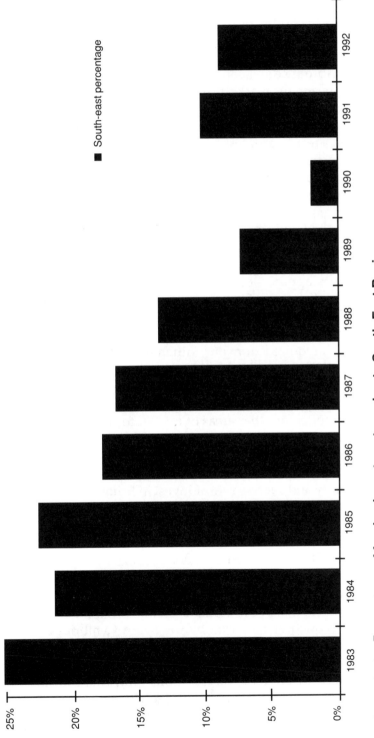

Figure 15.1   Percentage of foreign investment coming to South-East Region

marketing to 'place', unconstrained by tradition or national policy on regional development (Kotler *et al.*, 1993).

The local authorities were given a legal mandate to undertake economic development in their area in 1989 also, and are now required to produce an Economic Development Strategy. Few knew what this meant, the marketplace was confused and ill-defined, and much of the information was too oriented towards land use planning, and offered little guidance on industries, skills and people. As a result, progress has been slow, halting and is only now beginning to achieve a degree of coherence. The creation of unitary authorities is likely, in the medium to long term, to create a climate conducive to co-operative Economic Development.

One consequence is the move to form an Economic Development Forum and possibly a Regional Development Office for the six counties of the Eastern Region, following the Business in the Community recommendation (ibid.) and the moves to develop multi-agency approaches (the DTI's Business Links, for example). The existing Economic Development Agencies in the region are in excellent communication, and engage in a variety of cross-border programmes, as discussed below. Given that the needs, markets and approaches required for our differentiated and sophisticated economy differ from the traditional 'sunset' areas, we have an opportunity to create a unique marketing approach to this area which can take on the competition elsewhere in the world and provide a model for other areas of the UK to consider adapting for themselves. Now that the foundations for regional collaboration have been laid with the designation of parts of the region for Regional Selective Assistance and EU Objective 5b, it is likely that the suitability and success rate of Invest in Britain Bureau enquiries will increase.

■ BACKGROUND: FORMATION OF THE CAMBRIDGESHIRE UNIT IN 1991

The origins of The Cambridgeshire Unit lie in the extraordinary economic growth experienced by the South Cambridgeshire area during the middle and late 1980s. This is usually referred to as 'The Cambridge Phenomenon' after the famous book of that name by Nick Segal, which related the enormous growth to the outpouring of technology transfer from Cambridge University to local firms. Many other longer-term and wider economic and government issues also contributed on a regional basis, including the relocation of many Londoners into the region during the 50s and 60s; the re-orientation of the UK to face Europe, leading to the growth of commercial traffic through Felixstowe; and the general isolation of the area, which had allowed it to preserve the quality of life (and low property prices) which the incomers valued.

By the late 1980s, a further pressure was added — the attraction of Cambridge as a *regional* centre for professional and financial services. Over that period, the city became the regional head office for five of the six international firms of accountants, three national firms of solicitors, two merchant banks, four UK and two European commercial banks and two national insurance companies. All were attracted by the same characteristics which made Cambridge desirable to other market sectors: the cultural ambience associated with the presence of the university, the surrounding rurality, access both to London and the coast for leisure, excellent regional communications and the growing critical mass of professional services in the city.

The impact on the city of Cambridge was heightened by the Holford planning environment, which had imposed a green belt around the city to avoid over-development. By the late 1980s, this was exacerbating the city's difficulties by failing to encourage residential development and public transport to match the offices being built. This is well illustrated by Figure 15.2, taken from the City's Local Plan. The city's population grew by a mere 3 per cent over the decade, jobs by 25 per cent and traffic by nearly 50 per cent.

In an attempt to stop the flood, the city and county planners tried to enforce the Structure Plan, but were defeated by a combination of the economic boom, the usual short-termism of investors and the inadequacy of land use planning as a mechanism of economic regulation. The result was an imbalance: confrontation between the public and private sectors in the south, while the north of the county was welcoming any crumbs of economic growth on offer.

The local authorities and local business interests commissioned Professor Gordon Cameron, late head of the Department of Land Economy at the University of Cambridge, to produce an assessment of the scope for 'dispersing' this excess growth from the south towards the north and east of the county. The Cameron Report, published in 1989, supported the theory that the growth pressures on premises costs, labour costs and traffic congestion were causing Southern Cambridgeshire's employers to look at the north as possible relocation areas. The report recommended the formation of a

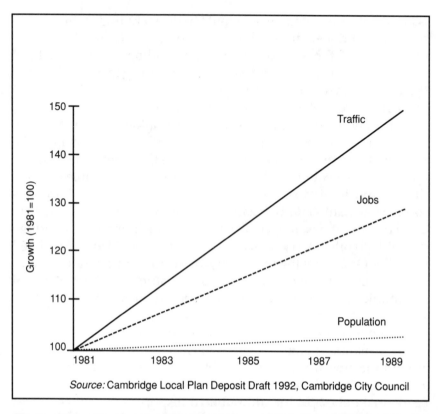

Figure 15.2   Traffic, housing and job growth in Cambridge 1980–89

'Dispersal and Relocation Agency' to identify and counsel those firms in the south of the county which were suffering growth pressures and assist them in making a decision to move north ('Dispersal') and to intercept enquiries about a Cambridgeshire location from prospective inward investors and see if they would consider a more northerly location ('Deflection'). As a consequence of this report, the local authorities established The Cambridgeshire Unit. This was a unique pact across ideological and political boundaries (urban/rural, developed/agricultural, north/south, all political parties).

A major initial (and current) difficulty was the multiplicity of organisations offering assistance to business in what appear to the client to be duplicating ways: the Training and Enterprise Councils (TECs), Confederation of British Industry (CBI), Department for Trade and Industry (DTI), Enterprise Agencies, Chambers of Commerce and local authority Economic Development Units all play an important part in creating a supportive environment for business, and roles range from the pure strategic and regional to the direct delivery of services on a local basis. So, an urgent requirement in late 1991 was to identify the key characteristics of The Cambridgeshire Unit concept, and differentiate it from the other players so that our respective roles could be seen as mutually supportive and complementary.

The information base of the average local authority is excellent, but strongly oriented towards land use planning and the strategic placement of schools, roads and other community services, and we have had to introduce more focused information collection and analysis. In addition, there was little in the way of marketing administration systems: little was known of where enquiries came from, what had happened to them, what the county's existing employers (the current customer base) thought, which sectors of industry prospered in the county and why, and where we might find other people like them to 'buy' the product.

The relationship between the public and private sectors was at an all-time low, primarily due to the adversarial positions adopted in the planning battles. Local authorities had an extremely negative image among the commercial sector, a situation which was made worse by the creation of the Uniform Business Rate. The county had neglected its existing clients, who (in marketing terms) represent the most cost-effective way of generating growth: existing customers have already bought the product, can tell us what it is that attracts them to it, and can point us towards others in their industry who may be interested in 'buying' it (that is, establishing an operation here). A key requirement is to develop relationships with employers whose companies are owned abroad, since they can act as absentee salespeople for the county and may need help in selling the idea of follow-up investment to their parent companies.

The fact that City and County shared the name of Cambridge was a double-edged sword in marketing terms: the City was well known internationally, but the commercial images associated with it were of research and high-tech and congestion and confrontation. Neither of these images conveyed a welcoming commercial community or an area of the country which was seeking to encourage industrialisation and had many engineering, financial and manufacturing skills.

Early consideration revealed that the concept of Dispersal/Deflection was over-simplistic. Many people making an enquiry to Cambridge were making a comparison with Munich, Sophia–Antipolis, Bologna or Montpellier, and would not be inclined to consider Wisbech, Chatteris or March, deep in the agricultural area of the county. We had to develop an arrangement which allowed the county to be welcoming to those who were important to the underpinning of 'strategic industries' in the south; identify very early in the process those who were using 'Cambridge' as a proxy for the area; and create an image of a county whose other towns had a unique and individual identity attractive to new customer segments.

Other issues were external: the world had moved on since the Cameron research had been done in 1989, at the peak of the economic boom. The economic recession meant that the volume of enquiries had dropped, firms were more choosy about where they went while thin margins and eagle-eyed bankers meant that relocations were harder to justify and finance. The recession also meant that an urgent priority was to protect what employment we already had and the world was becoming more competitive in this field. The regions of Europe, in particular, were gearing themselves up to market their attractions proactively in our backyard, and the opening up of eastern Europe had lent a whole new meaning to financial incentives.

■ MARKET ANALYSIS: WHAT WE FOUND

The most urgent first-year tasks were to develop a clear identity for the Unit, establish the key players in the game and decide what alliances and joint projects could be discussed with each. Only when this had been done, could the crucial operational issues be addressed — what were the Unique Selling Propositions of the product, how were the 'flavours' differentiated, who bought them now and why, where would we find others who would buy, what were the opportunities for the on-sale (further investment by an existing employer), how would we identify and communicate with our chosen client sectors.

The overriding constraint was finance — the Unit had been established with a three-year mandate and an annual budget of £120,000. This paid for staff of two and a half, an office, telephone and base level computer systems. Whatever was done had to be done with other people's money.

Competitor/ally analysis

The results of the first market analysis are shown in Figure 15.3; it seemed clear that the three primary parameters of the supplier set were (1) *client size*; (2) whether the service was of an *employment-* or *skill*-creating nature; and (3) whether the organisation's principal

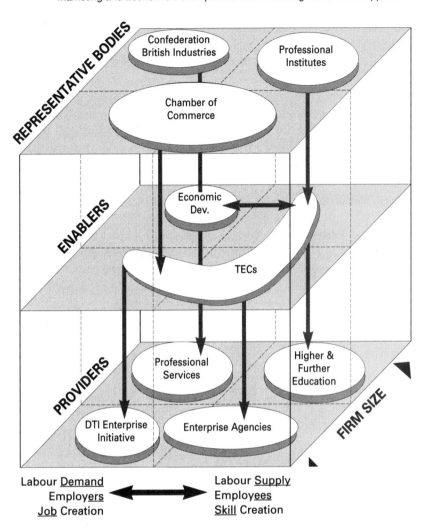

Figure 15.3   The business support network

role was of a *membership* kind (and thus primarily to represent the interests of its members), an *enabler* (organising service delivery from other players) or a direct service *provider*.

Given the size distribution of companies in the local economy, around 50 employees is regarded as the appropriate mid-point for the 'firm-size' axis.

The CBI and Chambers (and similar organisations such as the Institute of Directors and TUC) are seen as primarily *membership* organisations, lobbying on behalf of their particular client set. Economic   Development   Agencies   such   as   Peterborough

Development Agency and The Cambridgeshire Unit as well as the TECs are in the *'enabling'* business, since all depend upon organising other players to deliver the services for which they are responsible; Economic Development Agencies and TECs relate across the employment–skill polarity, since the former are primarily concerned with services to employers in creating *industries* and thus employment, while the latter are primarily concerned with creating and developing the skills in the *individuals* who will provide the labour for those employers.

On the third plane are the *service providers*, professional services (solicitors, accountants, bankers, property agents, etc.), educational institutions (Higher Educational Institutions and Further Education colleges), and Enterprise bodies. These interact directly with the client once the appropriate programme has been agreed.

This analysis has been remarkably effective in clarifying that the primary role of Economic Development Agencies is working with the larger employers (representing industries) to create new jobs, and interacting with the TECs to manage the demand–supply equation for skilled labour. In an ideal world, the TEC will be able to tell an Economic Development Agency where it can find the number of skilled welders bilingual in French required to meet a prospective employer's expressed need, and in what timescale existing workers (at present without these skills) can be trained. This, with similar information on premises and infrastructure, needs to be added to the overall presentation to the client. The analysis has also validated the intuitive feeling that the professional service suppliers are the natural allies of the Economic Development Agencies on the service provider plane.

The consequence of this analysis has been to allow the Unit to concentrate on upward relationships with the CBI and Chambers, peer relationships with the TECs, and operational relationships with the professional service suppliers. Relationships with Institute of Management, Institute of Directors, Higher Educational Institutions, Further Education colleges and Enterprise Agencies are close, but indirect and primarily mediated through the mutual direct relationships.

Product/market analysis

Commercial organisations are sadly very little concerned with local authority administrative boundaries, many of which skirt round major towns, leaving half the hinterland in another district or county. Travel to Work Areas are far more relevant, and they have developed identities of their own. Fortunately, the Employment Department uses these as the basis for its employment statistics and county councils base their Structure Planning subunits on them also. This gave rise to the concept of the Four Economies (see Figures 15.4 and 15.5), whose differentiating characteristics recognisable to the outside observer have now been identified and articulated.

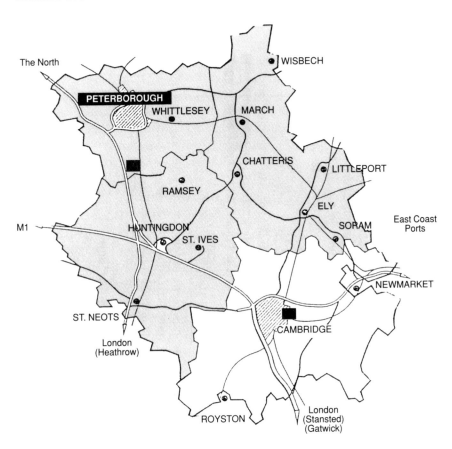

Figure 15.4   Cambridgshire's Four Economies

The northeast of the county is designated the 'Fens', predominantly rural and agricultural, most of it below sea-level, resulting from the draining of the marshes in the seventeenth century. While less than 10 per cent of the population now work on the land, around a third are dependent on agriculture, since many of the support industries in food processing, packaging, distribution and agricultural machinery have concentrated here. The area is well connected to the motorway network through the Fen Link Roads.

The Fens

- rural, agricultural base
- food processing, packaging, storage and distribution
- good communications to motorway network
- good living space and busines expansion potential
- five market towns, including Ely serving a large village population
- hard working, loyal and adaptable workforce

Ouse Valley

- river towns, excellent east/west connections
- distribution/logistics and light manufacturing
- consumer electronics, plastics, metal working

Peterborough

- new town, excellent north/south communications
- precision engineering, engines/machinery
- financial services, retailing
- leisure park and cathedral

South Cambridge

- city and villages; the colleges
- the universities, 'knowledge' industries
- pharmaceuticals, computers/telecoms, R&D

Figure 15.5   The Four Economies

This is a priority area since unemployment is high all over (in October 1993, male unemployment in March and Chatteris was 11 per cent and in Peterborough and Wisbech it was 15 per cent) and there are few alternative industries. The area has many attractive lifestyle features, with five market towns in which 80 per cent of the people live and the smallest cathedral city in the country, at Ely. The workforce is hardworking, loyal and adaptable, and readily takes to working with sophisticated equipment.

Driving from Ely to Huntingdon, one leaves the Fens and enters 'The Ouse Valley', with river towns and a predominance of distribution and light manufacturing industry. The 'crossroads of England' at Huntingdon and the main East Coast rail line make this a natural centre for national distribution centres while the proximity to Cambridge has ensured its popularity with the consumer electronics industry. In the past, it has been well able to rely upon its natural attractions and the centrifugal flow from London and Cambridge to sustain its industry, but now local pockets of unemployment are developing.

'Peterborough' has been successfully promoted under the New Towns banner for the past twenty years, growing from a town of 80,000 to the largest centre in the county (160,000) in this time. It has excellent infrastructure (internal roads, housing, schools, leisure facilities) and excellent north–south communications. It has a base in heavy engineering and has developed a financial services industry and mail order distribution. The city continues to expand, primarily through the recently designated Peterborough Southern Township.

It would be tempting to say that 'South Cambridge' needs no introduction, but its image, while well-known, is misleading. Much effort has gone into promoting it as a world-famous university city and publicising the 'high-tech' industry which has grown alongside. Less attention has been given to the substantial concentration of precision engineering and instrument-making, without which skills the clever ideas of the scientist could not have been translated into practice. Aircraft engineering, specialist vehicle manufacturers, scientific instruments, radio communications and the printing and publishing industry all add to the make-up of the city, while plant science, pharmaceuticals, contract research and telecommunications all create an 'appliance of science' character for the area.

The marketing issue devolved into collecting information on each of these four flavours, identifying the industries which prosper in each locality and building close relationships with the key players there. Although we were initially discouraged by the wide variety of characteristics exhibited by our four economies, we soon came to realise that diversity was a positive concept. Apart from deep-mined coal and inshore fisheries, we had an option for almost everyone.

In parallel, work was going on to identify the key characteristics which applied to the whole county, and which would be shared by all four of the flavours. Naturally, all have a workforce fluent in English, excellent road and rail communications, good air connections via Stansted, proximity to London and an educational culture of high standing. Internal road systems are of high standard so that Wisbech can share the benefit of Cambridge's technology resource base and Peterborough's manufacturing labour force. The result of this work was the message about the county, expressed in the promotional material we issue.

Marketing channels

The next most important priority was to define the marketing and 'distribution' channels we could use. The major constraint is financial: we do not have the money to engage in extensive advertising, expensive market research, promotional activities, exhibitions or overseas visits, nor (until recently) financial incentives or grants. We would have to rely upon our wits, our friends and the resolve of the community to tackle the issues we faced.

The Business Support Network analysis (*see* Figure 15.3, page 299) had shown that our 'nearest neighbours' were the CBI and Chamber of Commerce, the TECs (we have two in Cambridgeshire) and professional service suppliers as well as our major employers. The first priority was to establish our credentials and the need for joint activities with the fellow members of the Business Support Network, and this has proceeded through joint exhibitions, joint bidding for the Business Link and common approaches to economic research.

The next priority was the *professional service suppliers*. Naturally, the earliest likely beneficiaries would be the commercial property agents, and we had to tie them in as a matter of urgency. Accountants, solicitors, bankers and patent agents would benefit from the ongoing improvement of the business climate, but the property agents would benefit up-front from the letting of the buildings. We have developed a joint approach to property information with the agents, and a regional Joint Venture Panel to provide a forum for meeting the key accountants and solicitors. The main objectives of these programmes are to ensure a common approach to describing the county; encouraging these organisations to refer enquiries to The Cambridgeshire Unit; and, ultimately, finance for our activities on behalf of the county. The key relevance of this group is that they are likely to be the first to hear of a company's intention to move into, out of or within the county. The company will either approach their banker for finance, their solicitor for a view on their lease, their accountant as part of their long-term planning strategy or their property agent to find a buyer for their present premises.

Existing employers have long been overlooked in the marketing equation. Traditionally, in the business of economic development, the headlines and glory go to the organisation which captures Inward Investment; but even John Bridge, Managing Director of Northern Development Company and the prime mover behind the northeast's capture of the Nissan car plant for Tyne & Wear, acknowledges that 85 per cent of his effort goes into helping existing employers (both UK and foreign-owned) to grow and prosper (Bridge, 1991). Existing employers have demonstrated their commitment by 'buying' the product (a loyalty which has to be reinforced from time to time), and they can tell us what it is about the product that they like or dislike. In classic marketing terms, it is far more cost-effective to sell to an existing 'buyer' than to create a new market or client. A county's existing employers are in close contact with others in their industry through trade organisations, and can identify and probably speak to other firms who will appreciate the same values as they do themselves.

A further requirement in this area is a clear knowledge of the *industry structure*. In the traditional Regional Selective Assistance areas, the structure has been dominated by a single industry, be it coal, shipbuilding, steel or automotives. This has made it relatively easy to track the interactions between major industry groups and the sub-contractor networks, and between the industry groups and their customers. But Cambridgeshire (and most of the counties in the south-east of the UK) has a broadly differentiated economy, which has 'just growed'. The interactions are subtle and not easily identified, and sometimes it is difficult to decide which industries are represented. This has required the development of a whole new mechanism of industry analysis, based upon the mathematical technique of cluster analysis.

Some of the clusters so revealed are the obvious ones of Education, Health, Local Government, Food Processing,

Packaging, Retail and Construction; some others are obvious but were previously ill-defined (Plant Science, Pharmaceuticals, Consumer Electronics, Precision Engineering); others were completely unexpected (the county has a major group of companies producing Automotive Components, and the Plastics industry is much larger in this area than we had originally expected).

The final area of examination involved *overseas promotion*: traditionally, the UK government has used its consulates and embassies around the world to keep an eye open for possible inward investment in the UK, and this has been formalised and made more pro-active through the agency of the Invest in Britain Bureau. The traditional areas of Regional Selective Assistance (that is all but the South-east and East) have Regional Development Organisations to work alongside the local DTI office in managing the Government and EU aid being invested there and some of these have established overseas promotion posts to complement the activities of the Invest in Britain Bureau.

Cambridgeshire's budget does not permit any such investment, so our only approach was to use the existing, free (but 'noisy') channel provided by the DTI and Invest in Britain Bureau. We are now beginning to find ways in which the 'traditional' and 'marketing' approaches can coexist. Though enquiries received through the DTI/Invest in Britain Bureau channel represent less than half of our enquiry load and were (until the designation of Wisbech as an Assisted Area in 1993) the crumbs left after the priorities in Regional Policy have had their pick, we still felt that a close working relationship with DTI was the best way of getting our views represented at both national and international level.

Marketing systems

Economic development is a new and growing industry, and is only now developing the standards, procedures and products required to make it efficient and recognised for its professionalism. Most of the existing systems and customs were based upon either the traditional Regional Development Office markets or the land-use oriented systems used by the local authorities. Neither is ideal for the 'base-budgeting' approach of marketing a differentiated and sophisticated economy like ours, so (with our colleagues in adjacent counties) we have been developing modern computer-based solutions.

The first priority was the development of an *Enquiry Management System*, to record the receipt of an enquiry, allow us to track, chase and delegate to 'case-officers' in other organisations (mainly the district Economic Development Officers). The system also provides marketing information on the nature of our enquiry load and trends through time, plus providing half the measures we need for our performance appraisal system. Customer/industry information is derived from the *Employer and Training Database* maintained by the county on behalf of all the local authorities, but this has needed substantial 'civilising' to meet our needs, primarily because an in-house system is not ideal for shipping out to a demanding customer. The main development programme has concentrated on the *Property Database*, aimed at collating strands of information from commercial property agents, the land-use planners at the county council and economic information into a single PC-based system which can identify in seconds what existing premises and approved development sites exist in each geographical area to meet the client's needs.

The primary objectives of these and the other systems and procedures we have been involved in are:

- to reduce the labour intensiveness of the process by automating as much as possible of response

- to enhance the quality image of the product by ensuring that information is presented in a consistent and complementary fashion

- to facilitate quality control and staff training by providing our partners in the Business Support Network with systems and procedures which allow us all to perform in a consistent manner

- through the regional joint ventures to create and establish standards of information collection to allow exchange of information and cross-boundary comparisons.

■ ROLES, RELATIONSHIPS AND RESULTS

Objectives

The Unit's objectives are illustrated in Figure 15.6. The key points are that The Cambridgeshire Unit is a promotional agency for the whole of the county (working closely with our colleagues at the Peterborough Development Agency and the local authorities in Fenland and East Cambridgeshire, who have a direct sales responsibility in their districts); that our job is to inform the market place of what each part of the county has to offer commercial and industrial employers, taking advantage of the fact that many throughout the world have heard of Cambridge and Peterborough, and do not appreciate that other towns in the locality of each share many of their attractions; and that we have a responsibility to both existing employers and potential inward investors, using the clustering of existing strategic industries to attract more of the same and promoting the county's excellent professional services sector as a Unique Selling Proposition.

- focus for local authority/major employer contact
- promote expansion and growth of existing employers
- generate/capture/progress inward investment enquiries
- promote geographical/economic diversification
- promote welcoming image for county
- create/form alliances and partnerships

Chart 15.6   TCU Objectives

We act as a focus for local authority interaction in this field, and as a channel of communication between them as a group and the private sector, in such matters as Structure Plan review and approaches to a co-ordinated transport policy. We promote the image of Cambridgeshire as a place which welcomes and supports its commercial life, a crucial function in the aftermath of the confrontations of the 80s and the removal of direct contact between the local authorities and local business. We provide an enquiry response service, assembling the facts required to persuade those who we believe would benefit from a Cambridgeshire location that this is the place for them, and unbiased advice on which of Cambridgeshire's four economic areas and twenty towns would suit them best.

The key importance of existing employers is recognised by the second objective, while the importance of inward investment in bringing new capital, skills, products and processes to an area is seen in the third.

Services

Our main role is one of information, identifying industries which enjoy their location and looking for firms in those and other industries which share their values and needs. We share with all the country the advantages of language, an entrepreneurial culture, flexible employment law, and so on, but are unique in our position astride the 'crossroads of England' and our proximity to London, the Midlands and the East Coast ports.

We produce literature like 'The Case for Cambridgeshire', a sixty-page compendium of facts about the county as a business location, and its sister publication 'Living in Cambridgeshire'. We have fact sheets on the major industries, and collate information in the form of slides for presentations to interested parties.

Consistent with our market orientation, we have identified two key audiences: the first of these is the *professional service community* and other BSN members, whose services we promote as complementary to our own and with whom we will share in the prosperity resulting from the improvement in the county's economic performance. Our services to this community are illustrated in Figure 15.7, the key service being the last. While we do not charge this community for our services, we do expect joint venture activities, cross-referrals and occasional investment in joint publicity to compensate us for our efforts towards the mutual objective.

- focus for local authority contact
- liaison between local authorities
- focus for Business Support Network
- promotion of Cambridgeshire as a business location
- promotion of Cambridgeshire's businesses as a partner

Chart 15.7   TCU Services for the business community

A clear distinction has to be maintained between these Allies (who are often also Competitors from time to time) and the Client Market. Figure 15.8 illustrates the services we offer to the real client, *the employer (existing or prospective)* who wishes to expand an existing operation or establish a new one. Given our local authority provenance, we are uniquely placed to interpret local authority thinking and to convey the views of our major employer

- unbiased advice on Cambridgeshire's offering

- access to local authority thinking

- information on trends, structure and strategy

- one stop shop for local information

- signpost to other members of the Business Support Network

- introductions to professional service specialists

Chart 15.8   TCU services for the employer/inward investor

marketplace to both district and county authorities. But our 'Enabler' and 'Next Steps' Agency status provides us with an independence and objectivity not shared by our more commercial allies.

A key objective has been to create this overall image of a county which consists of four mutually complementary 'economies', each attractive to a different market sector. The key hypothesis was that we could use the international stature of Cambridge and Peterborough to 'float' and promote the other two economies, differentiating them from the two dominant images without either diminishing the dominant images or detracting from the subtlety of the two new images. Thus 'Cambridgeshire' needs to surround and reinforce 'South Cambridge' and 'Peterborough' as primary colours and supporting the more pastel images of the 'Fens' and 'Ouse Valley'. Though this view has only been marketed since early 1992, it is beginning to show an impact. The locational preferences expressed by our enquiry flow are illustrated in Figure 15.9.

Overall, only around 40% of the enquiries expressed a locational preference within Cambridgeshire, the remainder being the sort of general enquiries sent to every authority with a request to provide the relevant information on their area. This has remained fairly constant over the two and half years ("Aware"). However, the proportion expressing a non-Cambridge preference, asking specifically about March, Wisbech or Ely, demonstrating an awareness of the flavours which we seek to promote, has doubled to 40 l % over the period ("Direct").

Of those enquiries which express a preference for Cambridge, an average one third (when questioned further) are using 'Cambridge' as a proxy for the area ("Deflection"). Such enquirers do not require to be in the city itself, and are quite interested to be told that they can get many of the facilities they need at half the price twenty miles

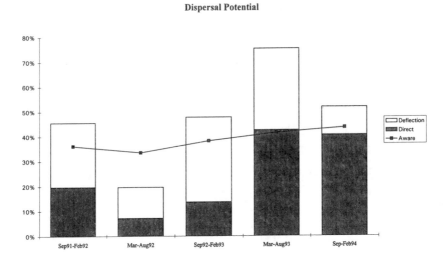

Dispersal Potential

Figure 15.9   **Locational preferences**

further north; many do not need (or particularly want) close proximity to the University or professional service suppliers, though they do wish to share in the general cultural ambience and transport communications. The remaining 'Cambridge only' enquiries really *did* want to be within fifteen miles of the City, though could often be encouraged to locate outside the city itself, where they could dip into the facilities on an 'as required' basis.

Apart from providing a reassurance that the image projection was beginning to work, this analysis underpins our Publicity Strategy. We must *inform* the 65 per cent who do not indicate a preference, so that they specify their requirements in a way which maximises the advantages of our product; we wish to *woo* the 16 per cent who ask about the individual flavours, since they are already half-way towards making a decision in our favour; we wish to *reinforce* the 13 per cent who ask about the area, but are conscious of the different flavours; and we need to *publicise* the interest of even the clients of 'South Cambridge', since this adds to the positive image we are projecting for the county as a whole.

As indicated in Figure 15.10, we have doubled the numbers of enquiries received, and find that 50 per cent of those enquirers who expressed a preference now specify a part of Cambridgeshire apart from the university city; we have created an identity for the county which is inclusive of and supported by the identities of its separate

Enquirer awareness:

- enquiry volume doubled
- 80 per cent advised about Fenland and East Cambs.
- 50 per cent of location requests are for Fenland and East Cambs

Promotion and Publicity:

- four separate areas
- individual identity
- county literature
- promotion of strategic industries

Stature:

- business-like image
- strategic alliances
- close co-operation

Chart 15.10   Value-added by TCU

parts, drawing on the high-tech and tertiary education image of Cambridge and the manufacturing and financial services strengths of Peterborough to develop a well-rounded image. We have broadened that image to include major industries like pharmaceuticals, packaging, consumer electronics, telecommunications, aircraft engineering and automotive components, all of which have been unsung in the past.

Two other consequences have contributed to this result. Organisational relationships have developed such that we can cross-refer work between the various agencies involved in the Business Support Network, and this will become even more effective with the formation of the *Greater Peterborough Partnership* in the north and the moves are made towards a Business Link bid in the south. This process has been reinforced by the growing public/private sector collaboration, evidenced by The Cambridgeshire Unit Steering Group (with equal representation from local authorities and commercial employers, and chaired by the county chairman of the CBI) and the local TEC board. Further development in each of these areas is crucial to the future success of integrated marketing of the county and the region.

■ MARKET TRENDS IN ECONOMIC DEVELOPMENT

The Economic Development Business is becoming more and more professional and competitive. However strong an area's offering, it is no longer sufficient to wait for enquirers to beat a path to your door. At best, you get flooded with employers who cannot use your existing labour force or require new types of buildings and infrastructure; more likely the local economy just stagnates.

The primary force is *regionalisation*; it is no longer sufficient to promote a single town or even county. One must retain the individual identity of the various parts, but present them as a range of 'flavours' from which the customer can choose the one which matches his needs best. The French Chambers of Commerce and regional Councils, the German Ländebüro and Dutch Development Agencies have created a strong concept of regional identity and industrial co-operation. This helps to bind in local employers, in both developing a vision of the local *industry structure* and acting as absentee salesmen in their industry. Reference has already been made (in the 'Introduction' section) to the pressure from Europe towards co-ordinated marketing of a region-sized area with critical mass, and this concept is already developing in other parts of the world.

Public/Private sector collaboration is becoming more important as the funding for infrastructure projects will increasingly rest on their commercial value. During 1993, the Government has taken steps to address this issue with the creation of the Business Links (the first ten of which will commence operations during 1994), in which all of the organisations mentioned will play a part. This will provide a platform for co-operation, but the strategic analysis of roles and relationships has still to be resolved at more than a local level. Birmingham has always been in the van in this field, having pioneered collaboration in the National Exhibition Centre, Birmingham Heartlands and now one of the first wave of Business Links.

The management of *EC/Government funding* is becoming increasingly sophisticated, and is a further reason for regionalisation, since many projects require both a strategic justification and cross-border collaboration. Finally, the east and south-east need to develop *Regional Development Organisations* similar to those in place in the rest of the country and elsewhere in Europe, to manage the liaison and collaboration on a regional basis. This is the only way in which to gain our rightful share of the limited national and international funding available, and is completely different from the traditional role of managing the investment of central government cash.

Regional collaboration in this region is at a very high level. Cambridgeshire, Suffolk and Norfolk already have the *Standing Conference of East Anglian Local Authorities*, a collaborative organisation with an extensive history in land use planning and transportation strategy and a key role in attracting EU funds to the area. This could provide the platform for an expanded organisation if broadened both *geographically* (to six counties) and *functionally* (to include economic development). The recent announcement by the Government of the formation of Integrated Regional Offices and a Single Regional Development Budget recognises that both the DTI and Department of Employment are on a six-county basis (including Bedfordshire, Essex and Hertfordshire), with headquarters in Cambridge, while Department of the Environment and Department of Transport have a seven-county region (including Buckinghamshire as well) centred on Bedford. The scene for this was set in June 1993 by a conference organised by the regional CBI at Duxford, just south of Cambridge.

The local authority Economic Development Agencies collaborate on joint projects; The Cambridgeshire Unit, for instance, has a joint venture with Hertfordshire and Bedfordshire in developing a *Property Database*, which is both an operational tool in our business and the basis for standardisation of data across the region and, perhaps, the country. The Higher Educational Institutions (as data producers), the local authority Research Departments, Economic Development Agencies (as data purchasers) and business organisations like the CBI, Chambers and TECs are all members of the *Regional Economic Research Observatory*, whose objective is to create a climate of co-operation in the collection and use of economic data, so that it can be aggregated and compared across the region and mean something at the end of it. At the end of 1993 Hertfordshire Development Organisation hosted a full-day conference of local authority Economic Development interests from across the region attended by the TECs, CBI and DTI which will provide a platform for wider collaboration in this field.

DTI East was responsible for gaining agreement for regional *Publicity Materials*, in the form of 'Profile east' a matched set of A4 folders for the region as a whole and for each individual county. This, with quarterly discussions of procedure and marketing issues, is leading to a commonality of approach across the region which bodes well for the future.

■ THE MARKETING LESSONS

The Cambridgeshire experience has provided a unique opportunity to apply the precepts of classic business-to-business marketing to the promotion of 'place' (Kotler *et al.*, 1993). The lack of dominant industries, the apparently undifferentiated economy, low level of traditional promotion and mature organisations have created the ideal blank sheet of paper for a marketing man.

The *Competitor/ally* analysis has gained new insights into the Business Support Network, and though this has yet to be translated into real formal alliances, there are a number of constructive movements which are leading in the right direction. The examination of roles and relationships has defined the supplier marketplace, and identified information sources and responsibilities.

The *Product/market* analysis has allowed us to define the product in the way that the client sees it, differentiating 'flavours' attractive to individual client segments. The process of image development has required us to be cautious, since it would have been very easy to end up with a confused message or to dilute the very strong images of the north and south flavours (Peterborough and Cambridge). Analysis of *industry structure* has given a new insight into the commercial relationships in our economy (the 'product' in client terms) and provided an opportunity to get close to our existing customer base, the major employers in the county.

Distribution and communication channels are crucial in any marketing strategy, and it has been very helpful to have the theoretical foundation of the Business Support Network to confirm the Professional Service Providers, our existing employers and DTI/Invest in Britain Bureau as the three major communication channels. This has further supported the importance of the existing employers in any policy of economic development, and this and the stream of DTI enquiries has enabled us to drive down the experience curve much faster than would have been the case otherwise. A clear knowledge of the traditions and hang-ups of the major players in your marketplace is crucial to successful marketing.

The importance of good *systems and procedures* cannot be over-emphasised. So long as responses are prepared on an individualised basis, the client cannot make a valid comparison. Providing the marketplace analysis is sufficiently sophisticated, competition will be between regions and countries, since, within each area, only one solution is likely to meet the precise client requirements. Systems are a means to achieve this standardisation: an industry standard system with proper information back-up reduces the performance difference between a small office and a large one and allows every response to contribute to the overall professional image. Quality control, common training, information and staff exchange then become possible.

Product Life Cycle theory states that, once a market has begun to develop, it behooves the market leaders to co-operate with their major 'competitors' in developing standards and services and products which satisfy the client set in a consistent and supportive fashion. By this stage of market development, the base product (an enquiry response) has become a commodity, and it is preferable for the dominant players to co-operate to build the overall market size. The individual player's strategy relies upon being selective about his market and competing on his product's specialist differentiating factors; the development of standards serves to increase the overall market size, the leader's strategy relying upon maintaining or improving market share.

Business forums/Conferences
Hertfordshire Development
Organisation
East Sussex

Sector Working Parties
Northern Development Company
Hertfordshire Development
Organisation

Data pooling
Essex/Anglia Polytechnic
Universities
Cambridgeshire
Yorks and Humberside

Economic development strategy
Norwich
East Susex
Birmingham

Development organisation
Cambridgeshire
Northern Development Company

Public/Private sector co-operation
Sheffield
Birmingham

Property databases
Lincolnshire
Cheshire
Cambridgeshire

Enquiry management
Lincolnshire
Cambridgeshire

Publicity material
Lincolnshire

Figure 15.11   Best practice

There is an excellent basis of raw material for this process: Figure 15.11 illustrates the range of specialist experience available in different Economic Development Agencies in early 1992. Once the industry has recognised itself as such and makes serious and co-ordinated attempts to develop a shared corpus of knowledge and procedures, the industry will be able to take on the world.

Acknowledgement

The views expressed in this paper are those of the author, and do not necessarily represent the views of the sponsors of The Cambridgeshire Unit; however, the author would like to acknowledge the assistance and helpful comments on the draft from colleagues in all of the organisations mentioned herein.

■ REFERENCES

BRIDGE J. (1991) Personal communication to the author.

COOPERS & LYBRAND (1992) 'Growing Business in the UK', *Business in the Community*, July 1992.

KOTLER P., HAIDER D. & REIN I. (1993) *Marketing Place*, Maxwell Macmillan.